LEO TOLSTOY

of God Is Within You

Mystical Teaching But As A New Concept Of Life

Translated from the Russian by Leo Wiener

INTRODUCTION BY KENNETH REXROTH

Library of Congress catalog card number 52–17628
SBN 374.5.0161.2
Manufactured in the United States of America
Fifth printing 1970

INTRODUCTION

By Kenneth Rexroth

EVERY DAY all states do things which, if they were the acts of individuals, would lead to summary arrest and often execution. By and large, organized society functions on the basis of an elaborate system of checks and balances. What is checked and balanced is not just the various "powers" of government, as we are taught in civics classes, but all the frauds and violence of institutionalized mankind. In the thousands of years since the Neolithic Revolution mankind has worked out an elaborate system of focusing and using its own destructive impulses, or, where they cannot be used, of neutralizing or aborting them. Machiavelli, Hobbes, the Social Darwinians, the Realpolitikers, and the vast majority of just the conventionally minded, the practically minded people who want to get something done, the majority has always accepted this situation, justified and even glorified it. When we speak of "civilization" this is always a big part of what we are talking about. These are the Emperor's new clothes—"The Social Lie."

From the beginning of organized society, or at least from the beginning of written documents, there have always been people who challenged and rejected this state of affairs. Usually they have been members of the Establishment themselves; Buddha and Tolstoy were both princes. Obviously the mute inglorious sufferers who have always borne the burden of "The System" are unknown to history, except in moments of social turmoil when some renegade from the ranks of the literate and privileged has spoken for them. It is hard to say of any given period of history or of any people, even our contemporaries, how acceptable the actual bulk of society finds the principles upon which it is organized. As a matter of fact, most people except politicians and authors work out for themselves, in secret, ways of living which ignore organized society as much as possible. After five or six thousand years much of life is still private, extraordinarily resistant to the mechanisms of civilization, even, or perhaps especially, in the most powerful and authoritarian states. What is called "growing up," "getting a little common sense," is largely the learning of techniques for outwitting the more destructive forces at large in the social order. The mature man lives quietly, does good privately, assumes personal responsibility for his actions, treats others with friendliness and courtesy, finds mischief boring and keeps out of it. Without this hidden conspiracy of good will, society would not endure an hour.

Tolstoy was the perfect type of discontented aristocrat. He had a great deal in common with Buddha, but he also shared many characteristics with Byron, with Bakunin, with Kropotkin. The thing that distinguishes men of this type is that they take their aristocratic profession seriously. They believe the Myth of the Aristocrat, the Platonic Guardian, responsible for the good and welfare of his fellows. Most members of the upper orders are "mature" enough to learn, early in life, that aristocracy is just another one of the many social hoaxes. The literature of the world from the Egyptians and Greeks to the present is full of guides and manuals, "The Mirrour of Princes," "The Regimen of Rulers," "The Courtier," "The Governour." There is little evidence that the class to which they were addressed ever took them very seriously. But a few always have. The vast majority are of course unknown, tragic noblemen who gave themselves to their people—who consumed them, or who consumed themselves with frustration and blew out their brains in tumble-down mansions. They are great favorites with Romantic novelists. Literature is full of them. A very few have been writers, able to articulate the utter contempt of the believing aristocrat for the cobwebs of vulgar lies and compromise which envelop society—the society which they feel they should have been permitted to govern or lead, strictly in the paths of their own noble idealism. Except for the tiny number who have managed to found religions, mankind has judged most of these people to be self-deluded fools.

In the eyes of the world, Tolstoy was such a fool. A hero of the siege of Sebastopol who became a pacifist, a passionate gambler who freed his serfs before the Emancipation, a young rake who in later life denounced the music of Beethoven, women's sweaters, and unchaperoned canoe trips as immoral in themselves and snares of still worse immorality—Tolstoy is not easy for the mature to take seriously. His religion is an expensive one—if it were literally put into practice, they say, organized society would collapse and it is open to question if it could ever be rebuilt afterwards.

The Kingdom of God Is Within You, like other specifically religious writings of Tolstoy's, attempts to "prove" that his religion was identical with that preached by Jesus Christ. These arguments have relatively little cogency with us today. We are not worried about the integrity of the original Gospel. We value Albert Schweitzer's Christology, not because of its historical soundness, its reconstruction of the

"True Christ," but because it has served as the symbolic vesture of Schweitzer's own world-transforming religion. So with Tolstoy, what is important about his religious writing is not his scholarship, which is make-believe, or his criticism of others, which is makeshift and utterly intolerant, but his vision.

Whatever the gospel of the authentic historic Jesus was, it was apocalyptic. The world as it is was weighed in the balance and found wanting. To this degree both Schweitzer and Tolstoy are "true Christians." But there is an essential difference between the two men. Committed to an ethics of apocalypse, a moral code of life lived always in the immanent eye of Judgment, Schweitzer has assumed the role of, to use the title of the Pope, a servant of the servants of God. Rather than attack society head on, he has preferred to subvert it with mercy. Tolstoy was closer to the pattern of his Master. He was intolerant of dogma, a compulsive anti-ritualist, militantly meek and aggressively mild, and, in spite of his professions of other-cheekism, unforgiving of the weaknesses and follies of his fellows . . . especially of his fellows in the ruling classes.

It is not the custom nowadays to take Tolstoy seriously as a thinker. Fiery apostles of nonviolence, loud denouncers of public and private hypocrisy do not make good colleagues or neighbors. Since all men are by nature fallible and foolish, society gets great delight in pointing out the hypocrisy and violence of such as Tolstoy. True he was a crank, with all the weaknesses of a crank, but, as cranks sometimes are, he was far more right than the majority of men who profess to speak for the majority of all the other inarticulate human beings. Furthermore, he was not a thinker in any substantial sense, he was a prophet. Prophets are supposed to be cranks. Nobody expects

Jeremiah to show the wisdom of Solomon. Unchallenged by the prophetic wrath of Jeremiah, the wisdom of all the Solomons of history leads only to perdition.

Tolstoy was also a great artist. Although he thought otherwise, he was singular among all the artist-prophets of modern times in being able to keep his prophecy from corrupting his art. His great novels are humane, lucid, all-knowing and all-forgiving. Yet they make no sacrifice of his principles. In contrast, Blake is turgid, Byron, who few people remember was once a prophet, is plain silly, D. H. Lawrence all too often bogs down in a mishmash of sentimentality that is neither art nor prophecy.

Possibly this is so because Tolstoy is more nearly right than they are. He may have been a crank, but he concentrated on essentials. Whatever the disputed teachings of Christ were, it is apparent that they have not been embodied in the practices of the organized Christian churches. "Do not resist evil with evil." "Respect the personal integrity of each man." "Assume direct personal responsibility for the moral world which surrounds yourself. Never delegate your moral responsibility." "Seek out all opportunities for direct, creative ethical action." "Avoid violence, anger, the invasion of others, refuse bloodshed, and all kinds of theft and lies, covert or open—especially in their approved and institutionalized forms." These are fairly simple commandments. Authority for them can certainly be found in the Sermon on the Mount and the great parables. What is more important, they are not at all difficult to carry out. The great churches have indisputably compromised the simple ethics of the Gospels, and yet, Protestant and Catholic, they have always represented the Christian ethic as extraordinarily difficult and even unpleasant. It is nothing of the sort. Many Buddhists and most Quakers, many simple monks and nuns, millions of humble housewives who attend daily Mass or Wednesday Prayer Meeting, live this way with ease and joy.

Untold numbers of people have lived like them, grinding corn in the adobe huts of Babylon, punching time clocks in Detroit. It is due to them that we have got as far as we have—that we are here at all. Over their heads their betters have fought the battles of the Social Lie and made history. This is the secret of Tolstoy's religion—in the final analysis, it is not cranky or odd at all. It is common. The significant thing is that, by and large, give and take a few pathetic sins, men do not behave in their daily relations with one another as states and churches and even abstractions like classes behave on the stage of history. If they had, we wouldn't be here.

THE KINGDOM OF GOD IS WITHIN YOU

THE KINGDOM OF GOD IS WITHIN YOU

Or, Christianity Not as a Mystical Teaching but as a New Concept of Life

And ye shall know the truth, and the truth shall make you free (John viii. 23).

And fear not them which kill the body, but are not able to kill the soul: but rather fear him which is able to destroy both soul and body in hell (Matt. x. 28).

Ye are bought with a price; be not ye the servants of men (1. Cor. vii. 23).

In the year 1884 I wrote a book under the title, *My Religion.* In this book I really expounded what my religion is.

In expounding my belief in Christ's teaching, I could not help but express the reason why I do not believe in the ecclesiastic faith, which is generally called Christianity, and why I consider it to be a delusion.

Among the many deviations of this teaching of Christ, I pointed out the chief deviation, namely, the failure to acknowledge the commandment of non-resistance to evil, which more obviously than any other shows the distortion of Christ's teaching in the church doctrine.

I knew very little, like the rest of us, as to what had

been done and preached and written in former days on this subject of non-resistance to evil. I knew what had been said on this subject by the fathers of the church, Origen, Tertullian, and others, and I knew also that there have existed certain so-called sects of the Mennonites, Herrnhuters, Quakers, who do not admit for a Christian the use of weapons and who do not enter military service, but what had been done by these so-called sects for the solution of this question was quite unknown to me.

My book, as I expected, was held back by the Russian censor, but, partly in consequence of my reputation as a writer, partly because it interested people, this book was disseminated in manuscripts and lithographic reprints in Russia and in translations abroad, and called forth, on the one hand, on the part of men who shared my views, a series of references to works written on the subject, and, on the other, a series of criticisms on the thoughts expressed in that book itself.

Both, together with the historical phenomena of recent times, have made many things clear to me and have brought me to new deductions and conclusions, which I wish to express.

First I shall tell of the information which I received concerning the history of the question of non-resistance to evil, then of the opinions on this subject which were expressed by ecclesiastic critics, that is, such as profess the Christian religion, and also by laymen, that is, such as do not profess the Christian religion; and finally, those deductions to which I was brought by both and by the historical events of recent times.

I.

Among the first answers to my book there came some letters from the American Quakers. In these letters, which express their sympathy with my views concerning the unlawfulness for Christianity of all violence and war, the Quakers informed me of the details of their so-called sect, which for more than two hundred years has in fact professed Christ's teaching about non-resistance to evil, and which has used no arms in order to defend itself. With their letters, the Quakers sent me their pamphlets, periodicals, and books. From these periodicals, pamphlets, and books which they sent me I learned to what extent they had many years ago incontestably proved the obligation for a Christian to fulfil the commandment about non-resistance to evil and had laid bare the incorrectness of the church teaching, which admitted executions and wars.

Having proved, by a whole series of considerations and texts, that war, that is, the maiming and killing of men, is incompatible with a religion which is based on love of peace and good-will to men, the Quakers affirm and prove that nothing has so much contributed to the obscuration of Christ's truth in the eyes of the pagans and impeded the dissemination of Christianity in the world as the non-acknowledgment of this commandment by men who called themselves Christians, — as the permission granted to a Christian to wage war and use violence.

"Christ's teaching, which entered into the consciousness of men, not by means of the sword and of violence," they say, "but by means of non-resistance to evil, can be disseminated in the world only through humility, meekness, peace, concord, and love among its followers.

"A Christian, according to the teaching of God Himself, can be guided in his relations to men by peace only, and so there cannot be such an authority as would compel a Christian to act contrary to God's teaching and contrary to the chief property of a Christian in relation to those who are near to him.

"The rule of state necessity," they say, "may compel those to become untrue to God's law, who for the sake of worldly advantages try to harmonize what cannot be harmonized, but for a Christian, who sincerely believes in this, that the adherence to Christ's teaching gives him salvation, this rule can have no meaning."

My acquaintance with the activity of the Quakers and with their writings, — with Fox, Paine, and especially with Dymond's book (1827), — showed me that not only had the impossibility of uniting Christianity with violence and war been recognized long ago, but that this incompatibility had long ago been proved so clearly and so incontestably that one has only to marvel how this impossible connection of the Christian teaching with violence, which has been preached all this time by the churches, could have been continued.

Besides the information received by me from the Quakers, I, at about the same time, received, again from America, information in regard to the same subject from an entirely different source, which had been quite unknown to me before.

The son of William Lloyd Garrison, the famous champion for the liberation of the negroes, wrote to me that, when he read my book, in which he found ideas resembling those expressed by his father in 1838, he, assuming that it might be interesting for me to know this, sent me the "Declaration of Non-resistance," which his father had made about fifty years ago.

This declaration had its origin under the following conditions: William Lloyd Garrison, in speaking before a society for the establishment of peace among men, which existed in America in 1838, about the measures for abolishing war, came to the conclusion that the establishment of universal peace could be based only on the obvious recognition of the commandment of non-resistance to evil (Matt. v. 39) in all its significance, as this was understood by the Quakers, with whom Garrison stood in friendly relations. When he came to this conclusion, he formulated and proposed to the society the following declaration, which was then, in 1838, signed by many members.

DECLARATION OF SENTIMENTS ADOPTED BY THE PEACE CONVENTION, HELD IN BOSTON IN 1838

"We, the undersigned, regard it as due to ourselves, to the cause which we love, to the country in which we live, and to the world, to publish a Declaration, expressive of the principles we cherish, the purposes we aim to accomplish, and the measures we shall adopt to carry forward the work of peaceful and universal reformation.

"We cannot acknowledge allegiance to any human government. . . . We recognize but one King and Lawgiver, one Judge and Ruler of mankind. . . .

"Our country is the world, our countrymen are all mankind. We love the land of our nativity, only as we love all other lands. The interests, rights, and liberties of American citizens are no more dear to us than are those of the whole human race. Hence we can allow no appeal to patriotism, to revenge any national insult or injury. . . .

"We conceive, that if a nation has no right to defend itself against foreign enemies, or to punish its invaders, no individual possesses that right in his own case. The unit cannot be of greater importance than the aggregate. . . . But if a rapacious and bloodthirsty soldiery, thronging these shores from abroad, with intent to commit rapine and destroy life, may not be resisted by the people or magistracy, then ought no resistance to be offered to domestic troublers of the public peace, or of private security. . . .

"The dogma, that all the governments of the world are approvingly ordained of God, and that the powers that be in the United States, in Russia, in Turkey, are in accordance with His will, is not less absurd than impious. It makes the impartial Author of human freedom and equality unequal and tyrannical. It cannot be affirmed that the powers that be, in any nation, are actuated by the spirit, or guided by the example of Christ, in the treatment of enemies: therefore, they cannot be agreeable to the will of God: and, therefore, their overthrow, by a spiritual regeneration of their subjects, is inevitable.

"We register our testimony, not only against all wars, whether offensive or defensive, but all preparations for war; against every naval ship, every arsenal, every fortification; against the militia system and a standing army; against all military chieftains and soldiers; against all monuments commemorative of victory over a foreign foe, all trophies won in battle, all celebrations in honour of military or naval exploits: against all appropriations for the defence of a nation by force and arms on the part of any legislative body; against every edict of government, requiring of its subjects military service. Hence, we deem it unlawful to bear arms, or to hold a military office.

"As every human government is upheld by physical strength, and its laws are enforced virtually at the point of the bayonet, we cannot hold any office which imposes upon its incumbent the obligation to do right, on pain of imprisonment or death. We therefore voluntarily exclude ourselves from every legislative and judicial body, and repudiate all human politics, worldly honours, and stations of authority. If we cannot occupy a seat in the legislasure, or on the bench, neither can we elect others to act as our substitutes in any such capacity.

"It follows that we cannot sue any man at law, to compel him by force to restore anything which he may have wrongfully taken from us or others; but, if he has seized our coat, we shall surrender up our cloak, rather than subject him to punishment.

"We believe that the penal code of the old covenant, An eye for an eye, and a tooth for a tooth, has been abrogated by Jesus Christ; and that, under the new covenant, the forgiveness, instead of the punishment of enemies, has been enjoined upon all His disciples, in all cases whatsoever. To extort money from enemies, or set them upon a pillory, or cast them into prison, or hang them upon a gallows, is obviously not to forgive, but to take retribution. . . .

"The history of mankind is crowded with evidences, proving that physical coercion is not adapted to moral regeneration; that the sinful disposition of man can be subdued only by love; that evil can be exterminated from the earth only by goodness; that it is not safe to rely upon an arm of flesh. . . . to preserve us from harm; that there is great security in being gentle, harmless, long-suffering, and abundant in mercy; that it is only the meek who shall inherit the earth, for the violent, who resort to the sword, shall perish with the sword. Hence, as a measure of sound policy, of safety to property, life, and liberty, of public quietude, and private enjoyment, as well as on the ground of allegiance to Him who is King of kings, and Lord of lords, we cordially adopt the non-resistance principle; being confident that it provides for all possible consequences, will ensure all things needful to us, is armed with omnipotent power, and must ultimately triumph over every assailing foe.

"We advocate no jacobinical doctrines. The spirit of jacobinism is the spirit of retaliation, violence, and murder. It neither fears God, nor regards man. We would be filled with the spirit of Christ. If we abide by our principles, it is impossible for us to be disorderly, or plot treason, or participate in any evil work: we shall submit to every ordinance of man, for the Lord's sake; obey all the requirements of government, except such as we deem contrary to the commands of the gospel; and in no wise resist the operation of law, except by meekly submitting to the penalty of disobedience.

"But, while we shall adhere to the doctrines of non-resistance and passive submission to enemies, we purpose, in a moral and spiritual sense, to speak and act boldly in the cause of God; to assail iniquity in high places and in low places; to apply our principles to all existing civil, political, legal, and ecclesiastical institutions; and to hasten the time when the kingdoms of this world shall become the kingdom of our Lord and of His Christ, and He shall reign for ever.

"It appears to us as a self-evident truth, that, whatever the gospel is designed to destroy, any period of the world, being contrary to it, ought now to be abandoned. If, then, the time is predicted, when swords shall be beaten into ploughshares, and spears into pruning-hooks, and men shall not learn the art of war any more, it follows that all who manufacture, sell, or wield these deadly weapons do thus array themselves against the peaceful dominion of the Son of God on earth.

"Having thus briefly, but frankly, stated our principles and purposes, we proceed to specify the measures we propose to adopt, in carrying our object into effect.

"We expect to prevail through the foolishness of preaching — striving to commend ourselves unto every man's conscience, in the sight of God. From the press, we shall promulgate our sentiments as widely as practicable. We shall endeavour to secure the coöperation of all persons, of whatever name or sect. . . . Hence we shall employ lectures, circulate tracts and publications, form societies, and petition our State and national governments in relation to the subject of universal peace. It will be our leading object to devise ways and means for effecting a radical change in the views, feelings, and practices of society respecting the sinfulness of war, and the treatment of enemies.

"In entering upon the great work before us, we are not unmindful that, in its prosecution, we may be called to test our sincerity, even as in a fiery ordeal. It may subject us to insult, outrage, suffering, yea, even death itself. We anticipate no small amount of misconception, misrepresentation, calumny. Tumults may arise against us. The ungodly and the violent, the proud and pharisaical, the ambitious and tyrannical, principalities and powers, and spiritual wickedness in high places, may combine to crush us. So they treated the Messiah, whose example we are humbly striving to imitate. . . . We shall not be afraid of their terror, neither be troubled. Our confidence is in the Lord Almighty, not in man. Having withdrawn from human protection, what can sustain us but that faith which overcomes the world? We shall not think it strange concerning the fiery ordeal which is to try us, as though some strange thing had happened unto us; but rejoice, inasmuch as we are partakers of Christ's sufferings. Wherefore, we commit the keeping of our souls to God, in well-doing, as unto a faithful Creator. 'For every one that forsakes houses, or brethren, or sisters, or father, or mother, or wife, or children, or lands, for Christ's sake, shall receive an hundredfold, and shall inherit everlasting life.'

"Firmly relying upon the certain and universal triumph of the sentiments contained in this Declaration, however formidable may be the opposition arrayed against them, in solemn testimony of our faith in their divine origin, we hereby affix our signatures to it; commending it to the reason and conscience of mankind, giving ourselves no anxiety as to what may befall us, and resolving, in the strength of the Lord God, calmly and meekly to abide the issue."

Immediately after this declaration Garrison founded a society of non-resistance, and a periodical, called *The Non-Resistant*, in which was preached the doctrine of non-resistance in all its significance and with all its consequences, as it had been expressed in the "Declaration." The information as to the later fate of the society and the periodical of non-resistance I received from the beautiful biography of William Lloyd Garrison, written by his sons.

The society and the periodical did not exist long: the majority of Garrison's collaborators in matters of freeing the slaves, fearing lest the too radical demands, as expressed in *The Non-Resistant*, might repel people from the practical work of the liberation of the negroes, refused to profess the principle of non-resistance, as it had been expressed in the "Declaration," and the society and the periodical ceased to exist.

This "Declaration" by Garrison, which so powerfully and so beautifully expressed such an important profession of faith, ought, it seems, to have startled men and to have become universally known and a subject of wide discussion. But nothing of the kind happened. It is not only unknown in Europe, but even among the Americans, who so highly esteem Garrison's memory, this declaration is almost unknown.

The same ingloriousness has fallen to the share of another champion of non-resistance to evil, the American Adin Ballou, who lately died, and who preached this doctrine for fifty years. How little is known of what refers to the question of non-resistance may be seen from the fact that Garrison's son, who has written an excellent biography of his father in four volumes, this son of Garrison, in reply to my question whether the society of non-resistance was still in existence, and whether there were any followers of it, answered me that so far as he knew the society had fallen to pieces, and there existed no followers of this doctrine, whereas at the time of his writing, there lived in Hopedale, Massachusetts, Adin Ballou, who had taken part in Garrison's labours and had devoted fifty years of his life to the oral and printed propaganda of the doctrine of non-resistance. Later on I received a letter from Wilson, a disciple and assistant of Ballou, and entered into direct communication with Ballou himself. I wrote to Ballou, and he answered me and sent me his writings. Here are a few extracts from them:

"Jesus Christ is my Lord and Master," says Ballou in one of the articles,[1] in which he arraigns the inconsistency of the Christians who recognize the right of defence and war. "I have covenanted to forsake all and follow Him, through good and evil report, until death. But I am nevertheless a Democratic-Republican citizen of the United States, implicitly sworn to bear true allegiance to my country, and to support its Constitution, if need be, with my life. Jesus Christ requires me to do unto others as I would that others should do unto me. The Constitution of the United States requires me to do unto twenty-seven hundred slaves" (there were slaves then, now we may put the working people in their place) "the very contrary of what I would have them do unto me, viz., assist to keep them in a grievous bondage. . . . But I am quite easy. I vote on. I help govern on. I am willing to hold any office I may be elected to under the Constitution. And I am still a Christian. I profess on. I find no difficulty in keeping covenant both with Christ and the Constitution. . . .

"Jesus Christ forbids me to resist evil-doers by taking 'eye for eye, tooth for tooth, blood for blood, and life for

[1] In *The Non-Resistant*, Vol. i., No. 4, Hopedale, Milford, Mass., Feb 15, 1845.

life. My government requires the very reverse, and depends, for its own self-preservation, on the halter, the musket, and the sword, seasonably employed against its domestic and foreign enemies. Accordingly, the land is well furnished with gibbets, prisons, arsenals, train-bands, soldiers, and ships-of-war. In the maintenance and use of this expensive life-destroying apparatus, we can exemplify the virtues of forgiving our injurers, loving our enemies, blessing them that curse us, and doing good to those that hate us. For this reason, we have regular Christian chaplains to pray for us, and call down the sins of God on our holy murderers. . . .

"I see it all; and yet I insist that I am as good a Christian as ever. I fellowship all; I vote on; I help govern on; I profess on; and I glory in being at once a devoted Christian, and a no less devoted adherent to the existing government. I will not give in to those miserable non-resistant notions. I will not throw away my political influence, and leave unprincipled men to carry on government alone. . . .

"The Constitution says, 'Congress shall have power to declare war.' . . . I agree to this. I endorse it. I swear to help carry it through. . . . What then, am I less a Christian? Is not war a Christian service? Is it not perfectly Christian to murder hundreds of thousands of fellow human beings; to ravish defenceless females, sack and burn cities, and exact all the other cruelties of war? Out upon these new-fangled scruples! This is the very way to forgive injuries, and love our enemies! If we only do it all in true love, nothing can be more Christian than wholesale murder!"

In another pamphlet, under the title, *How Many Does It Take?*[1] he says, "How many does it take to metamorphose wickedness into righteousness? One man must

[1] Not a pamphlet, but an article in *The Non-Resistant*, Vol. I, No. 4, and very imperfectly quoted by Tolstóy.

not kill. If he does, it is murder. Two, ten, one hundred men, acting on their own responsibility, must not kill. If they do, it is still murder. But a state or nation may kill as many as they please, and it is no murder. It is just, necessary, commendable, and right. Only get people enough to agree to it, and the butchery of myriads of human beings is perfectly innocent. But how many men does it take? This is the question. Just so with theft, robbery, burglary, and all other crimes. . . . But a whole nation can commit it. . . . But how many does it take?"[1]

Here is Ballou's catechism, composed for his flock (*The Catechism of Non-Resistance*[2]):

Q. Whence originated the term "non-resistance?"

A. From the injunction, "Resist not evil," Matt. v. 39.

Q. What does the term signify?

A. It expresses a high Christian virtue, prescribed by Christ.

Q. Is the word "resistance" to be taken in its widest meaning, that is, as showing that no resistance whatever is to be shown to evil?

A. No, it is to be taken in the strict sense of the Saviour's injunction; that is, we are not to retaliate evil with evil. Evil is to be resisted by all just means, but never with evil.

Q. From what can we see that Christ in such cases prescribed non-resistance?

A. From the words which He then used. He said,

[1] To this Tolstóy adds, on his own responsibility: "Why must one, ten, one hundred men not violate God's law, while very many may?"

[2] Translated freely, with some omissions. — *Author's Note.* I fail to find this *Catechism* in any of Ballou's writings accessible in and about Boston. The nearest approach to these questions and answers is found scattered throughout his *Christian Non-Resistance, in Its Important Bearings, Illustrated and Defended*, Philadelphia, 1846.

"Ye have heard that it hath been said, An eye for an eye, and a tooth for a tooth. But I say unto you that ye resist not evil; but whosoever shall smite thee on thy right cheek, turn to him the other also. And if any man will sue thee at the law, and take away thy coat, let him have thy cloak also."

Q. To whom does Jesus refer in the words, "It has been said?"

A. To the patriarchs and prophets, to what they said,— to what is contained in the writings of the Old Testament, which the Jews generally call the Law and the Prophets.

Q. What injunctions did Christ mean by "It hath been said?"

A. Those injunctions by which Noah, Moses, and other prophets authorize men to inflict personal injury on injurers, in order to punish and destroy evil.

Q. Quote these precepts.

A. Whoso sheddeth man's blood, by man shall his blood be shed: for in the image of God made He man (Gen. ix. 6). He that smiteth a man, so that he die, shall be surely put to death, and if any mischief follow, then thou shalt give life for life, eye for eye, tooth for tooth, hand for hand, foot for foot, burning for burning, wound for wound, stripe for stripe (Ex. xxi. 12, 23–25).

And he that killeth any man shall surely be put to death. And if a man cause a blemish in his neighbour; as he hath done, so shall it be done to him: breach for breach, eye for eye, tooth for tooth: as he hath caused a blemish in a man, so shall it be done to him again (Lev. xxiv. 17, 19, 20).

And the judges shall make diligent inquisition: and, behold, if the witness be a false witness, and hath testified falsely against his brother; then shall ye do unto him, as he had thought to have done unto his brother: and thine eye shall not pity; but life shall go for life, eye for eye, tooth for tooth, hand for hand, foot for foot (Deut. xix. 18, 19, 21). These are the precepts of which Jesus is speaking.

Noah, Moses, and the prophets taught that he who kills, maims, and tortures his neighbours does evil. To resist such evil and destroy it, the doer of evil is to be punished by death or maiming or some personal injury. Insult is to be opposed to insult, murder to murder, torture to torture, evil to evil. Thus taught Noah, Moses, and the prophets. But Christ denies it all. "But I say unto you," it says in the Gospel, "that ye resist not evil, resist not an insult with an insult, but rather bear the repeated insult from the doer of evil." What was authorized is prohibited. If we understand what kind of resistance they taught, we clearly see what we are taught by Christ's non-resistance.

Q. Did the ancients authorize the resistance of insult with insult?

A. Yes; but Jesus prohibited this. A Christian has under no condition the right to deprive of life or to subject to insult him who does evil to his neighbour.

Q. May a man kill or maim another in self-defence?

A. No.

Q. May he enter a court with a complaint, to have his insulter punished?

A. No; for what he is doing through others, he is in reality doing in his own person.

Q. May he fight with an army against enemies, or against domestic rebels?

A. Of course not. He cannot take any part in war or warlike preparations. He cannot use death-dealing arms. He cannot resist injury with injury, no matter whether he be alone or with others, through himself or through others.

Q. May he choose or fit out military men for the government?

A. He can do nothing of the kind, if he wishes to be true to Christ's law.

Q. May he voluntarily give money, to aid the government, which is supported by military forces, capital punishment, and violence in general?

A. No, if the money is not intended for some special object, just in itself, where the aim and means are good.

Q. May he pay taxes to such a government?

A. No; he must not voluntarily pay the taxes, but he must also not resist their collection. The taxes imposed by the government are collected independently of the will of the subjects. It is impossible to resist the collection, without having recourse to violence; but a Christian must not use violence, and so he must give up his property to the violence which is exerted by the powers.

Q. May a Christian vote at elections and take part in a court or in the government?

A. No; the participation in elections, in the court, or in the government, is a participation in governmental violence.

Q. In what does the chief significance of the doctrine of non-resistance consist?

A. In that it alone makes it possible to tear the evil out by the root, both out of one's own heart and out of the neighbour's heart. This doctrine forbids doing that by which evil is perpetuated and multiplied. He who attacks another and insults him, engenders in another the sentiment of hatred, the root of all evil. To offend another, because he offended us, for the specious reason of removing an evil, means to repeat an evil deed, both against him and against ourselves, — to beget, or at least to free, to encourage, the very demon whom we claim we wish to expel. Satan cannot be driven out by Satan, untruth cannot be cleansed by untruth, and evil cannot be vanquished by evil.

True non-resistance is the one true resistance to evil. It kills and finally destroys the evil sentiment.

Q. But, if the idea of the doctrine is right, is it practicable?

A. It is as practicable as any good prescribed by the Law of God. The good cannot under all circumstances be executed without self-renunciation, privation, suffering, and, in extreme cases, without the loss of life itself. But he who values life more than the fulfilment of God's will is already dead to the one true life. Such a man, in trying to save his life, shall lose it. Besides, in general, where non-resistance costs the sacrifice of one life, or the sacrifice of some essential good of life, resistance costs thousands of such sacrifices.

Non-resistance preserves, resistance destroys.

It is incomparably safer to act justly than unjustly; to bear an insult than to resist it with violence, — it is safer even in relation to the present life. If all men did not resist evil with evil, the world would be blessed.

Q. But if only a few shall act thus, what will become of them?

A. If only one man acted thus, and all the others agreed to crucify him, would it not be more glorious for him to die in the triumph of non-resisting love, praying for his enemies, than to live wearing the crown of Cæsar, bespattered with the blood of the slain? But one or thousands who have firmly determined not to resist evil with evil, whether among the enlightened or among savage neighbours, are much safer from violence than those who rely on violence. A robber, murderer, deceiver, will more quickly leave them alone than those who resist with weapons. They who take the sword perish with the sword, and those who seek peace, who act in a friendly manner, inoffensively, who forget and forgive offences, for the most part enjoy peace or, if they die, die blessed.

Thus, if all kept the commandment of non-resistance, it

is evident that there would be no offences, no evil deeds. If these formed a majority, they would establish the reign of love and good-will, even toward the ill-disposed, by never resisting evil with evil, never using violence. If there were a considerable minority of these, they would have such a corrective, moral effect upon society that every cruel punishment would be abolished, and violence and enmity would be changed to peace and love. If there were but a small minority of them, they would rarely experience anything worse than the contempt of the world, and the world would in the meantime, without noticing it, and without feeling itself under obligation, become wiser and better from this secret influence. And if, in the very worst case, a few members of the minority should be persecuted to death, these men, dying for the truth, would leave behind them their teaching, which is already sanctified by their martyr's death.

Peace be with all who seek peace, and all-conquering love be the imperishable inheritance of every soul, which voluntarily submits to the Law of Christ: "Resist not evil." In the course of fifty years, Ballou wrote and edited books dealing mainly with the question of non-resistance to evil. In these works, which are beautiful in their lucidity of thought and elegance of expression, the question is discussed from every possible side. He establishes the obligatoriness of this commandment for every Christian who professes the Bible as a divine revelation. He adduces all the customary retorts to the commandment of non-resistance, both from the Old Testament and from the New, as, for example, the expulsion from the temple, and so forth, and all these are overthrown; he shows, independently of Scripture, the practical wisdom of this rule, and adduces all the objections which are usually made to it, and meets all these objections. Thus one chapter of a work of his treats of non-resistance to evil in exclusive cases, and here he acknowledges that, if there were cases when the application of non-resistance to evil were impossible, this would prove that the rule is altogether untenable. In adducing these special cases, he proves that it is precisely in them that the application of this rule is necessary and rational. There is not a single side of the question, either for his followers or for his adversaries, which is not investigated in these works. I say all this, in order to show the unquestionable interest which such works ought to have for men who profess Christianity, and that, therefore, one would think Ballou's activity ought to have been known, and the thoughts expressed by him ought to have been accepted or refuted; but there has been nothing of the kind.

The activity of Garrison the father, with his foundation of a society of non-resistants and his declaration, convinced me even more than my relations with the Quakers, that the departure of state Christianity from Christ's law about non-resistance to evil is something that has been observed and pointed out long ago, and that men have without cessation worked to arraign it. Ballou's activity still more confirmed this fact to me. But the fate of Garrison and especially of Ballou, who is not known to any one, in spite of his fifty years of stubborn and constant work in one and the same direction, has also confirmed to me the other fact, that there exists some kind of unexpressed but firm understanding as to passing all such attempts in silence.

Ballou died in August, 1890, and his obituary was given in an American periodical with a Christian tendency (*Religio-Philosophical Journal*, August 23d).

In this eulogistic obituary it says that Ballou was a spiritual guide of a community, that he delivered between eight and nine thousand sermons, married one thousand pairs, and wrote about five hundred articles, but not a word is said about the aim to which he devoted all his life, — the word "non-resistance" is not even used.

Like all that which the Quakers have been preaching for two hundred years, like the activity of Garrison the father, the foundation of his society and periodical, and his declaration, so Ballou's whole activity does not seem to have existed at all.

A striking example of such an ingloriousness of writings intended to elucidate non-resistance to evil, and to arraign those who do not recognize this commandment, is found in the fate of the book by the Bohemian Chelcický, which has but lately become known and has so far not yet been printed.

Soon after the publication of my book in German, I received a letter from a professor of the Prague University, which informed me of the existence of a still unpublished work by the Bohemian Chelcický, of the fifteenth century, by the name of *The Drawnet of Faith.* In this work, as the professor wrote me, Chelcický about four centuries ago expressed the same view in regard to the true and the false Christianity, which I had expressed in my work, *My Religion.* The professor wrote to me that Chelcický's work was for the first time to be published in Bohemian in the periodical of the St. Petersburg Academy of Sciences. As I was unable to procure the work itself, I tried to become acquainted with what was known of Chelcický, and such information I got from a German book sent me by the same Prague professor, and from Pýpin's "History of Bohemian Literature." This is what Pýpin says:

"*The Drawnet of Faith* is that teaching of Christ which is to draw man out from the dark depths of the sea of life and its untruths. True faith consists in believing in God's words; but now there has come a time when men consider the true faith to be heresy, and so reason must show wherein the true faith consists, if one does not know it. Darkness has concealed it from men, and they do not know Christ's true law.

"To explain this law, Chelcický points out the original structure of Christian society, which, he says, is now regarded as rank heresy by the Roman Church.

"This primitive church was his own ideal of a social structure, based on equality, freedom, and brotherhood. Christianity, according to Chelcický, still treasures these principles, and all that is necessary is, that society should return to its pure teaching, and then any other order, in which kings and popes are needed, would seem superfluous: in everything the law of love alone is sufficient.

"Historically Chelcický refers the fall of Christianity to the times of Constantine the Great, whom Pope Sylvester introduced into Christianity with all the pagan customs and life. Constantine, in his turn, invested the Pope with worldly wealth and power. Since then both powers have been aiding one another and have striven after external glory. Doctors and masters and the clergy have begun to care only for the subjugation of the whole world to their dominion, have armed men against one another for the purpose of murdering and plundering, and have completely destroyed Christianity in faith and in life. Chelcický absolutely denies the right to wage war and administer capital punishment; every warrior and even 'knight' is only an oppressor, malefactor, and murderer."

The same, except for some biographical details and excerpts from Chelcický's correspondence, is said in the German book.

Having thus learned the essence of Chelcický's teaching, I with much greater impatience waited for the appearance of *The Drawnet of Faith* in the journal of the Academy. But a year, two, three years passed, and the book did not appear. Only in 1888 I learned that the printing of the book, which had been begun, had come to a stop. I got the proof-sheets of as much as had been printed, and I read the book. The book is in every respect remarkable.

The contents are quite correctly rendered by Pýpin.

Chelcický's fundamental idea is this, that Christianity, having united with the power in the time of Constantine and having continued to develop under these conditions, has become absolutely corrupt and has ceased to be Christianity. The title "The Drawnet of Faith," was given by Chelcický to his work, because, taking for his motto the verse of the Gospel about calling the disciples to become fishers of men, Chelcický, continuing this comparison, says, "Christ by means of His disciples caught in His drawnet of faith the whole world, but the larger fish, tearing the net, jumped out of it, and through the holes, which these larger fish had made, all the others went away, and the net was left almost empty."

The large fish that broke through the net are the rulers, emperors, popes, kings, who, in not renouncing their power, did not accept Christianity, but its semblance only.

Chelcický taught what has been taught until the present by the Mennonites and Quakers, and what in former years was taught by the Bogomils, Paulicians, and many others. He teaches that Christianity, which demands from its followers meekness, humility, kindness, forgiveness of sins, the offering of the other cheek when one cheek has been smitten, love of enemies, is incompatible with violence, which forms an indispensable condition of power.

A Christian, according to Chelcický's interpretation, can not only not be a chief or a soldier, but cannot even take part in the government, be a merchant or even a landowner; he can be only an artisan or an agriculturist.

This book is one of the extremely few that have survived the auto-da-fés of books in which the official Christianity is arraigned. All such books, which are called heretical, have been burned together with the authors, so that there are very few ancient works which arraign the departure of official Christianity, and so this book is especially interesting.

But besides being interesting, no matter how we look upon it, this book is one of the most remarkable productions of thoughts, as judged by the depth of its contents, and the wonderful force and beauty of the popular language, and its antiquity. And yet this book has for more than four centuries remained unprinted, and continues to be unknown, except to learned specialists.

One would think that all these kinds of works, by the Quakers, and Garrison, and Ballou, and Chelcický, which assert and prove, on the basis of the Gospel, that our world comprehends Christ's teaching falsely, ought to rouse interest, agitation, discussions, in the midst of the pastors and of the flock.

Works of this kind, which touch on the essence of the Christian teaching, ought, it seems, to be analyzed and recognized as true, or to be rejected and overthrown.

But nothing of the kind has happened. One and the same thing is repeated with all these works. People of the most different views, both those who believe and, what is most surprising, those who are unbelieving liberals, seem to have an agreement to pass them stubbornly in silence, and all that has been done by men to elucidate the true meaning of Christ's teaching remains unknown or forgotten.

But still more startling is the ingloriousness of two works, of which I learned also in connection with the appearance of my book. These are Dymond's book *On War*, published for the first time in London, in 1824, and Daniel Musser's book *On Non-Resistance*, written in 1864. The ignorance about these two books is particularly remarkable, because, to say nothing of their worth, both books treat not so much of the theory as of the practical application of the theory to life, of the relation of Christianity to military service, which is particularly important and interesting now, in connection with the universal liability to do military service.

People will, perhaps, ask: "What are the duties of a subject, who believes that war is incompatible with his religion, but of whom the government demands a participation in military service?"

It seems that this is a very living question, one, the answer to which is particularly important in connection with the military service of the present time. All, or a vast majority of men, — Christians, — all males, are called on to perform military service. What must a man, as a Christian, answer in reply to this demand? Dymond's answer is as follows:

"It is his duty, mildly and temperately, yet firmly, to refuse to serve.

"There are some persons, who, without any determinate process of reasoning, appear to conclude that responsibility for national measures attaches solely to those who direct them; that it is the business of governments to consider what is good for the community, and that, in these cases, the duty of the subject is merged in the will of the sovereign. Considerations like these are, I believe, often voluntarily permitted to become opiates of the conscience. 'I have no part,' it is said, 'in the councils of the government, and am not therefore responsible for its crimes.' We are, indeed, not responsible for the crimes of our rulers, but we are responsible for our own; and the crimes of our rulers are our own, if, whilst we believe them to be crimes, we promote them by our coöperation.

"But those who suppose that obedience in all things is required, or that responsibility in political affairs is transferred from the subject to the sovereign, reduce themselves to a great dilemma.

"It is to say that we must resign our conduct and our consciences to the will of others, and act wickedly or well, as their good or evil may preponderate, without merit for virtue, or responsibility for crime."

What is remarkable is this, that precisely the same is expressed in the instruction to the soldiers, which they are made to learn by rote: it says there that only the general is responsible for the consequences of his command. But this is not true. A man cannot shift the responsibility for his acts. And this may be seen from what follows:

"If the government direct you to fire your neighbour's property, or to throw him over a precipice, will you obey?[1] If you will not, there is an end of the argument, for if you may reject its authority in one instance, where is the limit to rejection? There is no rational limit but that which is assigned by Christianity, and that is both rational and practicable.

"We think, then, that it is the business of every man, who believes that war is inconsistent with our religion, respectfully, but steadfastly, to refuse to engage in it. Let such as these remember that an honourable and an awful duty is laid upon them. It is upon their fidelity, so far as human agency is concerned, that the cause of peace is suspended. Let them be willing to avow their opinions and to defend them. Neither let them be contented with words, if more than words, if suffering also, is required. If you believe that Jesus Christ has prohibited slaughter, let not the opinion or the commands of a world induce you to join in it. By this 'steady and determinate pursuit of virtue,' the benediction which attaches to those who hear the sayings of God and do them, will rest upon you, and the time will come when even the world will honour you, as contributors to the work of human reformation."

Musser's book is called *Non-Resistance Asserted; or,*

[1] Tolstóy's translation from the English, which is generally loose, here departs entirely from the text. Tolstóy writes: "If a chief direct you to kill your neighbour's child, or your father, or your mother, will you obey?"

Kingdom of Christ and Kingdom of This World Separated, 1864.[1]

The book is devoted to the same question, which it analyzes in relation with the demand made by the government of the United States on its citizens as regards military service during that Civil War, and it has the same contemporary importance, in that it analyzes the question as to how and under what conditions men must and can refuse to do military service. In the introduction the author says:

"It is well known that in the United States there are many people who consciously deny war. They are called 'non-resistant' or 'defenceless' Christians. These Christians refuse to defend their country or to bear arms, or to engage, at the request of the government, in war against its enemies. Until now this religious cause has been respected by the government, and those who professed it were excused from service. But with the beginning of our civil war public opinion has been wrought up by this state of affairs. Naturally, people who consider it their duty to bear all the burdens and perils of a military life for the defence of their country feel harsh toward those who for a long time have with them enjoyed the protection and the advantages of the government, but in time of necessity and danger do not wish to share in bearing the labours and dangers in its defence. It is also natural for the condition of such men to be considered irrational, monstrous, and suspicious.

"Many orators and writers," says the author, "have raised their voice against this state and have tried to prove the injustice of non-resistance from common sense and from Scripture; and this is quite natural, and in

[1] A thorough search through bibliographies, catalogues, and libraries has failed to reveal such a book or such an author, and as Tolstóy speaks above of the book as being written, it may be that Tolstóy had a manuscript before him.

many cases these authors are right, — they are right in relation to those persons who, declining the labours connected with military service, do not decline the advantages which they receive from the governments, — but they are not right in relation to the principle of non-resistance itself."

First of all the author proves the obligatoriness of the rule of non-resistance for every Christian in that it is clear and that it is given to a Christian beyond any possibility of misinterpretation. "Judge yourselves whether it is right to obey man more than God," said Peter and John. Similarly every man who wants to be a Christian must act in relation to the demand that he should go to war, since Christ has told him, "Resist not evil with violence."

With this the author considers the question as to principle itself completely solved. The author analyzes in detail the other question as to whether persons, who do not decline the advantages which are obtained through the violence of government, have a right to refuse to do military service, and comes to the conclusion that a Christian, who follows Christ's law and refuses to go to war, can just as little take part in any governmental affairs, — either in courts or in elections, — nor can he in private matters have recourse to power, police or court. Then the book proceeds to analyze the relation of the Old Testament to the New, — the significance of government for non-Christians; there are offered objections to the doctrine of non-resistance, and these are refuted. The author concludes his book with the following:

"Christ chose His disciples in the world," he says. "They do not expect any worldly goods or worldly happiness, but, on the contrary, everlasting life. The spirit in which they live makes them satisfied and happy in every situation. If the world tolerates them, they are always satisfied. But if the world will not leave them in peace, they will go elsewhere, since they are wanderers on the earth and have no definite place of abode. They consider that the dead can bury the dead, — they need but one thing, and that is to follow their teacher."

Without touching the question whether the duty of a Christian in relation to war, as established in these two books, is correct or not, it is impossible not to see the practical importance and urgency of the solution of this question.

There are some people, — hundreds of thousands of Quakers, — and all our Spirit Wrestlers and Milkers, and people belonging to no definite sects, who assert that violence — and so military service — is not compatible with Christianity, and therefore every year several recruits in Russia refuse to do military service on the basis of their religious convictions. What does the government do? Does it excuse them? No. Does it compel them to serve, and, in case of a refusal, punish them? No. In 1818 the government acted as follows. Here is an excerpt, which is almost unknown in Russia, from a diary by N. N. Muravév-Kárski, which was not sanctioned by the censor.

"TIFLIS, October 2, 1818.

"In the morning the commandant told me that lately five manorial peasants from the Government of Támbov had been sent to Georgia. These men had been sent to the army, but they refused to serve; they have been flogged several times and have been sent between the rows, but they gladly undergo the most cruel torments and are prepared for death, if only they can avoid serving. 'Send us away,' they say, 'and do not touch us; we shall not touch any one. All men are equal and the Tsar is just such a man as we are. Why should we pay him tribute? Why should I subject my life to danger in order to kill in war a man who has done me no wrong? You may cut us into small pieces, but we will not change our ideas, we will not put on the military cloak, and will not eat rations. He who will pity us will give us an alms, but we have nothing belonging to the Crown and we want nothing.' Such are the words of these peasants, who assert that there is a large number like them in Russia. They have four times been taken before the Committee of Ministers, and it was finally decided to refer the matter to the Tsar, who commanded that they be sent to Georgia to mend their ways, and ordered the commander-in-chief to report to him every month concerning the gradual success in turning these peasants to the proper ideas."

It is not known how this improvement ended, just as nothing is known of the whole episode, which was kept a profound secret.

Thus the government acted seventy-five years ago,— thus it has acted in the vast majority of cases, which are always cautiously concealed from the people. Thus it acts even at present, except in relation to the German Mennonites, who live in the Government of Khersón, for their refusal to do military service is heeded and they are made to serve their time in connection with forestry work.

In the late cases of refusal to do military service in consequence of religious convictions, other than those of the Mennonites, the authorities have acted as follows:

At first they use all means of violence employed in our time for the purpose of "mending" them and bringing them back to "the proper ideas," and the whole matter is kept a profound secret. I know that in the case of one man in Moscow, who in 1884 refused to serve, they wrote up voluminous documents two months after his refusal, and these were kept in the ministry as the greatest secret.

They generally begin by sending the one who refuses

to the priests, who, to their shame be it said, always admonish the person refusing. But since the admonition, in the name of Christ, to renounce Christ is generally fruitless, the refusing person is after the admonition by the clergy sent to the gendarmes. The gendarmes, finding nothing of a political nature in the case, generally return him, and then the refusing person is sent to the learned, to the physicians, and into the insane asylum. In all these recommitments the refuser, who is deprived of his liberty, undergoes all kinds of humiliations and sufferings, like a condemned criminal. (This was repeated in four cases.) The physicians dismiss the refuser from the insane asylum, and then begin all kinds of secret, cunning measures, in order not to dismiss the refuser and thus encourage others to refuse like him, and at the same time not to leave him amidst the soldiers, lest the soldiers might find out from him that the levy for military service does not at all take place in accordance with God's law, as they are assured, but contrary to it.

The most convenient thing for the government to do would be to have the refuser executed, beaten to death with sticks, as they used to do of old, or executed in some other manner. But it is impossible openly to execute a man for being true to a teaching which we all profess, and it is equally impossible to let a man alone, who refuses to serve. And so the government tries either through suffering to compel the man to renounce Christ, or in some way imperceptibly to get rid of the man, without having him publicly executed, — in some way to conceal this man's act and the man himself from other people. And so there begin all kinds of devices and cunning and tortures of this man. Either he is sent to some outlying region, or he is provoked to commit some act of insubordination, and then he is tried for breach of discipline and is locked up in prison, in a disciplinary battalion, where he is freely tortured in secret, or he is declared insane and is locked up in an insane asylum. Thus one man was sent to Tashként, that is, as though he were transferred to the Tashként army, another to Omsk, a third was tried for insubordination and sent to prison, and a fourth was put into a lunatic asylum.

Everywhere the same is repeated. Not only the government, but also the majority of liberals, of freethinkers, as though by agreement, carefully turn away from everything which has been said, written, and done by men to show the incompatibility of violence in its most terrible, rude, and lurid form, in the form of militarism, that is, the readiness to kill anybody, with the teaching, not only of Christianity, but even of humanitarianism, which society pretends to be professing.

Thus the information which I received concerning the extent to which the true significance of Christ's teaching has been elucidated and is being elucidated more and more, and concerning the attitude which the highest ruling classes, not only in Russia, but also in Europe and in America, take toward this elucidation and execution of the teaching, convinced me that in these ruling classes there existed a consciously hostile relation toward true Christianity, which found its expression mainly in the silence observed concerning all its manifestations.

II.

THE same impression of a desire to conceal, to pass in silence, what I attempted so carefully to express in my book, has been produced on me by the criticisms upon it.

When my book appeared, it was, as I had expected, prohibited, and according to the law it ought to have been burned. But, instead of being burned, it was distributed among the officials, and it was disseminated in a large number of written copies and lithographic reprints, and in translations printed abroad. Very soon there appeared criticisms upon the book, not only by the clergy, but also by the laity, which the government not only sanctioned, but even encouraged, so that the refutation of the book, which was assumed to be unknown to any one, was made a theme for theological essays in the academies.

The critics upon my books, both the Russian and the foreign critics, can be divided into two classes: into the religious critics, — people who consider themselves to be believers, — and lay critics, who are freethinkers.

I shall begin with the first:

In my book I accuse the church teachers of teaching contrary to Christ's commandments, which are clearly and definitely expressed in the Sermon on the Mount, and especially contrary to the commandment about non-resistance to evil, thus depriving Christ's teaching of all significance. The church teachers recognize the Sermon on the Mount with the commandment about non-resistance to evil as a divine revelation, and so, if they have found it necessary to write about my book at all, they ought, it would seem, first of all to answer this chief point of accusation and say outright whether they consider the teaching of the Sermon on the Mount and of the commandment about non-resistance to evil obligatory for a Christian, or not, — and they must not answer it as this is generally done, that is, by saying that, although on the one hand it cannot properly be denied, on the other it cannot be affirmed, the more so that, and so forth, — but must answer it just as the question is put by me in my book: did Christ actually demand from His disciples the fulfilment of what He taught in the Sermon on the Mount? and so, can a Christian, remaining a Christian, go to court, taking part in it and condemning people, or seeking in it defence by means of violence, or can he not? Can a Christian, still remaining a Christian, take part in the government, using violence against his neighbours, or not? And the chief question, which now, with the universal military service, stands before all men, — can a Christian, remaining a Christian, contrary to Christ's injunction, make any promises as to future acts, which are directly contrary to the teaching, and, taking part in military service, prepare himself for the murder of men and commit it?

The questions are put clearly and frankly, and, it would seem, they ought to be answered clearly and frankly. But nothing of the kind has been done in all the criticisms upon my book, just as nothing of the kind has been done in the case of all those arraignments of the church teachers for departing from Christ's law, with which history is filled since the time of Constantine.

Very much has been said in reference to my book about how incorrectly I interpret this or that passage in the Gospel, how I err in not acknowledging the Trinity, the redemption, and the immortality of the soul; very much has been said, but this one thing, which for every Christian forms the chief, essential question of life: how to harmonize what was clearly expressed in the teacher's words and is clearly expressed in the heart of every one of us, — the teaching about forgiveness, humility, renunciation, and love of all men, of our neighbours and of our enemies, — with the demand of military violence exerted against the men of one's own nation or another nation.

Everything which may be called semblances of answers to this question may be reduced to the five following divisions. I have tried in this respect to collect everything I could, not only in reference to the criticisms upon my book, but also in reference to what has been written upon the subject in former times.

The first, the rudest way of answering, consists in the bold assertion that violence does not contradict Christ's teaching, and that it is permitted and even prescribed by the Old and the New Testament.

Assertions of this kind issue for the most part from people high up in the governmental or ecclesiastic hierarchy, who are, therefore, quite convinced that no one will dare to contradict their assertions, and that if one actually dared to do so, they would not hear these objections. These men have, in consequence of their intoxication with their power, for the most part to such an extent lost the concept of what that Christianity is, in the name of which they occupy their places, that everything of a Christian nature in Christianity presents itself to them as sectarian; but everything which in the writings of the Old and the New Testament may be interpreted in an anti-Christian and pagan sense, they consider to be the foundation of Christianity. In favour of their assertion that Christianity does not contradict violence, these men with the greatest boldness generally bring forward the most offensive passages from the Old and the New Testament, and interpret them in the most non-Christian manner: the execution of Ananias and Sapphira, the execution of Simon Magus, and so forth. They adduce all those words of Christ which may be interpreted as a justification of cruelty, such as the expulsion from the temple, "It shall be more tolerable on that day for Sodom, than for that city," and so forth.

According to the concepts of these men, the Christian government is not in the least obliged to be guided by the spirit of humility, forgiveness of offences, and love of our enemies.

It is useless to refute such an assertion, because the men who assert this refute themselves, or rather, turn away from Christ, inventing their own Christ and their own Christianity in place of Him in whose name the church exists and also the position which they occupy in it. If all men knew that the church preaches Christ punishing, and not forgiving, and warring, no one would be believing in this church, and there would be no one to prove what it is proving.

The second method is a little less rude. It consists in asserting that, although Christ really taught to offer one's cheek and give up a shirt, and this is a very high moral demand, there are malefactors in the world, and if these are not curbed by the exercise of force, the whole world and all good men will perish. This proof I found for the first time in John Chrysostom and I pointed out its incorrectness in my book, *My Religion.*

This argument is ungrounded, because, in the first place, if we allow ourselves to recognize any men as special malefactors (Raca), we thus destroy the whole meaning of the Christian teaching, according to which we are all equal and brothers, as the sons of one heavenly Father; in the second place, because, even if God permitted the exertion of violence against malefactors, it is absolutely impossible to find that safe and indubitable sign by which a malefactor may be unerringly told from one who is not, and so every man, or society of men, would recognize another as a malefactor, which is the case now; in the third place, because even if it were possible unerringly to tell malefactors from those who are not malefactors, it would still not be possible in a Christian society to execute, or maim, or lock up these malefactors, because in Christian society there would be no one to do this, because every Christian, as a Christian, is enjoined not to use violence against a malefactor.

The third method of answering is still shrewder than the previous one. It consists in asserting that, although the commandment of non-resistance to evil is obligatory for a Christian when the evil is directed against him personally, it ceases to be obligatory when the evil is directed against his neighbours, and that then a Christian is not only not obliged to fulfil the commandments, but is also obliged in the defence of his neighbours, contrary to the commandment, to use violence against the violators.

This assertion is quite arbitrary, and in the whole of Christ's teaching no confirmation of such an interpretation can be found. Such an interpretation is not only a limitation of the commandment, but a direct negation and annihilation of it. If any man has a right to use violence when another is threatened by danger, then the question as to the use of violence reduces itself to the question of defining what constitutes a danger for another person. But if my private judgment decides the question of danger for another, then there does not exist such a case of violence that it could not be explained on the basis of a danger with which another is threatened. Wizards were executed and burned, aristocrats and Girondists were executed, and so were their enemies, because those who were in power considered them to be dangerous for others.

If this important limitation, which radically undermines the meaning of the commandment, entered Christ's mind, there ought somewhere to be mention made of it. But in all the preaching and the life of the teacher there is not only no such limitation, but, on the contrary, there is expressed a particular caution against such a false and offensive limitation, which destroys the commandment. The mistake and the blunder of such a limitation is with particular clearness shown in the Gospel in connection with the judgment of Caiaphas, who made this very limitation. He recognized that it was not good to execute innocent Jesus, but he saw in Him danger, not for himself, but for the whole nation, and so he said: "It is expedient for us that one man should die for the people, and that the whole nation perish not." And more clearly still was the negation of such a limitation expressed in the words said to Peter when he attempted with violence to resist the evil which was directed against Jesus (Matt. xxvi. 52). Peter was not defending himself, but his beloved and divine teacher. And Christ directly forbade him to do so, saying that he who takes the sword shall perish with the sword.

Besides, the justification of violence used against a neighbour for the sake of defending another man against worse violence is always incorrect, because in using violence against an evil which is not yet accomplished, it is impossible to know which evil will be greater, — whether the evil of my violence or of that against which I wish to defend my neighbour. We execute a criminal, thus freeing society from him, and we are positively unable to tell whether the criminal would not have changed on the morrow and whether our execution is not a useless cruelty. We lock up a man whom we suppose to be a dangerous member of society, but beginning with to-morrow this man may cease to be dangerous, and his incarceration is futile. I see that a man whom I know to be a robber is pursuing a girl, and I have a gun in my hand, — I kill the robber and save the girl; the robber has certainly been killed or wounded, but it is unknown to me what would happen if that were not the case. What an enormous amount of evil must take place, as it actually does, as the result of arrogating to ourselves the right to prevent an evil that may occur! Ninety-nine hundredths of the evil of the world, from the Inquisition to dynamite bombs and the executions and sufferings of tens of thousands of so-called political criminals, are based on this reflection.

The fourth, still more refined answer to the question as to how a Christian should act toward Christ's commandment of non-resistance to evil consists in asserting that the commandment of non-resistance to evil is not denied by them, but is accepted like any other; but that they do not ascribe to this commandment any special exclusive significance, as the sectarians do. To ascribe to this commandment an invariable condition of Christian life, as do Garrison, Ballou, Dymond, the Quakers, the Mennonites, the Shakers, and as did the Moravian brothers, the Waldenses, Albigenses, Bogomils, Paulicians, is one-sided sectarianism. This commandment has neither more nor less significance than all the others, and a man who in his weakness transgresses any one of the commandments about non-resistance does not cease to be a Christian, provided he believes correctly. This subterfuge is very clever, and men who wish to be deceived are easily deceived by it. The subterfuge consists in reducing the direct conscious negation of the commandment to an accidental violation of the same. But we need only compare the relation of the church teachers to this commandment and to others, which they actually recognize, in order that we may convince ourselves that the relation of the church teachers to the commandments which they recognize is quite different from their relation to this one.

They actually recognize the commandment against fornication, and so never, under any condition, admit that fornication is not an evil. The preachers of the church never point out any cases when the commandment against fornication ought to be broken, and they always teach that we must avoid the offences which lead to the temptation of fornication. But this is not the case with the commandment about non-resistance. All the church preachers know cases when this commandment may be broken. And thus they teach men. And they not only do not teach how to avoid these offences, of which the chief one is the oath, but themselves commit them. The church preachers never and under no condition preach the violation of any other commandment; but in relation to the commandment of non-resistance they teach outright that this prohibition must not be understood in too direct a sense, and not only that this commandment must not be carried out at all times, but that there are conditions, situations, when directly the opposite should be done, that is, that we should judge, wage war, execute. Thus, in reference to the commandment about non-resistance to evil, they in the majority of cases preach how not to fulfil it. The fulfilment of this commandment, they say, is very difficult and is characteristic only of perfection. But how can it help but be difficult, when its breach is not only not prohibited, but is also directly encouraged, when they directly bless the courts, prisons, guns, cannon, armies, battles? Consequently it is not true that this commandment is recognized by the church preachers as of equal significance with the other commandments. The church preachers simply do not recognize it, and only because they do not dare to confess it, try to conceal their failure to recognize it.

Such is the fourth method of answers.

The fifth method, the most refined, most popular, and most powerful one, consists in begging the question, in making it appear as though the question had long ago been decided by some one in an absolutely clear and satisfactory manner, and as though it were not worth while to speak of it. This method is employed by more or less cultivated ecclesiastic writers, that is, such as feel the laws of logic to be obligatory for them. Knowing that the contradiction which exists between Christ's teaching, which we profess in words, and the whole structure of our life cannot be solved with words, and that, by touching it, we can only make it more obvious, they with greater or lesser agility get around it, making it appear that the question about the connection of Christianity with violence has been decided or does not exist at all.[1]

The majority of the ecclesiastic critics of my book employ this method. I could adduce dozens of such criticisms, in which without exception one and the same thing is repeated: they speak of everything but the chief subject of the book. As a characteristic example of such criticisms, I shall quote an article by the famous, refined English writer and preacher, Farrar, a great master, like many learned theologians, of evasions and reticence. This article was printed in the American periodical, *Forum*, in October, 1888.

Having conscientiously given a short review of my book, Farrar says:

"Tolstóy came to the conclusion that a coarse deceit was palmed upon the world when these words were held by civil society to be compatible with war, courts of

[1] I know but one piece of writing, not a criticism in the strict sense of the word, but an article which treats the same subject, and which has my book in view, that departs from this common definition. It is Tróitski's pamphlet (Kazán) *The Sermon on the Mount.* The author obviously recognizes Christ's teaching in its real significance. He says that the commandment about non-resistance to evil means what it does, and the same is true of the commandment about swearing; he does not deny, as others do, the significance of Christ's teaching, but unfortunately he does not make from this recognition those inevitable deductions, which in our life beg for recognition in connection with such a comprehension of Christ's teaching. If it is not right to resist evil and to swear, every man will naturally ask: "How about military service?" And to this question the author gives no answer, though an answer is demanded. And if it cannot be answered, it is best not to speak at all, because silence produces error. —*Author's Note.*

justice, capital punishment, divorce, oaths, national prejudice, and indeed with most of the institutions of civil and social life. He now believes that the kingdom of God would come if all men kept these five commandments, . . . (1) Live in peace with all men; (2) be pure; (3) take no oaths; (4) never resist evil; (5) renounce national distinctions.

"Tolstóy," he says, "rejects the divine inspiration of the Old Testament and of the epistles; he rejects all the dogmas of the church, that of the atonement by blood, that of the Trinity, that of the descent of the Holy Ghost upon the apostles . . . and recognizes only the words and commandments of Christ.

"Is this interpretation of Christ a true one?" he asks. "Are all men bound, or is any man bound, to act as Tolstóy has taught, that is, to fulfil the five commandments of Christ?"

One just hopes that in reply to this essential question, which alone could have urged the man to write an article on the book, he will say that this interpretation of Christ's teaching is correct, or that it is not correct, and so will prove why, and will give another, a correct interpretation to the words which I interpret incorrectly. But nothing of the kind is done. Farrar only expresses his conviction that, "though actuated by the noblest sincerity, Tolstóy has been misled by partial and one-sided interpretations of the meaning of the Gospel and the mind and will of Christ."

No explanation is given as to what this error consists in, but all there is said, is:

"To enter into the proof of this is impossible in this article, for I have already exceeded the space at my command."

And he concludes with an easy mind:

"Meanwhile the reader who feels troubled lest it should be his duty also to forsake all conditions of his life, and to take up the position and work of a common labourer may rest for the present on the principle, *Securus judicat orbis terrarum.* With few and rare exceptions," he continues, "the whole of Christendom, from the days of the apostles down to our own, has come to the firm conclusion that it was the object of Christ to lay down great eternal principles, but not disturb the bases and revolutionize the institutions of all human society, which themselves rest on divine sanction as well as on inevitable conditions. Were it my object to prove how untenable is the doctrine of communism, based by Tolstóy upon the divine paradoxes (*sic !*), which can be interpreted on only historical principles in accordance with the whole method of the teaching of Jesus, it would require an ampler canvas than I have here at my disposal."

What a misfortune, — he has not any space! And, strange to say, space has been lacking for fifteen centuries, to prove that Christ, whom we profess, said something different from what He said. They could prove it, if they only wanted to. However, it does not pay to prove what everybody knows. It is enough to say: "*Securus judicat orbis terrarum.*"

And such are, without exception, all the criticisms of the cultivated believers, who, therefore, do not understand the perilousness of their position. The only way out for them is the hope that, by using the authority of the church, of antiquity, of holiness, they may be able to confuse the reader and draw him away from the thought of reading the Gospel for himself and of considering the question with his own mind. And in this they are successful. To whom, indeed, will it occur that all that which with such assurance and solemnity is repeated from century to century by all these archdeacons, bishops, archbishops, most holy synods, and Popes, is a base lie and calumny, which they foist on Christ in order to secure the money which they need for the purpose of leading a life of pleasure, while sitting on the backs of others, — a lie and a calumny, which is so obvious, especially now that the only possibility of continuing this lie consists in frightening men into belief by their assurance, their unscrupulousness? It is precisely the same that of late years has taken place in the Recruiting Sessions: at the head of the table, with the Mirror of Laws upon it, and beneath the full-sized portrait of the emperor, sit dignified old officials in their regalia, conversing freely and unreservedly, noting down, commanding, calling out. Here also, with the cross over his breast and in silk vestments, with his gray hair falling down straight over his scapulary, stands an imposing old man, the priest, in front of the pulpit, on which lies a gold cross and a gold-trimmed Gospel.

Iván Petróv is called out. A young man steps out. He is poorly and dirtily dressed and looks frightened, and the muscles of his face tremble, and his fugitive eyes sparkle, and in a faltering voice, almost in a whisper, he says: "I — according to the law I, a Christian — I cannot — "

"What is he muttering there?" impatiently asks the presiding officer, half-closing his eyes and listening, as he raises his head from the book.

"Speak louder!" shouts to him the colonel with the shining shoulder-straps.

"I — I — I — as a Christian — "

It finally turns out that the young man refuses to do military service, because he is a Christian.

"Talk no nonsense! Get your measure! Doctor, be so kind as to take his measure. Is he fit for the army?"

"He is."

"Reverend father, have him sworn in."

No one is confused; no one even pays any attention to what this frightened, pitiable young man is muttering.

"They all mutter something, but we have no time: we have to receive so many recruits."

The recruit wants to say something again.

"This is against Christ's law."

"Go, go, we know without you what is according to the law, — but you get out of here. Reverend father, admonish him. Next: Vasíli Nikítin."

And the trembling youth is taken away. And to whom — whether the janitor, or Vasíli Nikítin, who is being brought in, or any one else who witnessed this scene from the side — will it occur that those indistinct, short words of the youth, which were at once put out of court by the authorities, contain the truth, while those loud, solemn speeches of the self-possessed, calm officials and of the priest are a lie, a deception?

A similar impression is produced, not only by the articles of a Farrar but by all those solemn sermons, articles, and books, which appear on all sides, the moment the truth peeps out and arraigns the ruling lie. Immediately there begin long, clever, elegant conversations or writings about questions which touch closely upon the subject with a shrewd reticence concerning the question itself.

In this consists the fifth and most effective means for removing the contradiction in which the ecclesiastic Christianity has placed itself by professing Christ in words and denying His teaching in life, and teaching the same to others.

Those who justify themselves by the first method, asserting outright and rudely that Christ has permitted violence, — wars, murder, — withdraw themselves from Christ's teaching; those who defend themselves according to the second, the third, and the fourth methods get themselves entangled, and it is easy to point out their untruth; but these last, who do not discuss, who do not condescend to discuss, but hide themselves behind their greatness and make it appear that all this has been decided long ago by them, or by somebody else, and that it no longer is subject to any doubt, seem invulnerable, and they will be invulnerable so long as people will remain under the influence of hypnotic suggestion, which is induced in them by governments and churches, and will not shake it off.

Such was the attitude which the ecclesiastics, that is, those who profess Christ's faith, assumed toward me. Nor could they have acted otherwise: they are bound by the contradiction in which they live,—the faith in the divinity of the teacher and the unbelief in His clearest words,—from which they must in some way extricate themselves, and so it was not possible to expect from them any free opinion concerning the essence of the question, concerning that change in the lives of men which results from the application of Christ's teaching to the existing order. Such opinions I expected from the freethinking lay critics, who are in no way bound to Christ's teaching and who can look upon it without restraint. I expected that the freethinking writers would look upon Christ not only as the establisher of a religion of worship and personal salvation (as which the ecclesiastics understand him), but, to express myself in their language, as a reformer, who destroys the old, and gives the new foundations of life, the reform of which is not yet accomplished, but continues until the present.

Such a view of Christ and His teaching results from my book, but, to my surprise, out of the large number of criticisms upon my book, there was *not one*, either Russian or foreign, which treated the subject from the same side from which it is expounded in my book, that is, which looked upon Christ's teaching as a philosophical, moral, and social doctrine (again to speak in the language of the learned). This was not the case in a single criticism.

The Russian lay critics, who understood my book in

such a way that all its contents reduced themselves to non-resistance to evil, and who understood the teaching about non-resistance to evil itself (apparently for convenience of refutal) as meaning that it prohibited any struggle against evil, furiously attacked this teaching and very successfully proved for the period of several years that Christ's teaching was incorrect, since it taught us not to resist evil. Their refutals of this supposed teaching of Christ were the more successful, since they knew in advance that their views could neither be overthrown nor corrected, because the censorship, having failed to sanction the book itself, did not sanction the articles in its defence either.

What is remarkable in connection with the matter is this, that with us, where not a word may be said about the Holy Scripture without a prohibition by the censorship, the clearly and directly expressed commandment of Matt. v. 39 has for several years been openly contorted, criticized, condemned, and ridiculed in all the periodicals.

The Russian lay critics, who evidently did not know all that had been done in the development of the question as to non-resistance to evil, and who at times even seemed to assume that I personally invented the rule of not resisting evil with violence, attacked the idea itself, rejecting and contorting it, and with much fervour advancing arguments which have long ago been analyzed from every side and rejected, proved that a man is obliged (with violence) to defend all the insulted and the oppressed, and that, therefore, the doctrine about not resisting evil with violence is immoral.

The whole significance of Christ's preaching presented itself to the Russian critics as though maliciously interfering with a certain activity, which was directed against what they at a given moment considered to be an evil, so that it turned out that the principle of not resisting evil with violence was attacked by two opposite camps, —

by the conservatives, because this principle interfered with their activity of resisting the evil which was produced by the revolutionists, and with their persecutions and executions; and by the revolutionists, because this principle interfered with the resistance to the evil which was produced by the conservatives, and with the overthrow of the conservatives. The conservatives were provoked, because the doctrine of non-resistance to evil interfered with the energetic suppression of the revolutionary elements, who are likely to ruin the welfare of the nation; while the revolutionists were provoked, because the doctrine of non-resistance to evil interfered with the overthrow of the conservatives, who were ruining the well-being of the nation.

What is remarkable is, that the revolutionists attacked the principle of non-resistance, although it is most terrible and most dangerous for every despotism, because ever since the beginning of the world the opposite principle of the necessity of resisting evil with violence has been lying at the basis of all violence, from the Inquisition to the Schlüsselburg Fortress.

Besides, the Russian critics pointed out that the application to life of the commandment about non-resistance to evil would turn humanity away from the path of civilization, on which it was marching now; but the path of civilization, on which the European civilization is marching, is, in their opinion, the one on which all humanity must always march.

Such was the chief character of the Russian criticisms.

The foreign critics proceeded from the same bases, but their reviews of my book differed from those of the Russian critics not only in a lesser degree of irritability and a greater degree of culture, but also in the essence of the matter.

In discussing my book and the Gospel teaching in general, as it is expressed in the Sermon on the Mount, the foreign critics asserted that such a teaching is really not Christian (Christian in their opinion is Catholicism and Protestantism), and that the doctrine of the Sermon on the Mount is only a series of very charming, impracticable reveries "*du charmant docteur*," as Renan used to say, which were good enough for the naïve and half-wild inhabitants of Galilee, who lived eighteen hundred years ago, and for the Russian peasants, Syutáev and Bondarév, and the Russian mystic, Tolstóy, but can in no way be applied to the high degree of European culture.

The foreign lay critics tried, in a refined manner, without giving me any offence, to let me know that my opinion that humanity can be guided by such a naïve teaching as the Sermon on the Mount is due partly to my ignorance, lack of acquaintance with history, lack of knowledge of all those vain attempts to realize in life the principles of the Sermon on the Mount, which have been made in history, and have led to nothing, thanks to ignorance concerning the whole significance of that high degree of culture on which European civilization now stands, with its Krupp guns, smokeless powder, the colonization of Africa, the government of Ireland, parliaments, journalism, strikes, constitutions, and Eiffel Tower.

Thus wrote Vogüé, and Leroy Beaulieu, and Matthew Arnold, and the American writer Savage, and Ingersoll, a popular American preacher of free thought, and many others.

"Christ's teaching is no good, because it does not harmonize with our industrial age," naïvely says Ingersoll, thus expressing with absolute precision and naïveté what the refined and cultured men of our time think about Christ's teaching. The teaching is no good for our industrial age, as though the existence of the industrial age is something sacred which must not and cannot be changed. It is something like what drunkards would do, if, in response to advice about how to get themselves into a sober state, they should reply that the advice is out of place in connection with their present alcoholic state.

The discussions of all the lay writers, both Russian and foreign, no matter how different their tone and the manner of their arguments may be, in reality reduce themselves to one and the same strange misunderstanding, namely, that Christ's teaching, one of the consequences of which is non-resistance to evil, is useless to us, because it demands that our life be changed.

Christ's teaching is useless, because, if it were put into practice, our life could not continue; in other words,— if we began to live well, as Christ has taught us, we could not continue to live badly, as we live and are accustomed to live. The question of non-resistance to evil is not discussed, and the very mention of the fact that the demand for non-resistance to evil enters into Christ's teaching is considered a sufficient proof of the inapplicability of the whole teaching.

And yet, it would seem, it is indispensable to point out some kind of a solution to this question, because it lies at the foundation of nearly all affairs which interest us.

The question consists in this: how are we to harmonize the conflicts of men, when some consider an evil what others consider to be good, and vice versa? And so, to consider that an evil which I consider an evil, although my adversary may consider it good, is no answer. There can be but two answers: either we have to find a true and indisputable criterion of what an evil is, or we must not resist evil with violence.

The first solution has been tried since the beginning of historical times, and, as we all know, has so far led to no satisfactory results.

The second answer, not to resist with violence what we consider evil, so long as we have found no common criterion, was proposed by Christ.

It may be found that Christ's answer is not correct; it may be possible to put in its place another, better answer, by finding a criterion which would indubitably and simultaneously for all define the evil; we may simply not recognize the essence of the question, as it is not recognized by the savage nations, — but it is impossible, as the learned critics of the Christian teaching do, to make it appear that such a question does not at all exist, or that the relegation of the right to determine the evil and resist it with violence to certain persons or assemblies of men (much less, if we are these men), solves the question; whereas we all know that such a relegation does not at all solve the question, since there are some people who do not recognize this right as belonging to certain people or to assemblies of men.

But it is this recognition that what to us appears evil is evil, or an absolute failure to comprehend the question, which serves as a foundation for the judgment of the lay critics concerning the Christian teaching, so that the opinions concerning my book, both of the ecclesiastic and the lay critics, showed me that the majority of men absolutely fail to comprehend, not only Christ's very teaching, but even those questions to which it serves as an answer.

III.

THUS, both the information received by me after the publication of my book, as to how the Christian teaching in its direct and true sense has without interruption been understood by the minority of men, and the criticisms upon it, both the ecclesiastic and the lay criticisms, which denied the possibility of understanding Christ's teaching in the direct sense, convinced me that, while, on the one hand, the true comprehension of this teaching never ceased for the minority, and became clearer and clearer to them, on the other hand, for the majority, its meaning became more and more obscure, finally reaching such a degree of obscuration that men no longer comprehend the simplest propositions, which are expressed in the Gospel in the simplest words.

The failure to comprehend Christ's teaching in its true, simple, and direct sense in our time, when the light of this teaching has penetrated all the darkest corners of human consciousness; when, as Christ has said, that which He has spoken in the ear, they now proclaim upon the housetops; when this teaching permeates all the sides of human life, — the domestic, the economic, the civil, the political, and the international, — this failure to comprehend would be incomprehensible, if there were no causes for it.

One of these causes is this, that both the believers and the unbelievers are firmly convinced that Christ's teaching has been comprehended by them long ago, and so completely, indubitably, and finally, that there can be no other meaning in it than the one they ascribe to it. This cause is due to the duration of the tradition of the false comprehension, and so of the failure to understand the true teaching.

The most powerful stream of water cannot add a drop to a vessel that is full.

It is possible to explain the most intricate matters to a man of very hard comprehension, so long as he has not formed any idea about them; but it is impossible to explain the simplest thing to a very clever man, if he is firmly convinced that he knows, and, besides, incontestably knows, what has been transmitted to him.

The Christian teaching presents itself to the men of our world precisely as such a teaching, which has for a long time and in a most indubitable manner been known in its minutest details, and which cannot be comprehended in any other manner than it now is.

Christianity is now understood by those who profess the church doctrines as a supernatural, miraculous revelation concerning everything which is given in the symbol of faith, and by those who do not believe, as an obsolete manifestation of humanity's need of believing in something supernatural, as a historical phenomenon, which is completely expressed in Catholicism, Orthodoxy, Protestantism, and which has no longer any vital meaning for us. For the believers the meaning of the teaching is concealed by the church, for unbelievers by science.

I shall begin with the first:

Eighteen hundred years ago there appeared in the pagan Roman world a strange, new teaching, which resembled nothing which preceded it, and which was ascribed to the man Christ.

This new teaching was absolutely new, both in form and in contents, for the European world, in the midst of which it arose, and especially in the Roman world, where it was preached and became diffused.

Amidst the elaborateness of the religious rules of Judaism, where, according to Isaiah, there was rule upon rule, and amidst the Roman legislation, which was worked out to a great degree of perfection, there appeared a teaching which not only denied all the divinities, — every fear of them, every divination and faith in them, — but also all human institutions and every necessity for them. In the place of all the rules of former faiths, this teaching advanced only the model of an inner perfection of truth and of love in the person of Christ, and the consequences of this inner perfection, attainable by men, — the external perfection, as predicted by the prophets, — the kingdom of God, in which all men will stop warring, and all will be taught by God and united in love, and the lion will lie with the lamb. In place of the threats of punishments for the non-compliance with the rules, which were made by the former laws, both religious and political, in place of the enticement of rewards for fulfilling them, this teaching called men to itself only by its being the truth. John vii. 17: "If any man wants to know of this doctrine, whether it be of God, let him fulfil it." John viii. 46: "If I say the truth, why do ye not believe me?" Why do you seek to kill a man who has told you the truth? The truth alone will free you. God must be professed in truth only. The whole teaching will be revealed and will be made clear by the spirit of truth. Do what I say, and you will know whether what I say is true.

No proofs were given of the teaching, except the truth, except the correspondence of the teaching with the truth. The whole teaching consisted in the knowledge of the truth and in following it, in a greater and ever greater approximation to it, in matters of life. According to this teaching, there are no acts which can justify a man, make him righteous; there is only the model of truth which attracts all hearts, for the inner perfection — in the person of Christ, and for the outer — in the realization of the kingdom of God. The fulfilment of the teaching is only in the motion along a given path, in the approximation to perfection, — the inner, — the imitation of Christ, and the outer, — the establishment of the kingdom of God. A man's greater or lesser good, according to this teaching, depends, not on the degree of perfection which he attains, but on the greater or lesser acceleration of motion.

The motion toward perfection of the publican, of Zacchæus, of the harlot, of the robber on the cross, is, according to this teaching, a greater good than the immovable righteousness of the Pharisee. A sheep gone astray is more precious than ninety-nine who have not. The prodigal son, the lost coin which is found again, is more precious, more loved by God than those who were not lost.

Every condition is, according to this teaching, only a certain step on the road toward the unattainable inner and outer perfection, and so has no meaning. The good is only in the motion toward perfection; but the stopping at any stage whatsoever is only a cessation of the good.

"Let not thy left hand know what thy right hand doeth," and "No man, having put his hand to the plough, and looking back, is fit for the kingdom of God." "Rejoice not, that the spirits are subject unto you; but rather rejoice, because your names are written in heaven."

"Be ye perfect as your Father which is in Heaven is perfect." "Seek the kingdom of God and His righteousness."

The fulfilment of the teaching is only in unceasing motion, — in the attainment of a higher and ever higher truth, and in an ever greater realization of the same in oneself by means of an ever increasing love, and outside of oneself by an ever greater realization of the kingdom of God.

It is evident that, having appeared in the midst of the Jewish and the pagan world, this teaching could not have been accepted by the majority of men, who lived a life entirely different from the one which this teaching demanded; and that it could not even be comprehended in its full significance by those who accepted it, as it was diametrically opposed to their former views.

Only by a series of misconceptions, blunders, one-sided explanations, corrected and supplemented by generations of men, was the meaning of the Christian teaching made more and more clear to men. The Christian world-conception affected the Jewish and the pagan conceptions, and the Jewish and pagan conceptions affected the Christian world-conception. And the Christian, as being vital, penetrated the reviving Jewish and pagan conceptions more and more, and stood forth more and more clearly, freeing itself from the false admixture, which was imposed upon it. Men came to comprehend the meaning better and better, and more and more realized it in life.

The longer humanity lived, the more and more was the meaning of Christianity made clear to it, as indeed it could not and cannot be otherwise with any teaching about life.

The subsequent generations corrected the mistakes of their predecessors, and more and more approached the comprehension of its true meaning. Thus it has been since the earliest times of Christianity. And here, in the earliest times, there appeared men, who began to assert that the meaning which they ascribed to the teaching was the only true one, and that as a proof of it served the supernatural phenomena which confirmed the correctness of their comprehension.

It was this that was the chief cause, at first, of the failure to comprehend the teaching, and later, of its complete corruption.

It was assumed that Christ's teaching was not transmitted to men like any other truth, but in a special, supernatural manner, so that the truth of the comprehension of the teaching was not proved by the correspondence of what was transmitted with the demands of reason and of the whole human nature, but by the miraculousness of the transmission, which served as an incontrovertible proof of the correctness of the comprehension. This proposition arose from a lack of comprehension, and its consequence was an impossibility of comprehending.

This began with the very first times, when the teaching was still understood incompletely and often perversely, as we may see from the gospels and from the Acts. The less the teaching was understood, the more obscurely did it present itself, and the more necessary were the external proofs of its veracity. The proposition about not doing unto another what one does not wish to have done to oneself did not need any proof by means of miracles, and there was no need for demanding belief in this proposition, because it is convincing in itself, in that it corresponds to both man's reason and nature, but the proposition as to Christ being God had to be proved by means of miracles, which are absolutely incomprehensible.

The more obscure the comprehension of Christ's teaching was, the more miraculous elements were mixed in with it; and the more miraculous elements were mixed in, the more did the teaching deviate from its meaning and become obscure; and the more it deviated from its meaning and became obscure, the more strongly it was necessary to assert one's infallibility, and the less did the teaching become comprehensible.

We can see from the gospels, the Acts, the epistles, how from the earliest times the failure to comprehend the teaching called forth the necessity of proving its truth by means of the miraculous and the incomprehensible.

According to the Acts, this began with the meeting of the disciples at Jerusalem, who assembled to settle the question which had arisen as to baptizing or not baptizing the uncircumcised who were still eating meats offered to idols.

The very putting of the question showed that those who were discussing it did not understand the teaching of Christ, who rejected all external rites — ablutions, purifications, fasts, Sabbaths. It says directly that not the things which enter a man's mouth, but those which come out of his heart, defile him, and so the question as to the baptism of the uncircumcised could have arisen only among men who loved their teacher, dimly felt His greatness, but still very obscurely comprehended the teaching itself. And so it was.

In proportion as the members of the assembly did not understand the teaching, they needed an external confirmation of their incomplete understanding. And so, to solve the question, the very putting of which shows the failure to comprehend the teaching, the strange words, "It has seemed good to the Holy Ghost, and to us," which were in an external manner to confirm the justice of certain establishments, and which have caused so much evil, were, as described in the Book of Acts, for the first time pronounced at this meeting, that is, it was asserted that the justice of what they decreed was testified to by the miraculous participation of the Holy Ghost, that is, of God, in this solution. But the assertion that the Holy Ghost, that is, God, spoke through the apostles, had again to be proved. And for this it was necessary to assert that on the day of Pentecost the Holy Ghost came down in the shape of tongues of fire on those who asserted this. (In the description the descent of the Holy Ghost precedes the assembly, but the Acts were written down much later than either.) But the descent of the Holy Ghost had to be confirmed for those who had not seen the tongues of fire (though it is incomprehensible why a tongue of fire burning above a man's head should prove that what a man says is an indisputable truth), and there were needed new miracles, cures, resurrections, putting to death, and all those offensive miracles, with which the Acts are filled, and which not only can never convince a man of the truth of the Christian teaching, but can only repel him from it. The consequence of such a method of confirmation was this, that the more these confirmations of the truth by means of stories of miracles heaped up upon one another, the more did the teaching itself depart from its original meaning, and the less comprehensible did it become.

Thus it has been since the earliest times, and it has been increasingly so all the time, until it logically reached in our time the dogmas of the transubstantiation and of the infallibility of the Pope, or of the bishops, or of the writings, that is, something absolutely incomprehensible, which has reached the point of absurdity and the demand for a blind faith, not in God, not in Christ, not even in the teaching, but in a person, as is the case in Catholicism, or in several persons, as in Orthodoxy, or in a book, as in Protestantism. The more Christianity became diffused, and the greater was the crowd of unprepared men which it embraced, the less it was understood, the more definitely was the infallibility of the comprehension asserted, and the less did it become possible to understand the true meaning of the teaching. As early as the time of Constantine the whole comprehension of the teaching was reduced to a résumé, confirmed by the worldly power, — a résumé of disputes which took place in a council, — to a symbol of faith, in which it says, I believe in so and so, and so and so, and finally, in the one, holy, catholic, and apostolic church, that is, in the infallibility of those persons who call themselves the church, so that everything was reduced to this, that a man no longer believes in God, nor in Christ, as they have been revealed to him, but in what the church commands him to believe.

But the church is holy, — the church was founded by Christ. God could not have left it to men to give an arbitrary interpretation to His teaching, — and so He established the church. All these expositions are to such an extent unjust and bold that one feels some compunction in overthrowing them.

There is nothing but the assertion of the churches to show that God or Christ founded anything resembling what the churchmen understand by church.

In the Gospel there is an indication against the church, as an external authority, and this indication is most obvious and clear in that place where it says that Christ's disciples should not call any one teachers and fathers. But nowhere is there anything said about the establishment of what the churchmen call a church.

In the gospels the word "church" is used twice,— once, in the sense of an assembly of men deciding a dispute; the other time, in connection with the obscure words about the rock, Peter, and the gates of hell. From these two mentions of the word "church," which has the meaning of nothing but an assembly, they deduce what we now understand by the word "church."

But Christ could certainly not have founded a church, that is, what we now understand by the word, because neither in Christ's words, nor in the conceptions of the men of that time, was there anything resembling the concept of a church, as we know it now, with its sacraments, its hierarchy, and, above all, its assertion of infallibility.

The fact that men named what was formed later by the same word which Christ had used in respect to something else, does in no way give them the right to assert that Christ established the one, true church.

Besides, if Christ had really founded such an institution as the church, on which the whole doctrine and the whole faith are based, He would most likely have expressed this establishment in such definite and clear words, and would have given the one, true church, outside of the stories about the miracles, which are used in connection with every superstition, such signs as to leave no doubts concerning its authenticity; there is nothing of the kind, but there are now, as there have been, all kinds of institutions which, each of them, call themselves the one, true church.

The Catholic catechism says: "*L'église est la société de fidèles établie par notre Seigneur Jésus-Christ, répandue sur toute la terre et soumise à l'autorité des pasteurs légitimes, principalement notre Saint Père — le Pape,*" meaning by "*pasteurs légitimes*" a human institution, which has the Pope at its head and which is composed of certain persons who are connected among themselves by a certain organization.

The Orthodox catechism says: "The church is a society, established by Jesus Christ upon earth, united among themselves into one whole by the one, divine teaching and the sacraments, under the guidance and management of the God-established hierarchy," meaning by "God-established hierarchy" the Greek hierarchy, which is composed of such and such persons, who are to be found in such and such places.

The Lutheran catechism says: "The church is holy Christianity, or an assembly of all believers, under Christ, their chief, in which the Holy Ghost through the Gospel and the sacraments offers, communicates, and secures divine salvation," meaning, by this, that the Catholic Church has gone astray and has fallen away, and that the true tradition is preserved in Lutheranism.

For the Catholics the divine church coincides with the Roman hierarchy and the Pope. For the Greek Orthodox the divine church coincides with the establishment of the Eastern and the Russian Church.[1] For the Lutherans

[1] Khomyakóv's definition of the church, which has some currency among Russians, does not mend matters, if we recognize with Khomyakóv that the Orthodox is the one true church. Khomyakóv asserts that the church is an assembly of men (of all, both the clergy and the congregation) united in love, and that the truth is revealed only to those who are united in love (Let us love one another, so that in

the divine church coincides with the assembly of men who recognize the Bible and Luther's catechism.

Speaking of the origin of Christianity, men who belong to one or the other of the existing churches generally use the word "church" in the singular, as though there has been but one church. But this is quite untrue. The church, as an institution which asserts of itself that it is in possession of the unquestionable truth, appeared only when it was not alone, but there were at least two of them.

So long as the believers agreed among themselves, and the assembly was one, it had no need of asserting that it was the church. Only when the believers divided into opposite parties, which denied one another, did there appear the necessity for each side to assert its authenticity, ascribing infallibility to itself. The concept of the one church arose only from this, that, when two sides disagreed and quarrelled, each of them, calling the other a heresy, recognized only its own as the infallible church.

If we know that there was a church, which in the year 51 decided to receive the uncircumcised, this church made its appearance only because there was an-

agreement of thought, and so forth), and that such a church is the one which, in the first place, recognizes the Nicene symbol, and, in the second, after the division of the churches, does not recognize the Pope and the new dogmas. But with such a definition of the church there appears a still greater difficulty in harmonizing, as Khomyakóv wants to, the church which is united in love with the church which recognizes the Nicene symbol and the justice of Photius. Thus Khomyakóv's assertion that this church, which is united in love and so is holy, is the church as professed by the Greek hierarchy, is still more arbitrary than the assertions of the Catholics and of the ancient Orthodox. If we admit the concept of the church in the sense which Khomyakóv gives to it, that is, as an assembly of men united in love and in truth, then everything a man can say in relation to this assembly is, that it is very desirable to be a member of such an assembly, if such exists, that is, to be in love and truth; but there are no external signs by which it would be possible to count oneself or another in with this holy assembly, or to exclude oneself from it, as no external institution can correspond to this concept. — *Author's Note.*

other church, that of the Judaizing, which had decided not to receive the uncircumcised.

If there now is a Catholic Church, which asserts its infallibility, it does this only because there are the Græco-Russian, Orthodox, Lutheran Churches, each of which asserts its own infallibility, and thus rejects all the other churches. Thus the one church is only a fantastic conception, which has not the slightest sign of reality.

As an actual, historical phenomenon there have existed only many assemblies of men, each of which has asserted that it is the one church, established by Christ, and that all the others, which call themselves churches, are heresies and schisms.

The catechisms of the most widely diffused churches, the Catholic, the Orthodox, and the Lutheran, say so outright.

In the Catholic catechism it says: "*Quels sont ceux, qui sont hors de l'église? Les infidèles, les hérétiques, les schismatiques.*" As schismatics are regarded the so-called Orthodox. The Lutherans are considered to be heretics; thus, according to the Catholic catechism, the Catholics alone are in the church.

In the so-called Orthodox catechism it says: "By the one church of Christ is meant nothing but the Orthodox, which remains in complete agreement with the œcumenical church. But as to the Roman Church and the other confessions" (the church does not even mention the Lutherans and others), "they cannot be referred to the one, true church, since they have themselves separated from it."

According to this definition the Catholics and Lutherans are outside the church, and in the church are only the Orthodox.

But the Lutheran catechism runs as follows: "*Die wahre Kirche wird daran erkannt, dass in ihr das Wort Gottes lauter und rein ohne Menschenzusätze gelehrt und die Sacramente treu nach Christi Einsetzung gewahrt werden.*"

According to this definition, all those who have added anything to the teaching of Christ and the apostles, as the Catholic and Greek Churches have done, are outside the church. And in the church are only the Protestants.

The Catholics assert that the Holy Ghost has uninterruptedly operated in their hierarchy; the Orthodox assert that the same Holy Ghost has operated in their hierarchy; the Arians asserted that the Holy Ghost operated in their hierarchy (this they asserted with as much right as the now ruling churches assert it); the Protestants of every description, Lutherans, Reformers, Presbyterians, Methodists, Swedenborgians, Mormons, assert that the Holy Ghost operates only in their assemblies.

If the Catholics assert that the Holy Ghost during the division of the Arian and of the Greek Churches left the apostatizing churches and remained only in the one, true church, the Protestants of every denomination can with the same right assert that during the separation of their church from the Catholic the Holy Ghost left the Catholic Church and passed over to the one which they recognize. And so they do.

Every church deduces its profession through an uninterrupted tradition from Christ and the apostles. And, indeed, every Christian confession, arising from Christ, must have inevitably reached the present generation through a certain tradition. But this does not prove that any one of these traditions, excluding all the others, is indubitably the correct one.

Every twig on the tree goes uninterruptedly back to the root; but the fact that every twig comes from the same root does in no way prove that there is but one twig. The same is true of the churches. Every church offers precisely the same proofs of its succession and even of the miracles in favour of its own authenticity; thus there is but one strict and precise definition of what the church is (not as something fantastic, which we should like it to be, but as something which in reality exists), and this is: the church is an assembly of men, who assert that they, and they only, are in the full possession of the truth.

It was these assemblies, which later on, with the aid of the support of the temporal power, passed into mighty institutions, that were the chief impediments in the dissemination of the true comprehension of Christ's teaching.

Nor could it be otherwise: the chief peculiarity of Christ's teaching, as distinguished from all the former teachings, consisted in this, that the men who accepted it tried more and more to understand and fulfil the teaching, whereas the church doctrine asserted the full and final comprehension and fulfilment of this teaching.

However strange it may seem to us people educated in the false doctrine about the church as a Christian institution, and in the contempt for heresy, it was only in what is called heresy that there was true motion, that is, true Christianity, and it ceased to be such when it stopped its motion in these heresies and became itself arrested in the immovable forms of the church.

Indeed, what is a heresy? Read all the theological works which treat about heresies, a subject which is the first to present itself for definition, since every theology speaks of the true teaching amidst the surrounding false teachings, that is, heresies, and you will nowhere find anything resembling a definition of heresy.

As a specimen of that complete absence of any semblance of a definition of what is understood by the word "heresy" may serve the opinion on this subject expressed by the learned historian of Christianity, E. de Pressensé, in his *Histoire du Dogme*, with the epigraph

Ubi Christus, ibi Ecclesia" (Paris, 1869). This is what he says in his introduction: "*Je sais que l'on nous conteste le droit de califier ainsi,*" that is, to call heresies "*les tendances qui furent si vivement combattues par les premiers Pères. La désignation même d'hérésie semble une atteinte portée à la liberté de conscience et de pensée. Nous ne pouvons partager ces scrupules, car ils n'iraient à rien moins qu'à enlever au christianisme tout caractère distinctif.*"

And after saying that after Constantine the church actually misused its power in defining the dissenters as heretics and persecuting them, he passes judgment on the early times and says:

"*L'église est une libre association; il y a tout profit à se séparer d'elle. La polémique contre l'erreur n'a d'autres resources que la pensée et le sentiment. Un type doctrinal uniforme n'a pas encore été élaboré; les divergences secondaires se produisent en Orient et en Occident avec une entière liberté, la théologie n'est point liée à d'invariables formules. Si au sein de cette diversité apparait un fond commun de croyances, n'est-on pas en droit d'y voir non pas un système formulé et composé par les représentants d'une autorité d'école, mais la foi elle même, dans son instinct le plus sûr et sa manifestation la plus spontanée? Si cette même unanimité qui se revèle dans les croyances essentielles, se retrouve pour repousser telles ou telles tendances, ne seront-nous pas en droit de conclure que ces tendances étaient en désaccord flagrant avec les principes fondamentaux du christianisme? Cette présomption ne se transformera-t-elle pas en certitude si nous reconnaissons dans la doctrine universellement repoussée par l'église les traits caractéristiques de l'une des religions du passé? Pour dire que le gnosticisme ou l'ebionitisme sont les formes légitimes de la pensée chrétienne, il faut dire hardiment qu'il n'y a pas de pensée chrétienne, ni de caractère specifique qui la fasse reconnaître. Sous prétexte de l'élargir on la dissent. Personne, au temps de Platon, n'eut osé de couvrir de son nom une doctrine qui n'eut pas fait place à la théorie des idées, et l'on eut excité les justes moqueries de la Grèce, en voulant faire d'Epicure ou de Zénon un disciple de l'Académie. Reconnaissons donc que s'il existe une religion et une doctrine qui s'appelle le christianisme elle peut avoir ses hérésies."*

The whole discussion of the author reduces itself to this, that every opinion which is not in agreement with a code of dogmas professed by us at a given time is a heresy; but at a given time and in a given place people profess something, and this profession of something in some place cannot be a criterion of the truth.

Everything reduces itself to this, that "*Ubi Christus, ibi Ecclesia;*" but Christ is where we are. Every so-called heresy, by recognizing as the truth what it professes, can in a similar manner find in the history of the churches a consistent explanation of what it professes, using for itself all the arguments of De Pressensé and calling only its own confession truly Christian, precisely what all the heresies have been doing.

The only definition of heresy (the word αἵρεσις means *part*) is the name given by an assembly of men to every judgment which rejects part of the teaching, as professed by the assembly. A more particular meaning, which more frequently than any other is ascribed to heresy, is that of an opinion which rejects the church doctrine, as established and supported by the worldly power.

There is a remarkable, little known, very large work (*Unpartheyische Kirchen und Ketzer-Historia*, 1729), by Gottfried Arnold, which treats directly on this subject and which shows all the illegality, arbitrariness, senselessness, and cruelty of using the word "heresy" in the sense of rejection. This book is an attempt at describing the history of Christianity in the form of a history of the heresies

In the introduction the author puts a number of questions: (1) regarding those who make heretics (*von den Ketzermachern selbst*); (2) concerning those who were made heretics; (3) concerning the subjects of heresy; (4) concerning the method of making heretics, and (5) concerning the aims and consequences of making heretics.

In connection with each of these points he puts dozens of questions, answers to which he later gives from the works of well-known theologians, but he chiefly leaves it to the reader himself to make the deduction from the exposition of the whole book. I shall quote the following as samples of these questions, which partly contain the answers. In reference to the fourth point, as to how heretics are made, he says in one of his questions (the seventh): "Does not all history show that the greatest makers of heretics and the masters of this work were those same wise men from whom the Father has hidden His secrets, that is, the hypocrites, Pharisees, and lawyers, or entirely godless and corrupt people?" Questions 20 and 21: "And did not, in the most corrupt times of Christianity, the hypocrites and envious people reject those very men who were particularly endowed by God with great gifts, and who in the time of pure Christianity would have been highly esteemed? And, on the contrary, would not these men, who during the decadence of Christianity elevated themselves above everything and recognized themselves to be the teachers of the purest Christianity, have been recognized, in apostolic times, as the basest heretics and antichristians?"

Expressing in these questions this thought, among others, that the verbal expression of the essence of faith, which was demanded by the church, and a departure from which was considered a heresy, could never completely cover the world-conception of the believer, and that, therefore, the demand for an expression of faith by means of particular words was the cause of heresy, he says, in Questions 21 and 33:

"And if the divine acts and thoughts present themselves to a man as so great and profound that he does not find corresponding words in which to express them, must he be recognized as a heretic, if he is not able precisely to express his ideas? And is not this true, that in the early times there was no heresy, because the Christians did not judge one another according to verbal expressions, but according to the heart and acts, in connection with a complete liberty of expression, without fear of being recognized as a heretic? Was it not a very common and easy method with the church," he says in Question 21, "when the clergy wanted to get rid of a person or ruin him, to make him suspected as regards his doctrine and to throw over him the cloak of heresy, and thus to condemn and remove him?

"Though it is true that amidst the so-called heretics there were errors and sins, yet it is not less true and obvious from the numberless examples here adduced" (that is, in the history of the church and of heresy), he says farther on, "that there has not been a single sincere and conscientious man with some standing who has not been ruined by the churchmen out of envy or for other causes."

Thus, nearly two hundred years ago, was the significance of heresy understood, and yet this conception continues to exist until the present time. Nor can it fail to exist, so long as there is a concept of the church. Heresy is the reverse of the church. Where there is the church, there is also heresy. The church is an assembly of men asserting that they are in possession of the indisputable truth. Heresy is the opinion of people who do not recognize the indisputableness of the church truth.

Heresy is a manifestation of motion in the church, an attempt at destroying the ossified assertion of the church, an attempt at a living comprehension of the teaching. Every step of moving forward, of comprehending and fulfilling the teaching has been accomplished by the heretics;

such heretics were Tertullian, and Origen, and Augustine, and Luther, and Huss, and Savonarola, and Chelcický, and others. Nor could it be otherwise.

A disciple of Christ, whose teaching consists in an eternally greater and greater comprehension of the teaching and in a greater and greater fulfilment of it, in a motion toward perfection, cannot, for the very reason that he is a disciple of Christ, assert concerning himself or concerning any one else, that he fully understands Christ's teaching and fulfils it; still less can he assert this concerning any assembly.

No matter at what stage of comprehension and perfection a disciple of Christ may be, he always feels the insufficiency of his comprehension and of his fulfilment, and always strives after a greater comprehension and fulfilment. And so the assertion about myself or about an assembly, that I, or we, possess the complete comprehension of Christ's teaching, and completely fulfil it, is a renunciation of the spirit of Christ's teaching.

No matter how strange this may seem, the churches, as churches, have always been, and cannot help but be, institutions that are not only foreign, but even directly hostile, to Christ's teaching. With good reason Voltaire called the church "*l'infâme;*" with good reason all, or nearly all, the Christian so-called sects have recognized the church to be that whore of whom Revelation prophesies; with good reason the history of the church is the history of the greatest cruelties and horrors.

The churches, as churches, are not certain institutions which have at their base the Christian principle, though slightly deviated from the straight path, as some think; the churches, as churches, as assemblies, which assert their infallibility, are antichristian institutions. Between the churches, as churches, and Christianity there is not only nothing in common but the name, but they are two absolutely divergent and mutually hostile principles. One is pride, violence, self-assertion, immobility, and death; the other is meekness, repentance, humility, motion, and life.

It is impossible at the same time to serve both masters, — one or the other has to be chosen.

The servants of the churches of all denominations have tried, especially of late, to appear as advocates of motion in Christianity; they make concessions, wish to mend the abuses which have stolen into the church, and say that for the sake of the abuses we ought not to deny the principle of the Christian church itself, which alone can unite all men and be a mediator between men and God. But all this is not true. The churches have not only never united, but have always been one of the chief causes of the disunion of men, of the hatred of one another, of wars, slaughters, inquisitions, nights of St. Bartholomew, and so forth, and the churches never serve as mediators between men and God, which is, indeed, unnecessary and is directly forbidden by Christ, who has revealed the teaching directly to every man, and they put up dead forms in the place of God, and not only fail to reveal God to man, but even conceal Him from them. Churches which have arisen from the failure to comprehend, and which maintain this lack of comprehension by their immobility, cannot help persecuting and oppressing every comprehension of the teaching. They try to conceal this, but this is impossible, because every motion forward along the path indicated by Christ destroys their existence.

As one hears and reads the articles and sermons, in which the church writers of modern times of all denominations speak of Christian truths and virtues, as one hears and reads these clever discussions, admonitions, confessions, which have been worked out by the ages, and which sometimes look very much as though they were sincere, one is prepared to doubt that the churches could be hostile to Christianity: "It certainly cannot be that these people, who have produced such men as Chrysostom, Fénelon, Butler, and other preachers of Christianity, should be hostile to it." One feels like saying: "The churches may have deviated from Christianity, may be in error, but cannot be hostile to it." But as one looks at the fruits, in order to judge the tree, as Christ has taught us to do, and sees that their fruits have been evil, that the consequence of their activity has been the distortion of Christianity, one cannot help but feel that, no matter how good the men have been, the cause of the churches in which they have taken part has not been Christian. The goodness and the deserts of all these men, who served the churches, were the goodness and the deserts of men, but not of the cause which they served. All these good men — like Francis d'Assisi and Francis de Lobes, our Tíkhon Zadónski, Thomas à Kempis, and others — were good men, in spite of their having served a cause which is hostile to Christianity, and they would have been better and more deserving still, if they had not succumbed to the error which they served.

But why speak of the past, judge of the past, which may have been falsely represented to us? The churches with their foundations and with their activity are not a work of the past: the churches are now before us, and we can judge of them directly, by their activity, their influence upon men.

In what does the activity of the churches now consist? How do they act upon men? What do the churches do in our country, among the Catholics, among the Protestants of every denomination? In what does their activity consist, and what are the consequences of their activity?

The activity of our Russian, so-called Orthodox, Church is in full sight. It is a vast fact, which cannot be concealed, and about which there can be no dispute.

In what consists the activity of this Russian Church,

this enormous, tensely active institution, which consists of an army of half a million, costing the nation tens of millions?

The activity of this church consists in using every possible means for the purpose of instilling in the one hundred millions of the Russian population those obsolete, backward faiths, which now have no justification whatsoever, and which sometime in the past were professed by people that are alien to our nation, and in which hardly any one now believes, frequently even not those whose duty it is to disseminate these false doctrines.

The inculcation of these alien, obsolete formulas of the Byzantine clergy, which no longer have any meaning for the men of our time, about the Trinity, the Holy Virgin, the sacraments, grace, and so forth, forms one part of the activity of the Russian Church; another part of its activity consists in the activity of maintaining idolatry in the direct sense of the word, — worshipping holy relics and images, bringing sacrifices to them, and expecting from them the fulfilment of their wishes. I shall not speak of what is spoken and written by the clergy with a shade of learning and liberalism in the clerical periodicals, but of what actually is done by the clergy over the breadth of the Russian land among a population of one hundred million people. What do they carefully, persistently, tensely, everywhere without exception, teach the people? What is demanded of them on the strength of the so-called Christian faith?

I will begin with the beginning, with the birth of a child: at the birth of a child, the clergy teaches that a prayer has to be read over the mother and the child, in order to purify them, since without this prayer the mother who has given birth to a child is accursed. For this purpose the priest takes the child in his hands in front of the representations of the saints, which the masses simply call gods, and pronounces exorcising words, and thus purifies the mother. Then it is impressed on the parents, and even demanded of them under threat of punishment in case of non-fulfilment, that the child shall be baptized, that is, dipped three times in water by the priest, in connection with which incomprehensible words are pronounced and even less comprehensible acts performed, — the smearing of various parts of the body with oil, the shearing of the hair, and the blowing and spitting of the sponsors on the imaginary devil. All this is supposed to cleanse the child and make him a Christian. Then the parents are impressed with the necessity of giving the holy sacrament to the child, that is, of giving him under the form of bread and wine a particle of Christ's body to eat, in consequence of which the child will receive the grace of Christ, and so forth. Then it is demanded that this child, according to his age, shall learn to pray. To pray means to stand straight in front of the boards on which the faces of Christ, the Virgin, the saints, are represented, and incline his head and his whole body, and with his right hand, with fingers put together in a certain form, to touch his brow, shoulders, and stomach, and pronounce Church-Slavic words, of which all the children are particularly enjoined to repeat, "Mother of God, Virgin, rejoice!" etc. Then the pupil is impressed with the necessity of doing the same, that is, crossing himself, in presence of any church or image; then he is told that on holidays (holidays are days on which Christ was born, though no one knows when that was, and circumcised, on which the Mother of God died, the cross was brought, the image was carried in, a saintly fool saw a vision, etc.,) he must put on his best clothes and go to church, buy tapers there and place them in front of images of saints, hand in little notes and commemorations and loaves, that triangles may be cut in them, and then pray many times for the health and welfare of the Tsar and the bishops, and for himself and his acts, and then kiss the cross and the priest's hand.

Besides this prayer he is enjoined to prepare himself at least once a year for the holy sacrament. To prepare himself for the holy sacrament means to go to church and tell the priest his sins, on the supposition that his imparting his sins to a stranger will completely cleanse him of his sins, and then to eat from a spoon a bit of bread with wine, which purifies him even more. Then it is impressed upon a man and a woman, who want their carnal intercourse to be sacred, that they must come to church, put on metallic crowns, drink potions, to the sound of singing walk three times around a table, and that then their carnal intercourse will become sacred and quite distinct from any other carnal intercourse.

In life people are impressed with the necessity of observing the following rules: not to eat meat or milk food on certain days, on other certain days to celebrate masses for the dead, on holidays to receive the priest and give him money, and several times a year to take the boards with the representations out of the church and carry them on sashes over fields and through houses. Before death a man is enjoined to eat from a spoon bread with wine, and still better, if he has time, to have himself smeared with oil. This secures for him happiness in the next world. After a man's death, his relatives are enjoined, for the purpose of saving the soul of the defunct, to put into his hands a printed sheet with a prayer; it is also useful to have a certain book read over the dead body and the name of the dead man pronounced several times in church.

All this is considered an obligatory faith for everybody.

But if one wants to care for his soul, he is taught, according to this faith, that the greatest amount of blessedness is secured for the soul in the world to come by contributing money for churches and monasteries, by putting holy men thus under obligation to pray for him. Other soul-saving measures, according to this faith, are the visiting of monasteries and the kissing of miracle-working images and relics.

According to this faith, miracle-working images and relics concentrate in themselves particular holiness, strength, and grace, and nearness to these objects — touching, kissing them, placing tapers before them, crawling up to them — contributes very much to a man's salvation, and so do masses, which are ordered before these sacred objects.

It is this faith, and no other, which is called Orthodox, that is, the right faith, and which has, under the guise of Christianity, been impressed upon the people for many centuries by the exercise of all kinds of force, and is now being impressed with particular effort.

And let it not be said that the Orthodox teachers place the essence of the teaching in something else, and that these are only ancient forms which it is not considered right to destroy. That is not true: throughout all of Russia, nothing but this faith has of late been impressed upon the people with particular effort. There is nothing else. Of something else they talk and write in the capitals, but only this is being impressed on one hundred million of people, and nothing else. The churchmen talk of other things, but they enjoin only this with every means at their command.

All this, and the worship of persons and images, is introduced into theologies, into catechisms; the masses are carefully taught this theoretically, and, being hypnotized practically, with every means of solemnity, splendour, authority, and violence, are made to believe in this, and are jealously guarded against every endeavour to be freed from these savage superstitions.

In my very presence, as I said in reference to my book, Christ's teaching and his own words concerning non-resistance to evil were a subject of ridicule and circus jokes, and the churchmen not only did not oppose this, but even encouraged the blasphemy; but allow yourself to say a disrespectful word concerning the monstrous idol, which is blasphemously carried about in Moscow by drunken persons under the name of the Iberian Virgin, and a groan of indignation will be raised by these same churchmen. All that is preached is the external cult of idolatry. Let no one say that one thing does not interfere with the other, that "these ought ye to have done, and not to have left the other undone," that "all, therefore, whatsoever they bid you observe, that observe and do; but do not ye after their works: for they say, and do not" (Matt. xxiii. 23, 3). This is said of the Pharisees, who fulfilled all the external injunctions of the law, and so the words, "whatsoever they bid you observe, that observe," refer to works of charity and of goodness, and the words, "but do ye not after their works, for they say, and do not," refer to the execution of ceremonies and to the omission of good works, and have precisely the opposite meaning to what the churchmen want to ascribe to this passage, when they interpret it as meaning that ceremonies are to be observed. An external cult and serving charity and truth are hard to harmonize; for the most part one thing excludes the other. Thus it was with the Pharisees, and thus it is now with the church Christians.

If a man can save himself through redemption, sacraments, prayer, he no longer needs any good deeds.

The Sermon on the Mount, or the symbol of faith: it is impossible to believe in both. And the churchmen have chosen the latter: the symbol of faith is taught and read as a prayer in the churches; and the Sermon on the Mount is excluded even from the Gospel teachings in the churches, so that in the churches the parishioners never hear it, except on the days when the whole Gospel is read. Nor can it be otherwise: men who believe in a bad and senseless God, who has cursed the human race and who has doomed His son to be a victim, and has doomed a part of humanity to everlasting torment, cannot believe in a God of love. A man who believes in God-Christ, who will come again in glory to judge and punish the living and the dead, cannot believe in Christ, who commands a man to offer his cheek to the offender, not to judge, but to forgive, and to love our enemies. A man who believes in the divine inspiration of the Old Testament and the holiness of David, who on his deathbed orders the killing of an old man who has offended him and whom he could not kill himself, because he was bound by an oath (Book of Kings, ii. 3), and similar abominations, of which the Old Testament is full, cannot believe in Christ's moral law; a man who believes in the doctrine and the preaching of the church about the compatibility of executions and wars with Christianity, cannot believe in the brotherhood of men.

Above all else, a man who believes in the salvation of men through faith, in redemption, or in the sacraments, can no longer employ all his strength in the fulfilment in life of the moral teaching of Christ.

A man who is taught by the church the blasphemous doctrine about his not being able to be saved by his own efforts, but that there is another means, will inevitably have recourse to this means, and not to his efforts, on which he is assured it is a sin to depend. The church doctrine, any church doctrine, with its redemption and its sacraments, excludes Christ's teaching, and the Orthodox doctrine, with its idolatry, does so especially.

"But the masses have always believed so themselves, and believe so now," people will say to this. "The whole history of the Russian masses proves this. It is not right to deprive the masses of their tradition." In this does the deception consist. The masses at one time, indeed.

professed something like what the church professes now though it was far from being the same (among the masses, there has existed, not only this superstition of the images, house spirits, relics, and the seventh Thursday after Easter, with its wreaths and birches, but also a deep moral, vital comprehension of Christianity, which has never existed in the whole church, and was met with only in its best representatives); but the masses, in spite of all the obstacles, which the government and the church have opposed to them, have long ago in their best representatives outlived this coarse stage of comprehension, which is proved by the spontaneous birth of rationalistic sects, with which one meets everywhere, with which Russia swarms at the present time, and with which the churchmen struggle in vain. The masses move on in the consciousness of the moral, vital side of Christianity. And it is here that the church appears with its failure to support, and with its intensified inculcation of an obsolete paganism in its ossified form, with its tendency to push the masses back into that darkness, from which they are struggling with so much effort to get out.

"We do not teach the masses anything new, but only what they believe in, and that in a more perfect form," say the churchmen.

This is the same as tying up a growing chick and pushing it back into the shell from which it has come.

I have often been struck by this observation, which would be comical, if its consequences were not so terrible, that men, taking hold of each other in a circle, deceive one another, without being able to get out of the enchanted circle.

The first question, the first doubt of a Russian who is beginning to think, is the question about the miracle-working images and, above all, the relics: "Is it true that they are imperishable, and that they work miracles?" Hundreds and thousands of men put these questions to themselves and are troubled about their solution, especially because the bishops, metropolitans, and all the dignitaries kiss the relics and the miracle-working images. Ask the bishops and the dignitaries why they do so, and they will tell you that they do so for the sake of the masses, and the masses worship the images and relics, because the bishops and dignitaries do so.

The activity of the Russian Church, in spite of its external veneer of modernness, learning, spirituality, which its members are beginning to assume in their writings, articles, clerical periodicals, and sermons, consists not only in keeping the masses in that consciousness of rude and savage idolatry, in which they are, but also in intensifying and disseminating superstition and religious ignorance, by pushing out of the masses the vital comprehension of Christianity, which has been living in them by the side of the idolatry.

I remember, I was once present in the monastery bookstore of Óptin Cloister, when an old peasant was choosing some religious books for his grandson, who could read. The monk kept pushing the description of relics, holidays, miraculous images, psalters, etc., into his hands. I asked the old man if he had the Gospel. "No." "Give him the Russian Gospel," I said to the monk. "That is not proper for him," said the monk.

This is in compressed form the activity of our church.

"But this is only true in barbarous Russia," a European or American reader will say. And such an opinion will be correct, but only in the measure in which it refers to the government which aids the church in accomplishing its stultifying and corrupting influence in Russia.

It is true that nowhere in Europe is there such a despotic government and one to such a degree in accord with the ruling church, and so the participation of the power in the corruption of the masses in Russia is very strong; but it is not true that the Russian Church in its influence upon the masses in any way differs from any other church.

The churches are everything the same, and if the Catholic, the Anglican, and the Lutheran Churches have not in hand such an obedient government as is the Russian, this is not due to the absence of any desire to make use of the same.

The church, as a church, no matter what it may be, Catholic, Anglican, Lutheran, Presbyterian, — every church, insomuch as it is a church, cannot help but tend toward the same as the Russian Church, — toward concealing the true meaning of Christ's teaching and substituting in its place its own doctrine, which does not put a person under any obligations, excludes the possibility of understanding the true activity of Christ's teaching, and, above all else, justifies the existence of priests who are living at the expense of the nation.

Has Catholicism been doing anything else with its prohibition of the reading of the Gospel, and with its demand for unreasoning obedience to the ecclesiastic guides and the infallible Pope? Does Catholicism preach anything different from what the Russian Church preaches? We have here the same external cult, the same relics, miracles, and statues, the miracle-working Notre-Dames, and processions. The same elatedly misty judgments concerning Christianity in books and sermons, and, when it comes to facts, the same maintenance of a coarse idolatry.

And is not the same being done in Anglicanism, Lutheranism, and in every Protestantism which has formed itself into a church? The same demands from the congregation for a belief in dogmas which were expressed in the fourth century and have lost all meaning for the men of our time, and the same demand for idolatry, if not before relics and images, at least before the Sabbath and the letter of the Bible. It is still the same activity, which is directed upon concealing the real demands of Christianity and substituting for them externals, which do not put a man under any obligations, and "cant," as the English beautifully define the occupation to which they are particularly subject. Among the Protestants this activity is particularly noticeable, since they do not even have the excuse of antiquity. And does not the same take place in the modern Revivalism, — the renovated Calvinism, Evangelism, — out of which has grown up the Salvation Army? Just as the condition of all the church doctrines is the same in reference to Christ's teaching, so are also their methods.

Their condition is such that they cannot help but strain all their efforts, in order to conceal the teaching of Christ, whose name they use.

The incompatibility of all the church confessions with Christ's teaching is such that it takes especial efforts to conceal this incompatibility from men. Indeed, we need but stop and think of the condition of any adult, not only cultured, but even simple, man of our time, who has filled himself with conceptions, which are in the air, from the fields of geology, physics, chemistry, cosmography, history, when he for the first time looks consciously at the beliefs, instilled in him in childhood and supported by the churches, that God created the world in six days; that there was light before the sun; that Noah stuck all the animals into his ark, and so forth; that Jesus is the same God, the son, who created everything before this; that this God descended upon earth for Adam's sin; that He rose from the dead, ascended to heaven, and sits on the right of the Father, and will come in the clouds to judge the world, and so forth.

All these propositions, which were worked out by the men of the fourth century and had a certain meaning for the men of that time, have no meaning for the men of the present. The men of our time may repeat these words with their lips, but they cannot believe, because these words, like the statements that God lives in heaven, that the heavens opened and a voice said something from there, that Christ rose from the dead and flew somewhere to heaven and will again come from somewhere in the clouds, and so forth, have no meaning for us.

It was possible for a man, who regarded the heaven as a finite, firm vault, to believe, or not, that God created the heaven, that heaven was opened, that Christ flew to heaven; but for us these words have no meaning whatsoever. Men of our time can only believe that they must believe so; but they cannot believe in what has no meaning for them.

But if all these expressions are to have a figurative meaning and are emblems, we know that, in the first place, not all churchmen agree in this, but that, on the contrary, the majority insist on understanding Holy Scripture in a direct sense, and, secondly, that these interpretations are varied and not confirmed by anything,

But even if a man wishes to make himself believe in the doctrine of the churches, as it is imparted, — the general diffusion of knowledge and of the Gospels, and the intercourse of men of various denominations among themselves, form for this another, even more insuperable obstacle.

A man of our time need but buy himself a Gospel for three kopeks and read Christ's clear words to the woman of Samaria, which are not subject to any other interpretation, about the Father needing no worshippers in Jerusalem, neither in this mountain, nor in that, worshippers in spirit and in truth, or the words about a Christian's being obliged to pray, not in temples, as the pagans do, and in the sight of all, but in secret, that is, in his closet, or that a disciple of Christ must not call any one father or teacher, — a man needs but read these words, to become convinced that no ecclesiastic pastors, who call themselves teachers in opposition to Christ's teaching, and who quarrel among themselves, form an authority, and that that which the churchmen teach us is not Christianity. But more than that: if a man of our time continues to believe in miracles and does not read the Gospel, his mere intercourse with men of other denominations and faiths, which has become so easy in our time, will make him doubt in the authenticity of his faith. It was all very well for a man who never saw any men of another faith than his own to believe that his own faith was the correct one; but a thinking man need only come in contact, as he now does all the time, with equally good and equally bad men of various denominations, which condemn the doctrines of one another, in order to lose faith in the truth of the religion which he professes. In our time only a very ignorant man or one who is quite indifferent to the questions of life, which are sanctified by religion, can stay in the church faith.

What cunning and what effort must be exerted by the churches, if, in spite of all these conditions which are subversive of faith, they are to continue building churches, celebrating masses, preaching, teaching, converting, and, above all, receiving for it a fat income, like all these priests, pastors, intendants, superintendents, abbots, archdeacons, bishops, and archbishops.

Especial, supernatural efforts are needed. And such efforts, which are strained more and more, are used by the churches. With us, in Russia, they use (in addition to all other means) the simple, coarse violence of the civil power, which is obedient to the church. Persons who depart from the external expression of faith and who give expression to it are either directly punished or deprived of their rights; while persons who strictly adhere to the external forms of faith are rewarded and given rights.

Thus do the Orthodox; but even all other churches, without exception, use for this all such means, of which the chief is what now is called hypnotization.

All the arts, from architecture to poetry, are put into action, to affect the souls of men and to stultify them, and this action takes place without interruption. Particularly evident is this necessity of the hypnotizing action upon men, in order to bring them to a state of stupefaction, in the activity of the Salvation Army, which uses new, unfamiliar methods of horns, drums, songs, banners, uniforms, processions, dances, tears, and dramatic attitudes.

But we are startled by them only because they are new methods. Are not the old methods of the temples, with especial illumination, with gold, splendour, candles, choirs, organs, bells, vestments, lackadaisical sermons, and so forth, the same?

But, no matter how strong this action of hypnotization may be, the chief and most deleterious activity of the churches does not lie in this. The chief, most pernicious activity of the church is the one which is directed to the deception of the children, those very children of whom Christ said that it will be woe to him who shall offend one of these little ones. With the very first awakening of the child, they begin to deceive him and to impress upon him with solemnity what those who impress do not believe in themselves, and they continue to impress him, until the deception, becoming a habit, is engrafted on the child's nature. The child is methodically deceived in the most important matter of life, and when the deception has so grown up with his life that it is difficult to tear it away, there is revealed to him the whole world of science and of reality, which can in no way harmonize with the beliefs instilled in him, and he is left to make the best he can out of these contradictions.

If we should set ourselves the task of entangling a man in such a way that he should not be able with his sound reason to get away from the two opposite world-conceptions, which have been instilled in him since his childhood, we could not invent anything more powerful than what is accomplished in the case of every young man who is educated in our so-called Christian society.

What the churches do to people is terrible, but if we reflect on their condition, we shall find that those men who form the institution of the churches cannot act otherwise. The churches are confronted with a dilemma, — the Sermon on the Mount, or the Nicene Creed, — one excludes the other: if a man sincerely believes in the Sermon on the Mount, the Nicene Creed, and with it the church and its representatives, inevitably lose all meaning and significance for him; but if a man believes in the Nicene Creed, that is, in the church, that is, in those who call themselves its representatives, the Sermon on the Mount will become superfluous to him. And so the churches cannot help but use every possible effort to obscure the meaning of the Sermon on the Mount and to attract people toward itself. Only thanks to the tense activity of the churches in this direction has the influence of the churches held itself until now. Let a church for the shortest time arrest this action upon the masses by means of hypnotizing them and deceiving the children, and people will understand Christ's teaching. But the comprehension of the teaching destroys the churches and their significance. And so the churches do not for a moment interrupt the tense activity and hypnotization of the adults and the deception of the children. And it is this activity of the churches, which instils a false comprehension of Christ's teaching in men, and serves as an obstacle in its comprehension for the majority of so-called believers.

IV.

Now I will speak of another putative comprehension of Christianity, which interferes with the correct comprehension of it, — the scientific comprehension.

The churchmen regard as Christianity that conception of it which they have formed, and this comprehension of Christianity they regard as the one indubitably true one.

The men of science regard as Christianity only what the different churches have been professing, and, assuming that these professions exhaust the whole significance of Christianity, they recognize it as a religious teaching which has outlived its time.

To have it made clear how impossible it is with such a view to understand the Christian teaching, we must form an idea of the place which the religions in general and Christianity in particular have in reality occupied in the life of humanity, and of the significance which is ascribed to religion by science.

As an individual man cannot live without having a definite idea of the meaning of his life, and always, though often unconsciously, conforms his acts to this meaning which he ascribes to his life, even so aggregates of men living under the same conditions, — nations cannot help but have a conception about the meaning of their collective life and the activity resulting therefrom. And as an individual, entering into a new age, invariably changes his comprehension of life, and a grown man sees its meaning in something else than in what a child sees it, so an aggregate of people, a nation, inevitably, according to its age, changes its comprehension of life and the activity which results from it.

The difference between the individual and the whole of humanity in this respect consists in this, that while the individual in the determination of the comprehension of life, proper to the new stage of life into which he enters, and in the activity which arises from it, makes use of the indications of men who have lived before him and who have already passed through the period of life upon which he is entering, humanity cannot have these indications, because it all moves along an untrodden path, and there is no one who can tell how life is to be understood, and how one is to act under the new conditions into which it is entering, and in which no one has lived before.

And yet, as a married man with children cannot continue to understand life as he understood it when he was a child, so humanity cannot in connection with all the various changes which have taken place, — the density of the population, and the established intercourse between the nations, and the improvement of the means for struggling against Nature, and the accumulation of science, — continue to understand life as before, but must establish a new concept of life, from which should result the activity which corresponds to that new condition into which it has entered or is about to enter.

To this demand responds the peculiar ability of humanity to segregate certain people who give a new meaning to the whole of human life, — a meaning from which results the whole new activity which is different from the preceding one. The establishment of the new life-conception, which is proper for humanity under the new conditions into which it is entering, and of the activity resulting from it, is what is called religion.

And so religion, in the first place, is not, as science thinks, a phenomenon which at one time accompanied the evolution of humanity, and later became obsolete, but is a phenomenon always inherent in the life of humanity, and is in our time as inevitably inherent in humanity as at any other time. In the second place, religion is always a determination of the activity of the future and not of the past, and so it is obvious that the investigation of past phenomena can in no way include the essence of religion.

The essence of every religious teaching does not consist in the desire to express the forces of Nature symbolically, or in the fear of them, or in the demand for the miraculous, or in the external forms of its manifestation, as the men of science imagine. The essence of religion lies in the property of men prophetically to foresee and point out the path of life, over which humanity must travel, in a new definition of the meaning of life, from which also results a new, the whole future activity of humanity.

This property of foreseeing the path on which humanity must travel is in a greater or lesser degree common to all men, but there have always, at all times, been men, in whom this quality has been manifested with particular force, and these men expressed clearly and precisely what was dimly felt by all men, and established a new comprehension of life, from which resulted an entirely new activity, for hundreds and thousands of years.

We know three such conceptions of life: two of them humanity has already outlived, and the third is the one through which we are now passing in Christianity. There are three, and only three, such conceptions, not because we have arbitrarily united all kinds of life-conceptions into these three, but because the acts of men always have for their base one of these three life-conceptions, because we cannot understand life in any other way than by one of these three means.

The three life-conceptions are these: the first — the personal, or animal; the second — the social, or the pagan; and the third — the universal, or the divine.

According to the first life-conception, man's life is contained in nothing but his personality; the aim of his life is the gratification of the will of this personality. According to the second life-conception, man's life is not contained in his personality alone, but in the aggregate and sequence of personalities, — in the tribe, the family, the race, the state; the aim of life consists in the gratification of the will of this aggregate of personalities. According to the third life-conception, man's life is contained neither in his personality, nor in the aggregate and sequence of personalities, but in the beginning and source of life, in God.

These three life-conceptions serve as the foundation of all past and present religions.

The savage recognizes life only in himself, in his personal desires. The good of his life is centred in himself alone. The highest good for him is the greatest gratification of his lust. The prime mover of his life is his personal enjoyment. His religion consists in appeasing the divinity in his favour, and in the worship of imaginary personalities of gods, who live only for personal ends.

A pagan, a social man, no longer recognizes life in himself alone, but in the aggregate of personalities, — in the tribe, the family, the race, the state, — and sacrifices his personal good for these aggregates. The prime mover of his life is glory. His religion consists in the glorification of the heads of unions, — of eponyms, ancestors, kings, and in the worship of gods, the exclusive protectors of his family, his race, his nation, his state.[1]

[1] The unity of this life-conception is not impaired by the fact that so many various forms of life, as that of the tribe, the family, the race, the state, and even the life of humanity, according to the theoretical speculations of the positivists, are based on this social, or pagan, life-conception. All these various forms of life are based on the same concept that the life of the personality is not a sufficient aim of life and that the meaning of life can be found only in the aggregate of personalities. — *Author's Note.*

The man with the divine life-conception no longer recognizes life to consist in his personality, or in the aggregate of personalities (in the family, the race, the people, the country, or the state), but in the source of the everlasting, immortal life, in God; and to do God's will he sacrifices his personal and domestic and social good. The prime mover of his religion is love. And his religion is the worship in deed and in truth of the beginning of everything, of God.

The whole historical life of humanity is nothing but a gradual transition from the personal, the animal life-conception, to the social, and from the social to the divine. The whole history of the ancient nations, which lasted for thousands of years and which came to a conclusion with the history of Rome, is the history of the substitution of the social and the political life-conception for the animal, the personal. The whole history since the time of imperial Rome and the appearance of Christianity has been the history of the substitution of the divine life-conception for the political, and we are passing through it even now.

It is this last life-conception, and the Christian teaching which is based upon it and which governs our whole life and lies at the foundation of our whole activity, both the practical and the theoretical, that the men of so-called science, considering it in reference to its external signs only, recognize as something obsolete and meaningless for us.

This teaching, which, according to the men of science, is contained only in its dogmatic part, — in the doctrine of the Trinity, the redemption, the miracles, the church, the sacraments, and so forth, — is only one out of a vast number of religions which have arisen in humanity, and now, having played its part in history, is outliving its usefulness, melting in the light of science and true culture.

What is taking place is what in the majority of cases

serves as a source of the coarsest human errors, — men who are standing on a lower level of comprehension, coming in contact with phenomena of a higher order, instead of making efforts to understand them, instead of rising to the point of view from which they ought to look upon a subject, judge it from their lower point of view, and that, too, with greater daring and determination the less they understand what they are talking about.

For the majority of scientific men, who view Christ's vital, moral teaching from the lower point of the social conception of life, this teaching is only a very indefinite, clumsy combination of Hindoo asceticism, Stoical and Neoplatonic teachings, and Utopian antisocial reveries, which have no serious significance for our time, and its whole meaning is centred in its external manifestations, — in Catholicism, Protestantism, the dogmas, the struggle with the worldly power. In defining the significance of Christianity according to these phenomena, they are like deaf persons who should judge of the meaning and the worth of music according to the appearance of the motions which the musicians make.

The result of it is this, that all these men, beginning with Comte, Strauss, Spencer, and Renan, who do not understand the meaning of Christ's sermons, who do not understand why they are uttered and for what purpose, who do not even understand the question to which they serve as an answer, who do not even take the trouble to grasp their meaning, if they are inimically inclined, deny outright the rationality of the teaching; but if they wish to be condescending to it, they correct it from the height of their grandeur, assuming that Christ wanted to say precisely what they have in mind, but did not know how to say it. They treat his teaching as, in correcting the words of an interlocutor, self-confident men generally speak to one whom they regard as standing below them, "Yes, what you mean to say is this." This correction is always made in the sense of reducing the higher, divine life-conception to the lower, social conception.

People generally say that the moral teaching of Christianity is good, but exaggerated, — that, in order that it should be absolutely good, we must reject from it what is superfluous, what does not fit in with our structure of life. "For otherwise the teaching, which demands too much, which cannot be carried out, is worse than one which demands from men what is possible and in conformity with their strength," think and assert the wise interpreters of Christianity, repeating what was long ago affirmed and still is affirmed, and could not help but be affirmed, in relation to the Christian teaching, by those who, having failed to comprehend the teacher of it, crucified Him, — by the Jews.

It turns out that before the judgment of the learned of our time, the Jewish law, A tooth for a tooth, and an eye for an eye, — the law of just retaliation, which was known to humanity five thousand years ago, — is more useful than the law of love which eighteen hundred years ago was preached by Christ in place of this very law of justice.

It turns out that everything which has been done by the men who comprehended Christ's teaching in a direct manner and lived in conformity with such a comprehension, everything which all true Christians, all Christian champions, have done, everything which now transforms the world under the guise of socialism and communism, — is exaggeration, of which it is not worth while to speak.

Men who have been educated in Christianity for eighteen centuries have convinced themselves in the persons of their foremost men, the scholars, that the Christian teaching is a teaching of dogmas, that the vital teaching is a misconception, an exaggeration, which violates the true legitimate demands of morality, which correspond to man's nature, and that the doctrine of justice, which

Christ rejected and in the place of which he put his own teaching, is much more profitable for us.

The learned consider the commandment of non-resistance to evil an exaggeration and even madness. If it be rejected, it would be much better, they think, without observing that they are not talking of Christ's teaching at all, but of what presents itself to them as such.

They do not notice that to say that Christ's commandment about non-resistance to evil is an exaggeration is the same as saying that in the theory of the circle the statement about the equality of the radii of a circle is an exaggeration. And those who say so do precisely what a man, who did not have any conception as to what a circle is, would do if he asserted that the demand that all the points on the circumference should be equally distant from the centre is an exaggeration. To advise that the statement concerning the equality of the radii in a circle be rejected or moderated is the same as not understanding what a circle is. To advise that the commandment about non-resistance to evil in the vital teaching of Christ be rejected or moderated means not to understand the teaching.

And those who do so actually do not understand it at all. They do not understand that this teaching is the establishment of a new comprehension of life, which corresponds to the new condition into which men have been entering for these eighteen hundred years, and the determination of the new activity which results from it. They do not believe that Christ wanted to say what he did; or it seems to them that what he said in the Sermon on the Mount and in other passages He said from infatuation, from lack of comprehension, from insufficient development.[1]

[1] Here, for example, is a characteristic judgment of the kind in an article of an American periodical, *Arena*, October, 1890. The article is entitled "A New Basis of Church Life." In discussing the sig

Therefore I say unto you, Take no thought for your life, what ye shall eat, or what ye shall drink; nor yet for your body, what ye shall put on. Is not the life more than meat, and the body than raiment? Behold the fowls of the air: for they sow not, neither do they reap, nor gather into barns; yet your heavenly Father feedeth them. Are ye not much better than they? Which of you by taking thought can add one cubit unto his stature? And why take ye thought for raiment? Consider the lilies of the field, how they grow; they toil not, neither do they spin: and yet I say unto you, That even Solomon in all his glory was not arrayed like one of these. Wherefore, if God so clothe the grass of the field, which to-day is, and to-morrow is cast into the oven, shall He not much more clothe you, O ye of little faith? Therefore take no thought, saying, What shall we eat? or, What shall we drink, or, Wherewithal shall we be clothed? (For after all these things do the Gentiles seek:) for your heavenly Father knoweth that ye have need of all these things. But seek ye first the kingdom

nificance of the Sermon on the Mount, and especially its non-resistance to evil, the author, who is not obliged, like the ecclesiastic writers, to conceal its meaning, says: "Christ actually preached complete communism and anarchy; but we must know how to look upon Christ in His historical and psychologic significance." [This sentence is not in the English article. — *Tr.*] "Devout common sense must gradually come to look upon Christ as a philanthropic teacher who, like every enthusiast who ever taught, went to an Utopian extreme of His own philosophy. Every great agitation for the betterment of the world has been led by men who beheld their own mission with such absorbing intensity that they could see little else. It is no reproach to Christ to say that He had the typical reformer's temperament; that His precepts cannot be literally accepted as a complete philosophy of life; and that men are to analyze them reverently, but, at the same time, in the spirit of ordinary, truth-seeking criticism," and so forth. Christ would have liked to speak well, but He did not know how to express Himself as precisely and clearly as we, in the spirit of criticism, and so we will correct him. Everything He said about meekness, sacrifice, poverty, the thoughtlessness for the morrow, He said by chance, having been unable to express himself scientifically. — *Author's Note.*

of God, and His righteousness; and all these things shall be added unto you. Take therefore no thought for the morrow: for the morrow shall take thought for the things of itself. Sufficient unto the day is the evil thereof (Matt. vi. 25–34).

Sell that ye have, and give alms; provide yourselves bags which wax not old, a treasure in the heavens that faileth not, where no thief approacheth, neither moth corrupteth. For where your treasure is there will your heart be also (Luke xii. 33–34).

Go and sell that thou hast, and follow me, and who hath not forsaken father or mother, or children, or brethren, or fields, or house, cannot be my disciple.

Turn away from thyself, take thy cross for every day, and come after me. My meat is to do the will of Him that sent me, and to do His work. Not my will be done, but Thine; not what I want, but what Thou wantest, and not as I want, but as Thou wantest. The life is in this, not to do one's will, but the will of God.

All these propositions seem to men who are standing on a lower life-conception to be an expression of an ecstatic transport, which has no direct applicability to life. And yet these propositions just as strictly result from the Christian conception of life as the tenet about giving up one's labour for the common good, about sacrificing one's life in the defence of one's country, results from the social conception.

Just as a man of the social life-conception says to a savage, "Come to your senses, bethink yourself! The life of your personality cannot be the true life, because it is wretched and transitory. Only the life of the aggregate and of the sequence of personalities, of the tribe, the family, the race, the state, is continued and lives, and so a man must sacrifice his personality for the life of the family, the state." Precisely the same the Christian teaching says to a man of the aggregate, of the social conception of life. "Repent, μετανοεῖτε, that is, bethink yourselves, or else you will perish. Remember that this carnal, personal life, which originated to-day and will be destroyed to-morrow, cannot be made secure in any way, that no external measures, no arrangement of it, can add firmness and rationality to it. Bethink yourselves and understand that the life which you live is not the true life: the life of the family, the life of society, the life of the state will not save you from ruin." The true, rational life is possible for man only in proportion as he can be a participant, not in the family or the state, but in the source of life, the Father; in proportion as he can blend his life with the life of the Father. Such indubitably is the Christian life-comprehension, which may be seen in every utterance of the Gospel.

It is possible not to share this life-conception; it is possible to reject it; it is possible to prove its inexactness and irregularity; but it is impossible to judge of the teaching, without having first grasped the life-conception from which it results; still less possible is it to judge about a subject of a higher order from a lower point of view, to judge of the tower by looking at the foundation. But it is precisely this that the learned men of our time are doing. They do so because they abide in an error, which is like the one of the churchmen, the belief that they are in possession of such methods of the study of the subject that, as soon as these methods, called scientific, are used, there can be no longer any doubt as to the correctness of the comprehension of the subject under advisement.

It is this possession of an instrument of cognition, which they deem infallible, that serves as the chief obstacle in the comprehension of the Christian teaching by unbelievers and so-called scientific men, by whose opinion the vast majority of unbelievers, the so-called cultured men, are guided. From this imaginary comprehension of theirs arise all the errors of the scientific men in respect to the Christian teaching, and especially two strange misconceptions which more than any other impede the correct comprehension of it.

One of these misconceptions is this, that the Christian vital teaching is impracticable, and so is either entirely unobligatory, that is, need not be taken for a guide, or else must be modified and moderated to such an extent as to make it practicable in our society. Another misunderstanding is this, that the Christian teaching of love of God, and so the service of Him, is an obscure, mystical demand, which has no definite object of love, and so must give way to a more precise and comprehensible teaching about loving men and serving humanity.

The first misconception about the impracticableness of the teaching consists in this, that the men of the social comprehension of life, being unable to comprehend the method by means of which the Christian teaching guides men, and taking the Christian indications of perfection to be rules which determine life, think and say that it is impossible to follow Christ's teaching, because a complete fulfilment of this teaching destroys life.

"If a man fulfilled what was preached by Christ, he would destroy his life; and if all men should fulfil it, the whole human race would come to an end," they say.

"If we care not for the morrow, for what we shall eat and drink and be clothed in; if we do not defend our lives; if we do not resist evil with force; if we give our lives for our friends, and observe absolute chastity, no man, nor the whole human race, can exist," they think and say.

And they are quite correct, if we take the indications of perfection, as given by Christ, for rules, which every man is obliged to carry out, just as in the social teaching everybody is obliged to carry out the rule about paying the taxes, about taking part in court, etc.

The misconception consists in this, that Christ's teaching guides men in a different way from the way those teachings guide which are based on a lower life-conception. The teachings of the social life-conception guide only by demanding a precise execution of the rules or laws. Christ's teaching guides men by indicating to them that infinite perfection of the Father in heaven, toward which it is proper for each man to strive voluntarily, no matter at what stage of perfection he may be.

The misconception of people who judge about the Christian teaching from the social point of view consists in this, that they, assuming that the perfection pointed out by Christ may be attained completely, ask themselves (even as they question themselves, assuming that the social laws will be fulfilled) what will happen when all this shall be fulfilled. This assumption is false, because the perfection pointed out by Christ is infinite and can never be attained; and Christ gives His teaching with this in view, that complete perfection will never be attained, but that the striving toward complete, infinite perfection will constantly increase the good of men, and that this good can, therefore, be increased infinitely.

Christ does not teach angels, but men, who live an animal life, who are moved by it. And it is to this animal force of motion that Christ seems to apply a new, a different force of the consciousness of divine perfection, and with this He directs the motion of life along the resultant of two forces.

To assume that human life will go in the direction indicated by Christ is the same as assuming that a boatman, in crossing a rapid river and directing his boat almost against the current, will move in that direction.

Christ recognizes the existence of both sides of the parallelogram, of both the eternal, indestructible forces, of which man's life is composed, — the force of the animal nature and the force of the consciousness of a filial relation to God. Without saying anything of the animal force, which, asserting itself, always remains equal to itself and exists outside of man's power, Christ speaks only of the divine force, calling man to recognize it in the highest degree, to free it as much as possible from what is retarding it, and to bring it to the highest degree of tension.

In this liberation and increase of the force does man's true life, according to Christ's teaching, consist. The true life, according to the previous conditions, consisted in the execution of rules, of the law; according to Christ's teaching, it consists in the greatest approach to the divine perfection, as pointed out to every man and inwardly felt by him, in a greater and ever greater approach toward blending our will with the will of God, a blending toward which a man strives, and which would be a destruction of life as we know it.

Divine perfection is the asymptote of the human life, toward which it always tends and approaches, and which can be attained by it only at infinity.

The Christian teaching seems to exclude the possibility of life only when men take the indication of the ideal to be a rule. It is only then that the demands put forth by Christ's teaching appear to be destructive of life. Without these demands the true life would be impossible.

"Too much should not be demanded," people generally say, in discussing the demands of the Christian teaching. "It is impossible to demand that we should not care for the future, as it says in the Gospel; all that we should do is not to care too much. It is impossible to give everything to the poor; but we should give a certain, definite part to them. It is not necessary to strive after chastity; but debauchery should be avoided. We must not leave our wives and children; but we should not be too much attached to them," and so forth.

But to speak in this manner is the same as telling a man who is crossing a rapid river, and who is directing his course against the current, that it is impossible to cross the river by going against the current, but that to cross it he should row in the direction he wishes to go.

Christ's teaching differs from previous teachings in that it guides men, not by external rules, but by the internal consciousness of the possibility of attaining divine perfection. And in man's soul there are not moderated rules of justice and of philanthropy, but the ideal of the complete, infinite, divine perfection. Only the striving after this perfection deflects the direction of man's life from the animal condition toward the divine, to the extent to which this is possible in this life.

In order to land where you wish, you must direct your course much higher up.

To lower the demands of the ideal means not only to diminish the possibility of perfection, but to destroy the ideal itself. The ideal which operates upon people is not an invented one, but one which is borne in the soul of every man. Only this ideal of the complete, infinite perfection acts upon people and moves them to activity. A moderated perfection loses its power to act upon men's souls.

Christ's teaching only then has force, when it demands full perfection, that is, the blending of God's essence, which abides in the soul of every man, with the will of God, — the union of the son and the Father. Only this liberation of the son of God, who lives in every man, from the animal, and his approximation to the Father form life according to Christ's teaching.

The existence of the animal in man, of nothing but the animal, is not the human life. Life according to the will of God alone is also not the human life. The human life is the resultant from the animal and the divine lives, and the more this resultant approaches the divine life, the more there is of life.

Life, according to the Christian teaching, is a motion toward divine perfection. No condition, according to this teaching, can be higher or lower than another. Every condition, according to this teaching, is only a certain step, indifferent in itself, toward the unattainable perfection, and so in itself forms neither a greater nor a lesser degree of life. The increase of life, according to this teaching, is only an acceleration of motion toward perfection, and so the motion toward perfection of the publican Zacchæus, of the harlot, of the robber on the cross, forms a higher degree of life than the immovable righteousness of the Pharisee. And so there can be no obligatory rules for this teaching. A man who stands on a lower step, in moving toward perfection, lives more morally and better, and better performs the teaching, than a man who stands on a much higher stage of morality, but who does not move toward perfection.

In this sense the lost sheep is dearer to the Father than one which is not lost. The prodigal son, the lost coin which is found again, are dearer than those which were not lost.

The fulfilment of the teaching consists in the motion from oneself toward God. It is evident that for such a fulfilment of the teaching there can be no definite laws and rules. All degrees of perfection and all degrees of imperfection are equal before this teaching; no fulfilment of the laws constitutes a fulfilment of the teaching; and so, for this teaching there are, and there can be, no rules and no laws.

From this radical distinction of Christ's teaching as compared with previous teachings, which are based on the social conception of life, there results the difference between the social and the Christian commandments. The social commandments are for the most part positive, prescribing certain acts, justifying men, giving them righteousness. But the Christian commandments (the commandment of love is not a commandment in the strict sense of the word, but an expression of the very essence of the teaching) — the five commandments of the Sermon on the Mount — are all negative, and they all show only what men may not do at a certain stage of human development. These commandments are, as it were, signals on the infinite road to perfection, toward which humanity walks, signals of that stage of perfection which is possible at a given period of the development of humanity.

In the Sermon on the Mount Christ has expressed the eternal ideal toward which it is proper for men to tend, and that degree of its attainment which can be reached even in our time.

The ideal consists in having no ill-will against any one, in calling forth no ill-will, in loving all; but the commandment, below which, in the attainment of this ideal, it is absolutely possible not to descend, consists in not offending any one with a word. And this forms the first commandment.

The ideal is complete chastity, even in thought; the commandment which points out the degree of attainment, below which, in the attainment of this ideal, it is absolutely possible not to descend, is the purity of the marital life, the abstaining from fornication. And this forms the second commandment.

The ideal is not to care for the future, to live only in the present; the commandment which points out the degree of the attainment, below which it is absolutely possible not to descend is not to swear, not to promise anything to men. And this is the third commandment.

The ideal is never, under any condition, to make use of violence; the commandment which points out the degree below which it is absolutely possible not to descend is not to repay evil with evil, but to suffer insult, to give up one's cloak. And this is the fourth commandment.

The ideal is to love our enemies, who hate us; the commandment which points out the degree of the attainment, below which it is possible not to descend, is to do no evil to our enemies, to speak well of them, to make no distinction between them and our fellow citizens.

All these commandments are indications of what we are fully able not to do on the path of striving after perfection, of what we ought to work over now, of what we must by degrees transfer into the sphere of habit, into the sphere of the unconscious. But these commandments fail to form a teaching, and do not exhaust it, and form only one of the endless steps in the approximation toward perfection.

After these commandments there must and will follow higher and higher ones on the path to perfection, which is indicated by the teaching.

And so it is the peculiarity of the Christian teaching that it makes higher demands than those which are expressed in these commandments, but under no condition minimizes the demands, either of the ideal itself, or of these commandments, as is done by people who judge the teaching of Christianity free from the standpoint of the social conception of life.

Such is one misconception of the scientific men concerning the meaning and significance of Christ's teaching; the other, which flows from the same source, consists in the substitution of the love and service of men, of humanity, for the Christian demand for loving God and serving Him.

The Christian teaching of loving God and serving Him, and (only in consequence of this love and this service) of the love and service of our neighbour, appears obscure, mystical, and arbitrary to the men of science, and they completely exclude the demand of love of God and of serving Him, assuming that the teaching about this love of men, of humanity, is much more intelligible and firm and better grounded.

The men of science teach theoretically that the good

and sensible life is only the life of serving the whole of humanity, and in this alone do they see the meaning of the Christian teaching; to this teaching do they reduce the Christian teaching; for this their teaching do they seek a confirmation in the Christian teaching, assuming that their teaching and the Christian teaching are one and the same.

This opinion is quite faulty. The Christian teaching, and that of the positivists, communists, and all the preachers of a universal brotherhood of men, which is based on the profitableness of such a brotherhood, have nothing in common among themselves, and differ from one another more especially in this, that the Christian teaching has firm, clear foundations in the human soul, while the teaching of the love of humanity is only a theoretical deduction from analogy.

The teaching of the love of humanity alone has for its basis the social conception of life.

The essence of the social conception of life consists in the transference of the meaning of our personal lives into the life of the aggregate of personalities, — the tribe, the family, the race, the state. This transference has taken place easily and naturally in its first forms, in the transference of the meaning of life from the personality to the tribe, the family. But the transference to the race or nation is more difficult and demands a special education for it; and the transference of the consciousness to the state forms the limit of such a transference.

It is natural for any one to love himself, and every person loves himself without any special incitement; to love my tribe, which supports and defends me, to love my wife, the joy and helpmate of my life, my children, the pleasure and hope of my life, and my parents, who have given me life and an education, is natural: and this kind of love, though far from being as strong as the love of self, is met with quite frequently.

To love one's race, one's nation, for the sake of oneself, of one's pride, though not so natural, is still to be met with. The love of one's nation, which is of the same race, tongue, and faith with one, is still possible, though this sentiment is far from being as strong as the love of self, or even of family and race; but the love of a country, like Turkey, Germany, England, Austria, Russia, is almost an impossible thing, and, in spite of the intensified education in this direction, is only assumed and does not exist in reality. With this aggregate there ends for man the possibility of transferring his consciousness and of experiencing in this fiction any immediate sensation. But the positivists and all the preachers of a scientific brotherhood, who do not take into consideration the weakening of the sentiment in proportion as the subject is widened, continue the discussion theoretically along the same direction: "If," they say, "it was more advantageous for the personality to transfer its consciousness to the tribe, the family, and then to the nation, the state, it will be still more advantageous to transfer the consciousness to the whole aggregate of humanity, and for all to live for humanity, just as individuals live for the family, the state."

Theoretically it really comes out that way.

Since the consciousness and the love of personality are transferred to the family, from the family to the race, the nation, the state, it would be quite logical for men, to save themselves from struggle and calamities, which are due to the division of humanity into nations and states, most naturally to transfer their love to humanity. This would seem to be the most logical thing, and this is theoretically advocated by men, who do not observe that love is a sentiment which one may have, but cannot preach, and that, besides, for love there must be an object, whereas humanity is not an object, but only a fiction.

The tribe, the family, even the state, are not invented by men, but were formed naturally like a swarm of bees or ants, and actually exist. A man who loves his family for the sake of his animal personality, knows whom he loves: Anna, Mary, John, Peter, and so forth. A man who loves a race and is proud of it, knows that he loves the whole race of the Guelphs, or all the Ghibellines; he who loves the state knows that he loves France as far as the Rhine and the Pyrenees, and its capital, Paris, and its history, and so forth. But what does a man love, when he loves humanity? There is the state, the nation; there is the abstract conception — man; but there is not, and there cannot be, a real conception of humanity.

Humanity? Where is the limit of humanity? Where does it end and where does it begin? Does humanity stop short of a savage, an idiot, an alcoholic, an insane person? If we are going to draw a line of demarcation for humanity, so as to exclude the lower representatives of the human race, where are we going to draw it? Are we going to exclude the negroes, as the Americans do, and the Hindoos, as some English do, and the Jews, as some do? But if we are going to include all men without exception, why include men only, and not the higher animals, many of whom stand higher than the lower representatives of the human race?

We do not know humanity as an external object, — we do not know its limits. Humanity is a fiction, and it cannot be loved. It would indeed be very convenient, if men could love humanity just as they love the family; it would be very convenient, as the communists talk of doing, to substitute the communal for the competitive tendency of human activity, and the universal for the individual, so that every man may be for all, and all for every man, only there are no motives whatever for it. The positivists, the communists, and all the preachers of the scientific brotherhood preach the widening of that love which men have for themselves and for their families and for the state, so as to embrace all humanity, forgetting that the love which they advocate is the personal love, which, by spreading out thinner, could extend to the family; which, by spreading out still thinner, could extend to the natural country of birth, which completely vanishes as soon as it reaches an artificial state, as Austria, Turkey, England, and which we are not even able to imagine, when we come to humanity, an entirely mystical subject.

"Man loves himself (his animal life), loves his family, loves even his country. Why should he not love also humanity? How nice that would be! By the way, this is precisely what Christianity teaches."

Thus think the preachers of the positivist, communistic, socialistic brotherhoods. It would indeed be very nice, but it cannot be, because love which is based on the personal and the social conception of life cannot go beyond the state.

The error of judgment consists in this, that the social life-conception, on which is based the love of family and of country, is built on the love of personality, and that this love, being transferred from the personality to the family, the race, the nationality, the state, keeps growing weaker and weaker, and in the state reaches its extreme limit, beyond which it cannot go.

The necessity for widening the sphere of love is incontestable; but at the same time this very necessity for its widening in reality destroys the possibility of love and proves the insufficiency of the personal, the human love.

And here the preachers of the positivist, communistic, socialistic brotherhoods, to succour the human love, which has proved insufficient, propose the Christian love,— in its consequences alone, and not in its foundations: they propose the love of humanity alone, without the love of God.

But there can be no such love. There exists no motive for it. Christian love results only from the Christian conception of life, according to which the meaning of life consists in the love of God and in serving Him.

By a natural progression, from the love of self to the love of family, of the race, of the nation, of the state, the social conception of life has brought men to the consciousness of the necessity for a love of humanity, which has no limits and blends with everything in existence,—to something which evokes no sensations in man; it has brought them to a contradiction, which cannot be solved by the social conception of life.

Only the Christian teaching in all its significance, by giving a new meaning to life, solves it. Christianity recognizes the love of self, and of the family, and of the nation, and of humanity,—not only of humanity, but of everything living, of everything in existence; it recognizes the necessity for an endless widening of the sphere of love; but the object of this love it does not find outside of self, or in the aggregate of personalities,—in the family, the race, the state, humanity, in the whole external world, but in oneself, in one's personality,—which, however, is a divine personality, the essence of which is the same love, to the necessity of widening which the animal personality was brought, in saving itself from the consciousness of its perdition.

The difference between the Christian teaching and what preceded it is this, that the preceding social teaching said: "Live contrary to your nature (meaning only the animal nature), subordinate it to the external law of the family, the society, the state;" but Christianity says: "Live in accordance with your nature (meaning the divine nature), subordinating it to nothing,—neither to your own, nor to anybody else's animal nature,—and you will attain what you are striving after by subordinating your external nature to external laws."

The Christian teaching takes man back to the primitive consciousness of self, not of self—the animal, but of self — God, the divine spark, of self — the son of God, of just such a God as the Father himself, but included in an animal integument. And the recognition of self as this son of God, whose chief quality is love, satisfies also all those demands for the widening of the sphere of love, to which the man of the social conception of life was brought. There, with a greater and ever greater widening of the sphere of love for the salvation of the personality, love was a necessity and was applied to certain objects, — self, the family, society, humanity; with the Christian conception of life, love is not a necessity and is not adapted to anything, but is an essential quality of man's soul. Man does not love because it is advantageous for him to love this man or these men, but because love is the essence of his soul, — because he cannot help loving.

The Christian teaching consists in pointing out to man that the essence of his soul is love, that his good is derived not from the fact that he will love this or that man, but from the fact that he will love the beginning of everything, God, whom he recognizes in himself through love, and so will love everybody and everything.

In this does the fundamental difference between the Christian teaching and the teaching of the positivists and of all the theorists of the non-Christian universal brotherhood consist.

Such are the two chief misconceptions concerning the Christian teaching, from which originate the majority of the false opinions in regard to it. One is, that, like the preceding teachings, Christ's teaching inculcates rules, which men are obliged to follow, and that these rules are impracticable; the other is, that the whole significance of Christianity consists in the teaching about the advantageous cohabitation of humanity, as one family, for which, without mentioning the love of God, it is necessary only to follow the rule of love toward humanity.

The false opinion of the scientific men, that the teaching of the supernatural forms the essence of the Christian teaching, and that Christ's vital teaching is impracticable, together with the misconception which arises from this false opinion, forms the second cause why Christianity is not understood by the men of our time.

V.

THERE are many causes for the failure to comprehend Christ's teaching. One cause lies in this, that men assume that they understand the teaching, when they decide, as the churchmen do, that it was transmitted to us in a supernatural manner; or, as the scientific men do, that they understand it, when they have studied a part of those external phenomena in which it is expressed. Another cause of a failure to comprehend lies in the misconceptions as to the impracticability of the teaching and as to this, that it ought to give way to the teaching about the love of humanity; but the chief cause which has engendered all these misconceptions is this, that Christ's teaching is considered to be such as can be accepted, or not, without changing one's life.

The men who are accustomed to the existing order of things, who love it and are afraid to change it, try to comprehend the teaching as a collection of revelations and rules, which may be accepted, without changing their lives, whereas Christ's teaching is not merely a teaching about rules which a man may follow, but the elucidation of a new meaning of life, which determines the whole, entirely new activity of humanity for the period upon which it is entering.

Human life moves, passes, like the life of the individual, and every age has its corresponding life-conception, and this life-conception is inevitably accepted by men. Those men who do not consciously accept the life-conception proper for their age are brought to it unconsciously.

What takes place with the change of views on life in the case of individuals, takes place also with the change of the views on life in the case of nations and of all humanity. If a man with a family continues to be guided in his activity by a childish comprehension of life, his life will become so hard for him that he will involuntarily seek another comprehension of life, and will gladly accept the one which is proper for his age.

The same is now taking place in our humanity in the transition from the pagan conception of life to the Christian, which is now going on. The social man of our time is brought by life itself to the necessity of renouncing the pagan conception of life, which is no longer proper for the present age of humanity, and of submitting to the demands of the Christian teaching, the truths of which, no matter how distorted and misinterpreted they may be, are still known to him and alone furnish a solution to those contradictions in which he is losing himself.

If the demands of the Christian teaching seem strange and even perilous to the man of the social life-conception, the demands of the social teaching anciently seemed just as incomprehensible and perilous to a savage, when he did not yet fully comprehend them and was unable to foresee their consequences.

"It is irrational for me to sacrifice my peace or even my life," says the savage, "in order to defend something incomprehensible, intangible, conventional, — the family, the race, the country, and, above all else, it is dangerous to give myself over to the disposition of a foreign power."

But the time came when the savage, on the one hand, comprehended, however dimly, the significance of the social life, the significance of its prime mover, — the public approval or condemnation, — glory; on the other hand, when the sufferings of his personal life became so great that he no longer continued to believe in the truth of his former conception of life, and accepted the social, the political teaching and submitted to it.

The same now takes place with the social, the political man.

"It is irrational for me," says the social man, "to sacrifice my good, the good of my family, my country, for the fulfilment of the conditions of some higher law, which demands from me the renunciation of the most natural and the best sentiments of love for myself, my family, my country, and, above all, it is dangerous to reject the security of life, which is given by the political structure."

But the time comes when, on the one hand, the dim consciousness in his soul of a higher law of love for God and for his neighbour, and, on the other, the sufferings which arise from the contradictions of life, compel him to reject the social life-conception and to accept the new, Christian conception of life, which is offered to him, and which solves all the contradictions and removes the sufferings of his life. And this time has now come.

To us, who thousands of years ago experienced the transition from the animal, personal life-conception to the social one, it seems that that transition was necessary and natural, and this, the one through which we have been passing these eighteen hundred years, is arbitrary, unnatural, and terrible. But that only seems so to us, because the other transition is already accomplished, and its activity has already passed into the subconscious, while the present transition is not yet accomplished, and we have to accomplish it consciously.

The social life-conception entered into the consciousness of men through centuries and millenniums, passed through several forms, and has now passed for humanity into the sphere of the subconscious, which is transmitted through heredity, education, and habit, and so it seems natural to us. But five thousand years ago it seemed to men just as unnatural and terrible as now the Christian teaching seems to us in its true meaning.

It now seems to us that the demands of the Christian teaching for a universal brotherhood, abolition of nationalities, absence of property, the apparently so strange non-resistance to evil, are impossible demands. But just so strange, thousands of years ago, seemed the demands, not only of the state, but also of the family, as, for example, the demand that the parents should support their children, and the young — the old, and that husband and wife should be true to one another. Still more strange, even senseless, seemed the political demands, — that the citizens should submit to the powers that be, pay taxes, go to war in the defence of their country, and so forth. It now seems to us that all such demands are simple, intelligible, natural, and have nothing mystical or even strange about them; but five or three thousand years ago, these demands seemed impossible.

The social life-conception served as a basis for religions for the very reason that, when it manifested itself to men, it seemed to them quite unintelligible, mystical, and supernatural. Now, since we have outlived this phase of the life of humanity, we understand the rational causes of the union of men in families, communes, states; but in antiquity the demands for such a union were manifested in the name of the supernatural, and were confirmed by it.

The patriarchal religion deified the families, races, nations: the political religions deified kings and states. Even now the majority of the men of little culture, such as our peasants, who call the Tsar an earthly God, submit to the social laws, not from a rational consciousness of their necessity, not because they have a conception of the idea of the state, but from a religious sentiment.

Even so now the Christian teaching represents itself to the men of the social, or pagan, world-conception in the form of a supernatural religion, whereas in reality there is in it nothing mysterious, or mystical, or supernatural; it is nothing but the teaching about life, which corresponds to that stage of the material development, to that age, in which humanity is, and which must therefore inevitably be accepted by it.

The time will come, and is already at hand, when the Christian foundations of life, equality, brotherhood of men, community of possession, non-resistance to evil, will become as natural and as simple as the foundations of the family, the social, and the political life now appear to us.

Neither man nor humanity can in their motion turn back. The social, family, and political life-conceptions have been outlived by men, and it is necessary to go ahead and accept the higher life-conception, which indeed is being done now.

This motion takes place from two sides, consciously, in consequence of spiritual causes, and unconsciously, in consequence of material causes.

Just as the individual seldom changes his life merely in accordance with the indications of reason, but as a rule, in spite of the new meaning and the new aims indicated by reason, continues to live his former life and changes it only when his life becomes entirely contradictory to his consciousness, and, therefore, agonizing, so also humanity, having come through its religious guides to know the new meaning of life, the new aims, toward which it must tend, even after this knowledge continues for a long time, in the case of the majority of men, to live the previous life, and is guided to the acceptance of a new life-conception only through the impossibility of continuing the former life.

In spite of the demands for the change of life, as cognized and expressed by the religious guides and accepted by the wisest men, the majority of men, in spite of the religious relation to these guides, that is, the faith in their teaching, continue in the more complex life to be guided by the previous teaching, just as a man of a family would act, if, knowing how he ought to live at his age, he should from habit and frivolity continue to live a child's life.

It is this that takes place in the matter of the transition of humanity from one age to another, such as is now going on. Humanity has outgrown its social, political age, and has entered upon a new one. It knows the teaching which ought to be put at the foundation of the life of this new age, but from inertia continues to hold on to the previous forms of life. From this lack of correspondence between the life-conception and the practice of life there arises a series of contradictions and sufferings, which poison our life and demand its change.

We need only to compare the practice of life with its theory, in order that we may be frightened at the crying contradiction of the conditions of life and of our consciousness, in which we live.

Our whole life is one solid contradiction to everything we know and consider necessary and right. This contradiction is in everything, — in the economic, the political, the international life. As though forgetting what we know, and for a time putting aside what we believe in (we cannot help but believe, because this constitutes our only foundations of life), we do everything contrary to what our conscience and our common sense demand of us.

In economic, political, and international relations we are guided by those foundations which were useful to men three and five thousand years ago, and which directly contradict our present consciousness and those conditions of life in which we now are.

It was well enough for a man of antiquity to live amidst a division of men into slaves and masters, when he believed that this division was from God, and that it could not be otherwise. But is a similar division possible in our day?

A man of the ancient world could consider himself in the right to use the benefits of this world to the disadvantage of other men, causing them to suffer for generations, because he believed that men are born of various breeds, noble and base, of the generation of Japheth and of Ham. Not only the greatest sages of the world, the teachers of humanity, Plato, Aristotle, justified the existence of slaves and proved the legality of it, but even three centuries ago men who wrote of the imaginary society of the future, of Utopia, could not imagine it without slaves.

The men of antiquity, and even of the Middle Ages, believed, believed firmly, that men are not equal, that only the Persians, only the Greeks, only the Romans, only the French were real men. But those men who in our time champion aristocratism and patriotism do not believe, cannot believe, in what they say.

We all know, and we cannot help but know, even if we have never heard or read this thought clearly expressed and have never expressed it ourselves, we, having imbibed this consciousness, which is borne in the Christian atmosphere, know with our whole heart, and we cannot help but know, that fundamental truth of the Christian teaching, that we all are the sons of one Father, all of us, no matter where we may live or what language we may speak, — that we are all brothers and are subject only to the law of love, which by our common Father is implanted in our hearts.

No matter what the manner of thought and degree of culture of a man of our time may be, be he a cultured liberal of any shade whatever, be he a philosopher of any camp, be he a scientific man, an economist, of any school, be he an uncultured, even a religious man of any confession of faith, — every man of our time knows that all men have the same right to life and to the benefits of this world, that no man is better or worse than any one else, that all men are equal. Everybody knows this with absolute certainty and with his whole being, and at the same time not only sees all about him the division of men into two castes: one, which is working, is oppressed, in need, in suffering, and the other, idle, oppressing, and living in luxury and pleasure, — he not only sees this, but involuntarily from one side or another takes part in this division of men, which his reason rejects, and he cannot help but suffer from the consciousness of such a contradiction and from participation in it.

Be he master or slave, a man of our time cannot help but experience a constant agonizing contradiction between his consciousness and reality, and sufferings which arise from it.

The working masses, the great majority of people, suffering from the constant, all-absorbing, senseless, dawnless labour and sufferings, suffer most of all from the consciousness of the crying contradiction between what exists and what ought to be, as the result of everything which is professed by them and by those who have placed them in this position and maintain them in it.

They know that they are in slavery, and are perishing in want and darkness, in order to serve the lust of the minority, which keeps them in slavery. They know this and give expression to it. And this consciousness not only increases their sufferings, but even forms the essence of their sufferings.

The ancient slave knew that he was a slave by nature, but our workman, feeling himself to be a slave, knows that he should not be a slave, and so experiences the torments of Tantalus, eternally wishing for and not receiving what not only could, but even should be. The sufferings of the working classes which result from the contradiction between what is and what ought to be are increased tenfold by the envy and hatred which result from them.

A workman of our time, even though his work may be lighter than that of an ancient slave and he may have attained an eight-hour work-day and a wage of three dollars per day, will not cease suffering, because, in manufacturing articles which he will not make use of, and working, not for himself and at his pleasure, but from necessity, for whims of luxurious and idle people in general and for the enrichment of one man, the rich owner of the factory or plant, in particular, he knows that all this is taking place in a world in which not only they have accepted the scientific proposition that only work is wealth, that the exploitation of other men's labour is unjust, illegal, amenable to punishment by law, but also they profess Christ's teaching, according to which all are brothers, and a man's worth and merit consists only in serving his neighbour, and not in making use of him.

He knows all this, and he cannot help but suffer torments from this crying contradiction between what ought to be and what actually exists. "From all the data and from everything which I know all men profess," the labouring man says to himself, "I ought to be free, equal to all other men, and loved; but I am a slave, — I am humiliated and hated." And he himself hates and seeks for means to save himself from this position, to throw off his foe, who is pressing down on him, and himself to get on top of him. They say, "The working men are not right in their desire to take the place of the capitalists, nor the poor in their desire to take the place of the rich." This is not true: the working men and the poor would be in the wrong, if they wished for it in a world in which slaves and masters, the rich and the poor, are established by God; but they wish for it in a world in which is professed the Gospel teaching, the first proposition of which is the filial relation of men to God, and so the brotherhood and equality of all men. And no matter how much men may try, it is impossible to conceal the fact that one of the first conditions of a Christian life is love, not in words, but in work.

In a still greater contradiction and in still greater sufferings lives the man of the so-called cultured class. Every such man, if he believes in anything, believes, if not in the brotherhood of men, at least in humanitarianism; if not in humanitarianism, at least in justice; if not in justice, at least in science, — and with all that knows that his whole life is built on conditions which are quite the reverse of all that, of all the tenets of Christianity, and humanity, and justice, and science.

He knows that all the habits in which he is brought up, and the deprivation of which would be a torment for him, can be gratified only by the painful, often perilous labour of oppressed working men, that is, by the most palpable, coarse violation of those principles of Christianity, humanitarianism, justice, and even science (I mean the demands of political economy), which he professes. He professes the principles of brotherhood, humanitarianism, justice, science, and yet lives in such a way that he needs that oppression of the labouring men which he denies, and even in such a way that his whole life is an exploitation of this oppression, and not only does he live in this way, but also he directs his activity to the maintenance of this order of things, which is directly opposed to everything in which he believes.

We are all brothers, and yet every morning my brother or my sister carries out my vessel. We are all brothers, and I need every morning my cigar, sugar, a mirror, and so forth, objects in the manufacture of which my brothers and my sisters, who are my equals, have been losing their health, and I employ these articles and even demand them. We are all brothers, and I live by working in a bank, or in a business house, or a shop, in order to make all the wares which my brothers need more expensive for them. We are all brothers, and yet I live by receiving a salary for arraigning, judging, and punishing a thief or a prostitute, whose existence is conditioned by the whole composition of my life, and who, I know myself, ought not to be punished, but corrected. We are all brothers, and I live by receiving a salary for collecting the taxes from poor working men, to be used for the luxury of the idle and the rich. We are all brothers, and I receive a salary for preaching to people what is supposed to be the Christian religion, in which I do not believe myself, and which deprives them of the possibility of finding out the real faith. I receive a salary as a priest, a bishop, for deceiving people in what is the most important matter for them. We are all brothers, but I give to the poor my pedagogical, medical, literary labours for money only. We are all brothers, but I receive a salary for preparing myself to commit murder, studying how to kill, or making a gun, powder, fortresses.

The whole life of our higher classes is one solid contradiction, which is the more agonizing, the more sensitive man's conscience is.

The man with a sensitive conscience cannot help but suffer, if he lives this life. There is one means by which he can free himself from this suffering, — it consists in drowning his conscience; but even if such men succeed in drowning their conscience, they cannot drown their terror.

Insensitive people of the higher, the oppressing classes, and those who have drowned their consciences, if they do not suffer from their consciences, suffer from fear and hatred. Nor can they help but suffer. They know of that hatred against them which exists, and cannot help but exist, among the labouring classes; and they know that the working men know that they are deceived and outraged, and they are beginning to organize for the purpose of throwing off the oppression and retaliating upon the oppressors. The higher classes see the unions, strikes, the First of May, and they feel the calamity which is threatening them, and this terror poisons their life. They feel the calamity which is threatening them, and the terror which they experience passes into a feeling of self-defence and hatred. They know that if they weaken for a moment in their struggle with the slaves oppressed by them, they will themselves perish, because the slaves are enraged, and this rage is growing with every day of the oppression. The oppressors cannot stop oppressing, even if they should wish to do so. They know that they themselves will perish, the moment they stop or even weaken in their oppressions. And they do oppress, in spite of their seeming concern for the welfare of the labouring people, for an eight-hour day, for the prohibition to employ children and women, for pensions and rewards. All this is a deception or a provision for eliciting work from the slave; but the slave remains a slave, and the master, who could not live without the slave, is less than ever prepared to free him.

The ruling classes are, in relation to the workingmen, in the position of a man who is astride a man whom he holds down and does not let go of, not so much because he does not want to let go of him, as because he knows that he need but for a moment let go of the subdued man, and the subdued man will cut his throat, because the subdued man is enraged and has a knife in his hand. And so, whether they be sensitive or not, our wealthy classes cannot enjoy the good things which they have taken from the poor, as the ancients did, who believed in their right. Their whole life and all their pleasures are poisoned by rebukes of conscience or by terror.

Such is the economical contradiction. More striking still is the political contradiction.

All men are above all else educated in the habits of obedience to the laws of the state. The whole life of the men of our time is determined by the law of the state. A man marries or gets a divorce, educates his children, even professes a faith (in many states) in accordance with the law. What is this law, which determines the whole life of men? Do the men believe in this law? Do they consider it to be true? Not in the least. In the majority of cases, the men of our time do not believe in the justice of this law, despise it, and yet obey it. It was all very well for the men of antiquity to carry out their laws. They believed firmly that their law (which for the most part was also religious) was the one true law which all men must obey. But we? We know, and we cannot help but know, that the law of our state is not only not the one eternal law, but that it is only one of many laws of various countries, equally imperfect, and frequently and palpably false and unjust, and widely discussed in the newspapers. It was all very well for a Jew to submit to his laws, when he had no doubt but that they were written by God's finger; or, for a Roman, when he thought that the nymph Egeria had written his laws; or even when they believed that the kings who gave the laws were the anointed of the Lord, or even that the legislative bodies had a desire to find the best laws, and were able to do so. But we know how laws are made; we have all been behind the scenes; we all know that laws are the results of greed, deception, the struggle of parties, — that in them there is and there can be no true justice. And so the men of our time cannot believe that obedience to civil or political laws would satisfy the demands of the rationality of human nature. Men have known for a long time that it is not sensible to obey a law of the correctness of which there can be any doubt, and so they cannot help but suffer, if they obey a law the rationality and obligatoriness of which they do not acknowledge.

A man cannot help but suffer, when his whole life is determined in advance by laws which he must obey under the menace of punishment, and in the rationality and justice of which he does not believe, and the unnaturalness, cruelty, injustice of which he clearly recognizes. We recognize the uselessness of custom-houses and import duties, and we must pay the duties; we recognize the uselessness of the expenses for the support of royal courts and many governmental offices; we recognize the harmfulness of the church propaganda, and we must contribute to the support of these institutions; we recognize the cruelty and unscrupulousness of the penalties imposed by courts of justice, and we must take part in them; we recognize the irregularity and harmfulness of the distribution of land-ownership, and we must submit to it; we do not recognize the indispensableness of armies and of war, and must bear terrible burdens for the maintenance of armies and the waging of wars, and so forth.

But these contradictions are as nothing in comparison with the contradiction which has now arisen among men in their international relations, and which, under threat of ruining both human reason and human life, demands a solution. This is the contradiction between the Christian conscience and war.

We are all Christian nations, who live the same spiritual life, so that every good, fruitful thought, which springs up in one corner of the earth, is at once communicated to the whole Christian world, evoking similar sensations of joy and pride, independently of nationality; we, who not only love the thinkers, benefactors, poets, scholars of other nations, but also pride ourselves on the exploit of a Damien, as though it were our own; we, who just love the men of other nationalities, — the French, the Germans, the Americans, the English; we, who not only respect their qualities, but rejoice when we meet them, who give them a smile of recognition, who not only could not regard a war with them as something to be proud of, but who could not even think without horror that any disagreement may arise between these men and us, — we are all called to take part in murder, which must inevitably take place, to-morrow, if not to-day.

It was all very well for a Jew, a Greek, a Roman not

only to defend the independence of his nation by means of murder, but by the means of murder also to cause other nations to submit to him, for he believed firmly that his nation was the one true, good, kind nation, which was loved by God, and that all the other nations were Philistines, barbarians. Even the men of the Middle Ages and the men of the end of the last and the beginning of this century could have believed so. But we, no matter how much we may be teased to do so, can no longer believe in this, and this contradiction is so terrible for the men of our time that it is impossible to live, if we do not destroy it.

"We live in a time which is full of contradictions," Count Komárovski, professor of international law, writes in his learned treatise. "In the press of all countries there is constantly shown a universal tendency toward peace, toward its necessity for all nations. In the same sense express themselves the representatives of governments, as private individuals and as official organs, in parliamentary debates, in diplomatic exchanges of opinion, and even in international treaties. At the same time, however, the governments annually increase the military forces of their countries, impose new taxes, make loans, and leave to future generations, as a legacy, the obligation to bear the blunders of the present senseless politics. What a crying contradiction between words and deeds!

"Of course, the governments, to justify these measures, point to the exclusively defensive character of all these expenditures and armaments, but none the less it remains a puzzle for every unbiassed man, whence we are to expect attacks, since all the great powers unanimously in their politics pursue the one aim of defence. In reality this looks as though each of these powers waited every moment to be attacked by another, and these are the consequences, — universal distrust and a preternatural endeavour of one power to surpass the force of the others

Such an emulation in itself increases the danger of war; the nations cannot for any length of time stand the intensified arming, and sooner or later will prefer war to all the disadvantages of the present condition and constant menace. Thus the most insignificant cause will be sufficient to make the fire of a universal war flame up in the whole of Europe. It is incorrect to think that such a crisis can cure us of the political and economical calamities which oppress us. Experience from the wars which have been waged in recent years teaches us that every war has only sharpened the hostility of the nations, increased the burden and the unendurableness of the pressure of militarism, and made the politico-economic condition of Europe more hopeless and complex."

"Modern Europe keeps under arms an active army of nine millions of men," writes Enrico Ferri, "and fifteen millions of reserves, expending on them four milliards of francs per year. By arming itself more and more, it paralyzes the sources of the social and the individual welfare, and may easily be compared to a man who, to provide himself with a gun, condemns himself to anæmia, at the same time wasting all his strength for the purpose of making use of the very gun with which he is providing himself, and under the burden of which he will finally fall."

The same was said by Charles Butt,[1] in his speech which he delivered in London before the Association for the Reform and Codification of the Law of Nations, July 26, 1887. After pointing out the same nine millions and over of the active armies and seventeen millions of reserves, and the enormous expenses of the governments for the support of these armies and equipments, he says: "But this forms only a small part of the actual cost, for besides the figures mentioned, which constitute merely the war budgets of the nations, we have to take into account the enormous loss to society by the withdrawal of so

[1] Not Charles Butt, but Henry Richard.

many able-bodied men . . . from the occupations of productive industry, together with the prodigious capital invested in all warlike preparations and appliances, and which is absolutely unproductive. . . . One necessary result of the expenditure on wars and preparations for war is the steady growth of national debts. . . . The aggregate national debts of Europe, by far the larger proportion of which has been contracted for war purposes, amount at the present time to £4,680,000,000."

The same Komárovski says in another place: "We are living in a hard time. Everywhere do we hear complaints as to the slackness of business and industry and in general as to the bad economic conditions: people point out the hard conditions of the life of the labouring classes and the universal impoverishment of the masses. But, in spite of it, the governments, in their endeavour to maintain their independence, reach the extreme limits of madness. Everywhere they invent new taxes and imposts, and the financial oppression of the nations knows no limits. If we look at the budgets of the European states for the last one hundred years, we shall first of all be struck by their constantly progressive and rapid growth. How can we explain this extraordinary phenomenon, which sooner or later threatens us with inevitable bankruptcy?

"This is incontestably due to the expenditures caused by the maintenance of an army, which swallow one-third and even one-half of the budgets of the European states. What is most lamentable in connection with it is this, that no end can be foreseen to this increase of the budgets and impoverishment of the masses. What is socialism, if not a protest against this abnormal condition, in which the greater part of the population of our part of the world finds itself?"

"We ruin ourselves," says Frederic Passy, in a note read at the last Congress (1890) of Universal Peace, at

London, "in preparing the means for taking part in the mad butcheries of the future, or in paying the interests of debts bequeathed to us by the mad and culpable butcheries of the past. We die of starvation, in order to be able to kill one another off."

Farther on, speaking of how France looks upon this subject, he says: "We believe that one hundred years after the *Declaration of the rights of man and of a citizen* it is time to recognize the rights of nations and to renounce for ever all these enterprises of force and violence, which, under the name of conquests, are real crimes against humanity, and which, whatever the ambition of the sovereigns or the pride of the races . . . weaken even those who seem to profit from them."

"I am always very much surprised at the way religion is carried on in this country," says Sir Wilfrid Lawson, at the same Congress. "You send a boy to the Sunday school, and you tell him, 'My dear boy, you must love your enemies; if any boy strikes you, don't strike him again; try to reform him by loving him.' Well, the boy stays in the Sunday school till he is fourteen or fifteen years of age, and then his friends say, 'Put him in the army.' What has he to do in the army? Why, not to love his enemies, but whenever he sees an enemy to run him through the body with a bayonet. That is the nature of all religious teaching in this country. I do not think that that is a very good way of carrying out the precepts of religion. I think if it is a good thing for the boy to love his enemy, it is a good thing for the man to love his enemy."

And farther: "The nations of Europe . . . keep somewhere about twenty-eight millions of armed men to settle quarrels by killing one another, instead of by arguing. That is what the Christian nations of the world are doing at this moment. It is a very expensive way also; for this publication which I saw made out that since the year

1872 these nations had spent the almost incredible amount of £1,500,000,000 of money in preparing, and settling their quarrels by killing one another. Now it seems to me that with that state of things one of two positions must be accepted: either that Christianity is a failure or, that those who profess to expound Christianity have failed in expounding it properly."

"Until our ironclads are withdrawn, and our army disbanded, we are not entitled to call ourselves a Christian nation," says Mr. J. Jowet Wilson.

In a discussion which arose in connection with the question of the obligatoriness of Christian pastors to preach against war, Mr. G. D. Bartlett said, among other things: "If I understand the Scriptures, I say that men are only playing with Christianity when they ignore this question," that is, say nothing about war. "I have lived a longish life, I have heard many sermons, and I can say without any exaggeration that I never heard universal peace recommended from the pulpit half a dozen times in my life. . . . Some twenty years ago I happened to stand in a drawing-room where there were forty or fifty people, and I dared to moot the proposition that war was incompatible with Christianity. They looked upon me as an arrant fanatic. The idea that we could get on without war was regarded as unmitigated weakness and folly."

In the same sense spoke the Catholic Abbé Defourny: "One of the first precepts of this eternal law which burns in the consciences of men is the one which forbids taking the life of one's like, shedding human blood without just cause, and without being constrained by necessity. It is one of those laws which are most indelibly engraved in the human heart. . . . But if it is a question of war, that is, of the shedding of human blood in torrents, the men of the present do not trouble themselves about a just cause. Those who take part in it do not think of asking themselves whether these innumerable murders are justified or not, that is, if the wars, or what goes by that name, are just or iniquitous, legal or illegal, permissible or criminal . . . whether they violate, or not, the primordial law which prohibits homicide and murder . . . without just cause. But their conscience is mute in this matter.

"War has ceased for them to be an act which has anything to do with morality. They have no other joy, in the fatigue and perils of the camp, than that of being victorious, and no other sadness than that of being vanquished. . . . Do not tell me that they serve their country. A long time ago a great genius told you these words, which have become proverbial, 'Reject justice, and what are the empires but great societies of brigands?' And are not a band of brigands themselves small empires? Brigands themselves have certain laws or conventions by which they are ruled. There, too, they fight for the conquest of booty and for the honour of the band. . . . The principle of the institution" (he is talking of the establishment of an international tribunal) "is this, that the European nations should stop being a nation of thieves, and the armies gangs of brigands and of pirates, and, I must add, of slaves. Yes, the armies are gangs of slaves, slaves of one or two rulers, or one or two ministers, who dispose of them tyrannically, without any other guarantee, we know, than a nominal one.

"What characterizes the slave is this, that he is in the hands of his master like a chattel, a tool, and no longer a man. Just so it is with a soldier, an officer, a general, who march to murder and to death without any care as to justice, by the arbitrary will of ministers. . . . Thus military slavery exists, and it is the worst of slaveries, particularly now, when by means of enforced military service it puts the chain about the necks of all free and strong men of the nations, in order to make of them tools of murder, killers by profession, butchers of human flesh, for this is the only *opus servile* for which they are chained up and trained. . . .

"Rulers, to the number of two or three . . . united into a secret cabinet, deliberate without control and without minutes which are intended for publicity . . . consequently without any guarantee for the conscience of those whom they send out to be killed."

"The protests against the heavy arming do not date from our day," says Signor E. T. Moneta. "Listen to what Montesquieu wrote in his time.

"'France' (you may substitute the word 'Europe') 'will be ruined by the military. A new malady has spread through Europe; it has infected our princes and has made them keep a disproportionate number of troops. It has its exacerbations, and it necessarily becomes contagious, because, as soon as one state increases what it calls its troops, the others suddenly increase theirs, so that nothing is gained by it but the common ruin.

"'Every monarch keeps on a war footing all the troops which he might need in case his people were in danger of being exterminated, and this state of tension, of all against all, is called peace. As a result, Europe is so ruined that if private individuals were in the condition in which the powers are in this part of the world, the richest of them would not have anything to live on. We are poor with the riches and the commerce of the whole universe.'

"This was written almost 150 years ago; the picture seems to be made for to-day. One single thing has changed, — the system of government. In the time of Montesquieu, and also afterward, they used to say that the cause for the maintenance of great armies lay in the absolute kings, who waged war in the hope of finding in the conquests the means for enriching their private budgets and passing down to history in the aureole of glory.

"Then they said, 'Oh, if the peoples could choose themselves those who have the right to refuse the governments soldiers and money, for then the politics of war would come to an end.'

"We have to-day representative governments in nearly all of Europe, and none the less the expenditures for war and for its preparation are increased in a frightful proportion.

"Evidently the folly of the princes has passed down to the governing classes. At the present time they no longer make war because a prince was disrespectful to a courtesan, as such things happened in the time of Louis XIV., but by exaggerating the respectable sentiments, like that of the national dignity and of patriotism, by exciting public opinion against a neighbouring nation, there will come a day when it will be sufficient to say, though the information may not be true, that the ambassador of your government was not received by the chief of a state, in order to make break forth the most terrible and disastrous of wars ever seen.

"At the present time Europe keeps under arms more soldiers than there were in the time of Napoleon's great wars. All citizens, with few exceptions, are obliged on our continent to pass several years in the barracks. They build fortresses, construct arsenals and ships, constantly manufacture arms, which after awhile have to be replaced by others, because science, which ought always to be directed toward the well-being of men, unfortunately lends its aid to works of destruction, invents at every instant new engines for killing great masses of men as rapidly as possible.

"And in order to maintain so many soldiers and to make such vast preparations for murder, they spend yearly hundreds of millions, that is, what would be sufficient for the education of the people, for the execution of the greatest works of public utility, and would furnish the means for solving pacifically the social question.

"Europe, therefore, finds itself, in spite of the scientific conquests, in a condition as though it were still living in the worst times of the ferocious Middle Ages. All men complain of this situation, which is not yet war, but which is not peace either, and everybody would like to get out of it. The chiefs of governments protest that they want peace, and it is a matter of emulation between them as to who will make the most solemn pacific declarations. But on the same day, or the day following, they present to the legislative chambers propositions for increasing the standing army, and they say that it is for the purpose of maintaining and assuring peace that they take so many precautions.

"But it is not the kind of peace we like; nor are the nations deceived. True peace has reciprocal confidence for its basis, while these enormous preparations betray a profound distrust, if not a concealed hostility, between the states. What would we say of a man who, wishing to prove his sentiments of friendship for his neighbour, should invite him to discuss some question with him, while he himself is holding a revolver in his hand? It is this flagrant contradiction between the pacific declarations and the warlike policy of the governments that all good citizens want to see stopped at any price and as quickly as possible."

They marvel why annually sixty thousand suicides are committed in Europe, and those only the ones that are recorded, which excludes Russia and Turkey; but what we ought to marvel at is not that there are so many suicides, but so few. Every man of our time, if he grasps the contradiction between his consciousness and his life, is in a very desperate condition. To say nothing of all the other contradictions between life and consciousness, which fill the life of a man of our time, the contradiction between this last military condition, in which Europe is, and the Christian profession of Europe is enough to make a man despair, doubt the rationality of human nature, and put an end to his life in this mad and beastly world. This contradiction, the military contradiction, which is the quintessence of all others, is so terrible that a man can live and take part in it only by not thinking of it, by being able to forget it.

How is this? We are all Christians, — we not only profess love of one another, but actually live one common life, the pulse of our life beats with the same beats, we aid one another, learn from one another, more and more approach one another, for a common joy! In this closer union lies the meaning of the whole of life, — and to-morrow some maddened head of a government will say something foolish, another man like him will answer him, and I shall go, making myself liable to be killed, to kill men who not only have done me no harm, but whom I love. And this is not a distant accident, but what we are preparing ourselves for, and it is not only a possible, but even an inevitable event.

It is enough to understand this clearly, in order to lose our mind and shoot ourselves. And it is precisely what happens with especial frequency among the military. We need but think for a moment, in order that we may come to the necessity of such an ending. It is only thus that we can explain that terrible tension with which the men of our time incline to intoxicate themselves with wine, tobacco, opium, cards, the reading of newspapers, travelling, all kinds of spectacles, and amusements. All these things are done like serious, important affairs. They are indeed important affairs. If there existed no external means for dimming their consciences, one-half of the men would at once shoot themselves, because to live contrary to one's reason is a most intolerable state, and all men of our time are in such a state. All men of our time live in a constant crying contradiction between consciousness and life. These contradictions are expressed in the economic and political relations, but most startling is this contradiction between the recognition of the law of the brotherhood of men, as professed by Christians, and the necessity, in which all men are placed by the universal military service, of being prepared for hostility, for murder, — of being at the same time a Christian and a gladiator.

VI.

THE removal of the contradiction between life and consciousness is possible in two ways, — by a change of life or by a change of consciousness, and in the choice of one of the two there can be no doubt.

A man may stop doing what he considers bad, but he cannot stop considering bad what is bad.

Even so the whole of humanity may stop doing what it considers bad, but is powerless, not only to change, but even for a time to retard the all-elucidating and expanding consciousness of what is bad and what, therefore, ought not to be. It would seem that the choice between the change of life and that of the consciousness ought to be clear and above doubt.

And so, it would seem, it is indispensable for the Christian humanity of our time to renounce the pagan forms of life, which it condemns, and to build up its life on the Christian foundations, which it professes.

But so it would be, if there did not exist the law of inertia, which is as invariable in the lives of men and nations as in inanimate bodies, and which is for men expressed by the psychological law, so well stated in the Gospel with the words, " and did not walk toward the light, because their deeds were evil." This law consists in this, that the majority of men do not think in order to know the truth, but in order to assure themselves that the life which they lead, and which is agreeable and habitual to them, is the one which coincides with the truth.

Slavery was contrary to all the moral principles which were preached by Plato and Aristotle, and yet neither the one nor the other saw this, because the negation of slavery destroyed all that life which they lived. The same happens in our world.

The division of men into two castes, like the violence of the state and of the army, is repugnant to all those moral principles by which our world lives, and at the same time the leading men of culture of our time do not seem to see it.

The majority, if not all, of the cultured people of our time unconsciously try to maintain the previous social concept of life which justifies their position, and to conceal from themselves and from men its inadequacy, and, above all, the necessity of the condition of the Christian life-conception, which destroys the whole structure of the existing life. They strive to maintain the orders that are based on the social life-conception, but themselves do not believe in it, because it is obsolete, and it is impossible to believe in it any longer.

All literature, the philosophic, the political, and that of the *belles-lettres*, of our time is striking in this respect. What a wealth of ideas, forms, colours, what erudition, elegance, abundance of thoughts, and what total absence of serious contents, and even what fear of every definiteness of thought and of its expression! Circumlocutions, allegories, jests, general, extremely broad reflections, and nothing simple, clear, pertinent to the matter, that is, to the question of life.

But it is not enough that they write and say graceful vapidities; they even write and say abominable, vile things, they in the most refined manner adduce reflections which take men back to primeval savagery, to the foundations, not only of pagan, but even of animal life, which we outlived as far back as five thousand years ago.

It can, indeed, not be otherwise. In keeping shy of the Christian life-conception, which for some impairs only the habitual order, and for others both the habitual and the advantageous order, men cannot help but return to the pagan concept of life, and to the teachings which are based on them. In our time they not only preach patriotism and aristocratism, as it was preached two thousand years ago, but they even preach the coarsest epicurism, animality, with this one difference, that the men who then preached it believed in what they preached, while now the preachers themselves do not believe in what they say, and they cannot believe, because what they preach no longer has any meaning. It is impossible to remain in one place, when the soil is in motion. If you do not go ahead, you fall behind. And, though it is strange and terrible to say so, the cultured people of our time, the leaders, with their refined reflections, in reality are dragging society back, not even to the pagan state, but to the state of primeval savagery.

In nothing may this direction of the activity of the leading men of our time be seen so clearly as in their relation to the phenomenon in which in our time the whole inadequacy of the social concept of life has been expressed in a concentrated form, — in their relation to war, to universal armaments, and to universal military service.

The indefiniteness, if not the insincerity, of the relation of the cultured men of our time to this phenomenon is striking. The relation to this matter in our cultured society is threefold: some look upon this phenomenon as something accidental, which arose from the peculiar political condition of Europe, and consider it corrigible, without the change of the whole structure of life, by means of external, diplomatic, international measures; others look upon this phenomenon as upon something terrible and cruel, but inevitable and fatal, like a disease or death; others again calmly and coolly look upon war as an indispensable, beneficent, and therefore desirable phenomenon.

These people look differently at the matter, but all of

them discuss war as an incident which is quite independent of the will of men who take part in it, and so do not even admit that natural question, which presents itself to every simple man, "Must I take part in it?" According to the opinion of all these men, these questions do not even exist, and every person, no matter how he himself may look upon war, must in this respect slavishly submit to the demands of the government.

The relation of the first, of those who see a salvation from wars in diplomatic, international measures, is beautifully expressed in the result of the last Congress of Peace in London, and in an article and letters concerning war by prominent authors in No. 8 of the *Revue des Revues* for 1891.

Here are the results of the Congress: having collected the personal or written opinions from learned men all over the world, the Congress began by a Te Deum in the Cathedral, and ended with a dinner with speeches, having for the period of five days listened to a large number of speeches, and having arrived at the following resolutions:

1. "The Congress affirms its belief that the brotherhood of man involves as a necessary consequence a brotherhood of nations, in which the true interests of all are acknowledged to be identical.

2. "The Congress recognizes the important influence which Christianity exercises upon the moral and political progress of mankind, and earnestly urges upon ministers of the Gospel, and other teachers of religion and morality, the duty of setting forth the principles of Peace and Good-will, and recommends that the third Sunday in December in each year be set apart for that purpose.

3. "This Congress expresses its opinion that all teachers of history should call the attention of the young to the grave evils inflicted on mankind in all ages by war, and to the fact that such war has been waged, as a rule, for most inadequate causes.

4. "The Congress protests against the use of military exercises in connection with the physical exercises of school, and suggests the formation of brigades for saving life rather than any of a quasi-military character; and it urges the desirability of impressing on the Board of Examiners, who formulate the questions for examination, the propriety of guiding the minds of children into the principles of Peace.

5. "The Congress holds that the doctrine of the universal rights of man requires that aboriginal and weaker races shall be guarded from injustice and fraud when brought into contact with civilized peoples, alike as to their territories, their liberties, and their property, and that they shall be shielded from the vices which are so prevalent among the so-called advanced races of men. It further expresses its conviction that there should be concert of action among the nations for the accomplishment of these ends. The Congress desires to express its hearty appreciation of the conclusions arrived at by the late Anti-Slavery Conference, held in Brussels, for the amelioration of the condition of the peoples of Africa.

6. "The Congress believes that the warlike prejudices and traditions which are still fostered in the various nationalities, and the misrepresentations by leaders of public opinion in legislative assemblies, or through the press, are not infrequently indirect causes of war. The Congress is therefore of opinion that these evils should be counteracted by the publication of accurate statements and information that would tend to the removal of misunderstanding among nations, and recommends to the Inter-Parliamentary Committee the importance of considering the question of commencing an international newspaper, which should have such a purpose as one of its primary objects.

7. "The Congress proposes to the Inter-Parliamentary Conference that the utmost support should be given to

every project for the unification of weights and measures, of coinage, tariffs, postal and telegraphic arrangements, means of transport, etc., which would assist in constituting a commercial, industrial, and scientific union of the peoples.

8. "The Congress, in view of the vast moral and social influence of woman, urges upon every woman throughout the world to sustain the things that make for peace; as otherwise she incurs grave responsibilities for the continuance of the systems of war and militarism.

9. "This Congress expresses the hope that the Financial Reform Association, and other Similar Societies in Europe and America, should unite in convoking at an early date a Conference to consider the best means of establishing equitable commercial relations between states by the reduction of import duties. The Congress feels that it can affirm that the whole of Europe desires Peace, and is impatiently waiting for the moment when it shall see the end of those crushing armaments which, under the plea of defence, become in their turn a danger, by keeping alive mutual distrust, and are at the same time the cause of that economic disturbance which stands in the way of settling in a satisfactory manner the problems of labour and poverty, which should take precedence of all others.

10. "The Congress, recognizing that a general disarmament would be the best guarantee of Peace, and would lead to the solution, in the general interest, of those questions which must now divide states, expresses the wish that a Congress of Representatives of all the states of Europe may be assembled as soon as possible, to consider the means of accepting a gradual general disarmament.

11. "The Congress, considering the timidity of the single Powers or other causes might delay indefinitely the convocation of the above-mentioned Congress, is of

opinion that the Government which should first dismiss any considerable number of soldiers would confer a signal benefit on Europe and mankind, because it would oblige other Governments, urged on by public opinion, to follow its example, and by the moral force of this accomplished fact, would have increased rather than diminished the condition of its national defence.

12. "This Congress, considering the question of disarmament, as well as the Peace question generally, depends upon public opinion, recommends the Peace Societies here represented, and all friends of Peace, to carry on an active propaganda among the people, especially at the time of Parliamentary elections, in order that the electors should give their vote to those candidates who have included in their programme Peace, Disarmament, and Arbitration.

13. "The Congress congratulates the friends of Peace on the resolution adopted by the International American Conference at Washington in April last, by which it was recommended that arbitration should be obligatory in all controversies concerning diplomatic and consular privileges, boundaries, territories, indemnities, right of navigation, and the validity, construction, and enforcement of treaties, and in all other cases, whatever their origin, nature, or occasion, except only those which, in the judgment of any of the nations involved in the controversy, may imperil its independence.

14. "The Congress respectfully recommends this resolution to the attention of the statesmen of Europe, and expresses the ardent desire that treaties in similar terms be speedily entered into between the other nations of the world.

15. "The Congress expresses its satisfaction at the adoption by the Spanish Senate, on June 16th last, of a project of law authorizing the Government to negotiate general or special treaties of arbitration for the settlement of all disputes, except those relating to the independence

and internal government of the state affected; also at the adoption of resolutions to a like effect by the Norwegian Storthing, and by the Italian Chamber, on July 11th.

16. "The Congress addresses official communications to the principal religious, political, commercial, labour, and peace organizations in civilized countries, requesting them to send petitions to governmental authorities of their respective countries, praying that measures be taken for the formation of suitable tribunals for the adjudicature of any international questions, so as to avoid the resort to war.

17. "Seeing (*a*) that the object pursued by all Peace Societies is the establishment of juridical order between nations; (*b*) that neutralization by international treaties constitutes a step toward this juridical state, and lessens the number of districts in which war can be carried on; the Congress recommends a larger extension of the rule of neutralization, and expresses the wish: (*a*) that all treaties which at present assure to a certain state the benefit of neutrality remain in force, or, if necessary, be amended in a manner to render the neutrality more effective, either by extending neutralization to the whole of the state, of which a part only may be neutralized, or by ordering the demolition of fortresses which constitute rather a peril than a guarantee of neutrality; (*b*) that new treaties, provided they are in harmony with the wishes of the population, be concluded for the establishment of the neutralization of other states.

18. "The Sub-Committee of the Congress recommends:

"I. That the next Congress be held immediately before or immediately after the next session of the Inter-Parliamentary Conference, and at the same place.

"II. That the question of an international Peace Emblem be postponed *sine die*.

"III. The adoption of the following resolution:

"(*a*) Resolved, that we express our satisfaction at the

formal and official overtures of the Presbyterian Church in the United States of America, addressed to the highest representatives of each church organization in Christendom, inviting the same to unite with itself in a general conference, the object of which shall be to promote the substitution of international arbitration for war; (*b*) that this Congress, assembled in London from the 14th to the 19th July, desires to express its profound reverence for the memory of Aurelio Saffi, the great Italian jurist, a member of the Committee of the International League of Peace and Liberty.

"IV. That the Memorial to the various Heads of Civilized States, adopted by this Congress and signed by the President, should so far as practicable be presented to each power, by an influential deputation.

"V. That the Organization Committee be empowered to make the needful verbal emendations in the papers and resolutions presented.

"VI. That the following resolutions be adopted:

"(*a*) A resolution of thanks to the Presidents of the various sittings of the Congress; (*b*) a resolution of thanks to the Chairman, the Secretary, and the Members of the Bureau of the Congress; (*c*) a resolution of thanks to the conveners and members of Sectional Committees; (*d*) a resolution of thanks to Rev. Cannon Scott Holland, Rev. Doctor Reuen, and Rev. J. Morgan Gibbon, for their pulpit addresses before the Congress, and that they be requested to furnish copies of the same for publication; and also to the Authorities of St. Paul's Cathedral, the City Temple, and Stamford Hill Congregational Church for the use of those buildings for public services; (*e*) a letter of thanks to Her Majesty for permission to visit Windsor Castle; (*f*) and also a resolution of thanks to the Lord Mayor and Lady Mayoress, to Mr. Passmore Edwards, and other friends, who had extended their hospitality to the members of the Congress.

19. "This Congress places on record a heartfelt expression of gratitude to Almighty God for the remarkable harmony and concord which have characterized the meetings of the Assembly, in which so many men and women of varied nations, creeds, tongues, and races have gathered in closest coöperation, and in the conclusion of the labours of the Congress; it expresses its firm and unshaken belief in the ultimate triumph of the cause of Peace and of the principles which have been advocated at these meetings."

The fundamental idea of the Congress is this, that it is necessary, in the first place, to diffuse by all means possible the conviction among men that war is very unprofitable for people and that peace is a great good, and in the second, to act upon the governments, impressing them with the superiority of the international tribunal over wars, and, therefore, the advantages and the necessity of disarmament. To attain the first end, the Congress turns to the teachers of history, to the women, and to the clergy with the advice that the evil of war and the good of peace be preached to men on every third Sunday in December; to attain the second end, the Congress addresses the governments, proposing that they disarm and substitute arbitration for war.

To preach the evil of war and the good of peace to men! But the evil of war and the good of peace are so well known to men that, so long as we have known men, the best greeting has been, "Peace be with you." What need is there, then, in preaching?

Not only the Christians, but all the pagans thousands of years ago knew the evil of war and the good of peace, — consequently the advice given to the preachers of the Gospel to preach on the evil of war and the good of peace on every third Sunday in December is quite superfluous.

A Christian cannot help but preach this at all times, on all the days of his life. If Christians and preachers of Christianity do not do so, there must be causes for this.

and so long as these causes are not removed, no advice will be effective. Still less effective can be the advice given to the governments, to dismiss the armies and substitute international tribunals for them. The governments themselves know very well all the difficulty and burdensomeness of collecting and maintaining armies, and if, in spite of it, they continue with terrible efforts and tension to collect and maintain armies, they obviously cannot do otherwise, and the advice of the Congress cannot change anything. But the learned do not want to see this, and all hope to find a combination by which the governments, who produce the wars, will limit themselves.

"Is it possible to be freed from war?" writes a learned man in the *Revue des Revues*. "All admit that when it breaks loose in Europe, its consequences will be like a great incursion of the barbarians. In a forthcoming war the existence of whole nationalities will be at stake, and so it will be sanguinary, desperate, cruel.

"It is these considerations, combined with those terrible implements of war which are at the disposal of modern science, that are retarding the moment of the declaration of war and are maintaining the existing temporary order of things, which might be prolonged for an indefinite time, if it were not for those terrible expenses that oppress the European nations and threaten to bring them to no lesser calamities than those which are produced by war.

"Startled by this idea, the men of the various countries have sought for a means for stopping or at least mitigating the consequences of the terrible slaughter which is menacing us.

"Such are the questions that are propounded by the Congress soon to be held in Rome and in pamphlets dealing with disarmament.

"Unfortunately it is certain that with the present structure of the majority of the European states, which are removed from one another and are guided by various interests, the complete cessation of war is a dream with which it would be dangerous to console ourselves. Still, some more reasonable laws and regulations, accepted by all, in these duels of the nations might considerably reduce the horrors of war.

"Similarly Utopian would be the hope of disarmament, which is almost impossible, from considerations of a national character, which are intelligible to our readers." (This, no doubt, means that France cannot disarm previous to avenging its wrongs.) "Public opinion is not prepared for the adoption of projects of disarmament, and, besides, the international relations are not such as to make their adoption possible.

"Disarmament, demanded by one nation of another, is tantamount to a declaration of war.

"It must, however, be admitted that the exchange of views between the interested nations will to a certain extent aid in the international agreement and will make possible a considerable diminution of the military expenses, which now oppress the European nations at the expense of the solution of social questions, the necessity of which is felt by every state individually, threatening to provoke an internal war in the effort to avert one from without.

"It is possible at least to assume a diminution of the enormous expenses which are needed in connection with the present business of war, which aims at the possibility of seizing the adversary's possessions within twenty-four hours and giving a decisive battle a week after the declaration of war."

What is needed is, that states should not be able to attack other states and in twenty-four hours to seize the possessions of others.

This practical idea was expressed by Maxime du Camp, and to this the conclusion of the article is reduced.

M. du Camp's propositions are these:

"(1) A diplomatic congress ought to meet every year.

"(2) No war can be declared sooner than two months after the incident provoking it. (The difficulty will be to determine which incident it is that provokes the war, because with every war there are a very large number of such incidents, and it would be necessary to decide from which incident the two months are to be counted.)

"(3) War cannot be declared before it is submitted to the vote of the nations preparing for it.

"Military action cannot begin sooner than a month after the declaration of war."

"War cannot be begun . . . must . . ." and so forth.

But who will see to it that war cannot be begun? Who will see to it that men must do so and so? Who will compel the power to wait until the proper time? All the other powers need just as much to be moderated and placed within bounds and compelled. Who will do the compelling? and how? — Public opinion. — But if there is a public opinion which can compel a power to wait for a given time, the same public opinion can compel the power not to begin the war at all.

But, they reply to all this, we can have such a balance of forces, *ponderation des forces*, that the powers will support one another. This has been tried and is being tried even now. Such were the Holy Alliance, the League of Peace, and so forth.

"But if all should agree to it?" we are told. If all should agree to it, there would be no war, and there would be no need for supreme tribunals and courts of arbitration.

"Arbitration will take the place of war. The questions will be decided by a court of arbitration. The *Alabama* question was decided by a court of arbitration, it was proposed to have the question about the Caroline Islands submitted to the arbitration of the Pope. Switzerland

and Belgium, and Denmark, and Holland, — all have declared that they prefer the decisions of a court of arbitration to war." Monaco, it seems, also declared itself in this way. What is a pity is, that Germany, Russia, Austria, France have not yet made such declarations.

It is wonderful how men can deceive themselves.

The governments will decide to submit their differences to a court of arbitration and so will disband their armies. The differences between Russia and Poland, between England and Ireland, between Austria and Bohemia, between Turkey and the Slavs, between France and Germany will be decided by voluntary consent.

This is the same as though it should be proposed that merchants and bankers should not sell anything at a higher price than at what they have bought the articles, should busy themselves with the distribution of wealth without profit, and should abolish the money which has thus become useless.

But commerce and the banking industry consist in nothing but selling at a higher price than that at which the purchases are made, and so the proposition that articles should not be sold except at a purchase price, and that money should be abolished, is tantamount to a proposition that they should abolish themselves. The same is true of the governments. The proposition made to the governments that no violence be used, and that the differences be decided on their merits, is a proposition that the government as such should abolish itself, and to this no government can consent.

Learned men gather in societies (there are many such societies, more than a hundred of them), congresses are called (lately such met at Paris and London, and one will soon meet at Rome), speeches are made, people dine, make toasts, publish periodicals, which are devoted to the cause, and in all of them it is proved that the tension of the nations, who are compelled to support millions of troops, has reached the utmost limit, and that this armament contradicts all the aims, properties, and desires of all the nations, but that, if a lot of paper is covered with writing, and a lot of speeches are made, it is possible to make all people agree and to cause them not to have any opposing interests, and then there will be no war.

When I was a little fellow, I was assured that to catch a bird it was just necessary to pour some salt on its tail. I went out with the salt to the birds, and immediately convinced myself that, if I could get near enough to pour the salt on a bird's tail, I could catch it, and I understood that they were making fun of me.

It is the same that must be understood by those who read books and pamphlets on courts of arbitration and disarmament.

If it is possible to pour salt on a bird's tail, this means that it does not fly, and that there is no need of catching it. But if a bird has wings and does not want to be caught, it does not allow any one to pour salt on its tail, because it is the property of a bird to fly. Even so the property of a government does not consist in being subjected, but in subjecting, and a government is a government only in so far as it is able, not to be subjected, but to subject, and so it strives to do so, and can never voluntarily renounce its power; but the power gives it the army, and so it will never give up the army and its use for purposes of war.

The mistake is based on this, that learned jurists, deceiving themselves and others, assert in their books that the government is not what it is, — a collection of one set of men, doing violence to another, — but, as science makes it out to be, a representation of the aggregate of citizens. The learned have for so long a time assured others of this fact that they have come themselves to believe in it, and they often think seriously that justice can be obligatory for the governments. But history shows that from Cæsar to

Napoleon, both the first and the third, and Bismarck, the government has by its essence always been a justice-impairing force, as, indeed, it cannot be otherwise. Justice cannot be obligatory for a man or for men, who keep in hand deceived men, drilled for violence, — the soldiers, — and by means of them rule others. And so the governments cannot agree to the diminution of the number of these drilled men, who obey them and who form all their strength and significance.

Such is the relation of one set of learned men to the contradiction which weighs heavily on our world, and such are the means for its solution. Tell these men that the question is only in the personal relation of every man to the moral, religious question, now standing before all, of the legitimacy and illegitimacy of his participation in the universal military service, and these savants will only shrug their shoulders, and will not even deign to give you an answer, or pay attention to you. The solution of the question for them consists in reading addresses, writing books, choosing presidents, vice-presidents, secretaries, and meeting and talking, now in this city, and now in that. From these talks and writings there will, in their opinion, come this result, that the governments will cease drafting soldiers, on whom their whole power is based, but will listen to their speeches and will dismiss their soldiers, will remain defenceless, not only against their neighbours, but even against their subjects, — like robbers who, having bound defenceless men, for the purpose of robbing them, upon hearing speeches about the pain caused to the bound men by the rope, should immediately set them free.

But there are people who believe in it, who busy themselves with peace congresses, deliver addresses, write little books; and the governments, of course, express their sympathy with this, let it appear that they are supporting this, just as they make it appear that they are supporting a temperance society, whereas they for the most part live by the drunkenness of the masses; just as they make it appear that they are supporting education, whereas their strength is based on ignorance; just as they make it appear that they are supporting the liberty of the constitution, whereas their strength is based only on the absence of a constitution; just as they make it appear that they are concerned about the betterment of the labouring classes, whereas it is on the oppression of the labourer that their existence is; just as they make it appear that they are supporting Christianity, whereas Christianity destroys every government.

To be able to do this, they have long ago worked out such provisions for temperance, that drunkenness is not impaired; such provisions for education, that ignorance is not only not interfered with, but is even strengthened; such provisions for liberty and for the constitution, that despotism is not impeded; such provisions for the labourers, that they are not freed from slavery; such Christianity as does not destroy, but maintains the governments.

Now they have also added their concern about peace. The governments, simply the kings, who travel about with their ministers, of their own accord deciding the questions as to whether they shall begin the slaughter of millions this year or next, know full well that their talks about peace will not keep them, whenever they feel like it, from sending millions to slaughter. The kings even listen with pleasure to these talks, encourage them, and take part in them.

All this is not only harmless, but even useful to the governments, in that it takes people's minds away from the most essential question, as to whether each individual man, who is called to become a soldier, should perform the universal military service or not.

"Peace will soon be established, thanks to alliances and congresses and in consequence of books and pamphlets, but in the meantime go, put on uniforms, and be prepared to oppress and torture yourselves for our advantage," say the governments. And the learned authors of congresses and of writings fully agree to this.

This is one relation, the most advantageous one for the governments, and so it is encouraged by all wise governments.

Another relation is the tragic relation of the men who assert that the contradiction between the striving and love for peace and the necessity of war is terrible, but that such is the fate of men. These for the most part sensitive, gifted men see and comprehend the whole terror and the whole madness and cruelty of war, but by some strange turn of mind do not see and do not look for any issue from this condition, and, as though irritating their wound, enjoy the desperate plight of humanity.

Here is a remarkable specimen of such a relation to war, by a famous French author (Maupassant). As he looks from his yacht at the exercises and target-shooting of the French soldiers, the following ideas come to him:

"War! When I but think of this word, I feel bewildered, as though they were speaking to me of sorcery, of the Inquisition, of a distant, finished, abominable, monstrous, unnatural thing.

"When they speak to us of cannibals, we smile proudly, as we proclaim our superiority to these savages. Who are the savages, the real savages? Those who struggle in order to eat those whom they vanquish, or those who struggle to kill, merely to kill?

"The little soldiers of the rank and file who are running down there are destined for death, like flocks of sheep, whom a butcher drives before him on the highway. They will fall in a plain, their heads cut open by a sword-stroke, or their chests pierced by bullets; and these are young men who might have worked, produced, been useful. Their fathers are old and poor; their mothers, who have loved them for twenty years and adored them as only mothers can, will learn in six months or, perhaps, in a year that their son, their child, their grandchild, who had been reared with so much love, was thrown into a hole, like a dead dog, after he had been eviscerated by a ball, trampled underfoot, crushed, mashed into pulp by the charges of cavalry. Why did they kill her boy, her fine boy, her only hope, her pride, her life? She does not know. Yes, why?

"War! To fight! To butcher! To massacre people! And to-day, at our period of the world, with our civilization, with the expansion of science and the degree of philosophy which we deem the human genius to have attained, we have schools in which they teach how to kill; to kill at a great distance, with perfection, a lot of people at the same time,—to kill poor innocent fellows, who have the care of a family and are under no judicial sentence.

"And what is most startling is the fact that the people do not rise against the governments! What difference is there really between the monarchies and the republics? It is most startling that society does not rise in a body and revolt at the very mention of the word 'war.'

"Oh, we shall always live under the burden of the ancient and odious customs, criminal prejudices, and savage ideas of our barbarous ancestors, because we are beasts, and shall remain beasts, who are dominated by instinct and do not change.

"Would not any other man than Victor Hugo have been disgraced, if he sent forth this cry of deliverance and truth?

"'To-day force is called violence and is about to be judged; war is summoned to court. Civilization, at the instigation of the human race, institutes proceedings and prepares the great criminal brief of the conquerors and captains. The nations are coming to understand that the increase of an offence cannot be its diminution; that if it is a crime to kill, killing much cannot be an extenuating circumstance; that if stealing is a disgrace, forcible seizing cannot be a glory. Oh, let us proclaim these absolute verities, — let us disgrace war!'

"Vain fury and indignation of a poet! War is honoured more than ever.

"A versatile artist in these matters, a gifted butcher of men, Mr. von Moltke, one day spoke the following words to some delegates of peace:

"'War is sacred and divinely instituted, it is one of the sacred laws of the world; it nurtures in men all the great and noble sentiments, — honour, disinterestedness, virtue, courage, — and, to be short, keeps men from falling into the most hideous materialism.'

"Thus, uniting into herds of four hundred thousand men, marching day and night without any rest, not thinking of anything, nor studying anything, nor learning anything, nor reading anything, not being useful to a single person, rotting from dirt, sleeping in the mire, living like the brutes in a constant stupor, pillaging cities, burning villages, ruining peoples, then meeting another conglomeration of human flesh, rushing against it, making lakes of blood and fields of battered flesh, mingled with muddy and blood-stained earth and mounds of corpses, being deprived of arms or legs, or having the skull crushed without profit to any one, and dying in the corner of a field, while your old parents, your wife, and your children are starving, — that's what is called not to fall into the most hideous materialism.

"The men of war are the scourges of the world. We struggle against Nature, against ignorance, against obstacles of every sort, in order to make our miserable life less hard. Men, benefactors, savants use their existence in order to work, to find what may help, may succour, may ease their brothers. They go with vim about their useful business, accumulate discovery upon discovery, increasing the human spirit, expanding science, giving every day a sum of new knowledge to the intelligence of man, giving every day well-being, ease, and force to their country.

"War arrives. In six months the generals destroy twenty years of effort, of patience, and of genius.

"This is what is called not to fall into the most hideous materialism.

"We have seen what war is. We have seen men turned into brutes, maddened, killing for the sake of pleasure, of terror, of bravado, of ostentation. Then, when law no longer exists, when law is dead, when every notion of right has disappeared, we have seen men shoot innocent people who are found on the road and who have roused suspicion only because they showed fear. We have seen dogs chained near the doors of their masters killed, just to try new revolvers on them; we have seen cows lying in the field shot to pieces, for the sake of pleasure, only to try a gun on them, to have something to laugh at.

"This is what is called not to fall into the most hideous materialism.

"To enter a country, to kill a man who is defending his home, simply because he wears a blouse and has no cap on his head, to burn the habitations of wretched people who have no bread, to smash the furniture, to steal some of it, to drink the wine which is found in the cellars, to rape the women who are found in the streets, to burn millions of dollars' worth of powder, and to leave behind them misery and the cholera, — this is what is called not to fall into the most hideous materialism.

"What have the men of war done to give evidence of even a little intelligence? Nothing. What have they invented? Cannon and guns. That is all.

"What has Greece left to us? Books, marbles. Is she great because she has conquered, or because she has produced?

"Is it the invasion of the Persians that kept her from falling into the most hideous materialism?

"Is it the invasions of the barbarians that saved Rome and regenerated her?

"Was it Napoleon I. who continued the great intellectual movement which was begun by the philosophers at the end of the last century?

"Oh, well, if the governments arrogate to themselves the right to kill the nations, there is nothing surprising in the fact that the nations now and then take upon themselves the right to do away with the governments.

"They defend themselves. They are right. Nobody has the absolute right to govern others. This can be done only for the good of the governed. Whoever rules is as much obliged to avoid war as a captain of a boat is obliged to avoid a shipwreck.

"When a captain has lost his boat, he is judged and condemned, if he is found guilty of negligence or even of incapacity.

"Why should not the governments be judged after the declaration of a war? If the nations understood this, if they themselves sat in judgment over the death-dealing powers, if they refused to allow themselves to be killed without reason, if they made use of their weapons against those who gave them to them for the purpose of massacring, war would be dead at once! But this day will not come!" (*Sur l'Eau*, pp. 71–80.)

The author sees all the horror of war; he sees that its cause is in this, that the governments, deceiving people, compel them to go out to kill and die without any need; he sees also that the men composing the armies might turn their weapons against the governments and demand accounts from them. But the author thinks that this will never happen, and that, therefore, there is no way out of this situation. He thinks that the business of war is terrible, but that it is inevitable and that the demands of the governments that the soldiers shall go and fight are as inevitable as death, and that, since the governments will always demand it, there will always exist wars.

Thus writes a talented, sincere author, who is endowed with that penetration into the essence of the matter which forms the essence of the poetical genius. He presents to us all the cruelty of the contradiction between men's conscience and their activity, and, without solving it, seems to recognize that this contradiction must exist and that in it consists the tragedy of life.

Another, not less gifted author (E. Rod), describes the cruelty and madness of the present situation in still more glaring colours, and similarly, recognizing the tragical element in it, does not offer or foresee any way out of it.

"What good is there in doing anything? What good is there in undertaking anything?" he says. "How can we love men in these troubled times, when the morrow is but a menace? Everything we have begun, our maturing ideas, our incepted works, the little good which we shall have been able to do, — will it not all be carried away by the coming hurricane? Everywhere the earth is trembling under our feet, and the clouds that are gathering upon our horizon will not pass by us.

"Oh, if it were only the Revolution, with which we are frightened, that we had to fear! As I am incapable of imagining a more detestable society than is ours, I have more mistrust than fear for the one which will succeed it. If I were to suffer from the transformation, I should console myself with the thought that the executioners of to-day are the victims of yesterday, and the expectation of what is better would make me put up with what is worse. But it is not this distant peril that frightens me, — I see another, nearer, above all, a more cruel peril, more cruel, because it has no excuse, because it is absurd, because no good can result from it. Every day men weigh the chances of war for the morrow, and every day they are more merciless.

"Thought staggers before the catastrophe which appears at the end of the century as the limit of the progress of our era, — but we must get used to it: for twenty years all the forces of science have been exhausting themselves to invent engines of destruction, and soon a few cannon-shots will suffice to annihilate a whole army; they no longer arm, as formerly, a few thousands of poor devils, whose blood was paid for, but whole nations, who go out to cut each others' throats; they steal their time, in order later more surely to steal their lives; to prepare them for the massacre, their hatred is fanned, by pretending that they are hated. And good people are tricked, and we shall see furious masses of peaceful citizens, into whose hands the guns will be placed by a stupid order, rush against one another with the ferocity of wild animals, God knows for the sake of what ridiculous incident of the border or of what mercantile colonial interests! They will march, like sheep, to the slaughter, — but knowing whither they are going, knowing that they are leaving their wives, knowing that their children will be hungry, and they will go with anxious fear, but none the less intoxicated by the sonorous, deceptive words that will be trumpeted into their ears. They will go without revolt, passive and resigned, though they are the mass and the force, and could be the power, if they wished and if they knew how to establish common sense and brotherhood in the place of the savage trickeries of diplomacy. They will go, so deceived, so duped, that they will believe the carnage to be a duty, and will ask God to bless their sanguinary appetites. They will go, trampling on the crops which they have sown, burning the cities which they have built, with enthusiastic songs, joyous cries, and festive music. And their sons will erect statues to those who shall have massacred them better than any one else!

"The fate of a whole generation depends on the hour at which some sombre politician will give the signal, which will be followed. We know that the best among us will be mowed down and that our work will be destroyed in the germ. We know this, and we tremble from anger, and we are unable to do anything. We are caught in the net of offices and red tape, which it would take too violent an effort to break. We belong to the laws which we have called into life to protect us, but which oppress us. We are only things of this Antinomian abstraction, the state, which makes every individual a slave in the name of the will of all, who, taken separately, would want the very opposite of what they are compelled to do.

"If it were only one generation that is to be sacrificed! But there are other interests as well.

"All these salaried shouters, these ambitious exploiters of the evil passions of the masses and the poor in spirit, who are deceived by the sonority of words, have to such an extent envenomed the national hatreds that the war of to-morrow will stake the existence of a race: one of the elements which have constituted the modern world is menaced, — he who will be vanquished must disappear morally, — and, whatever it be, we shall see a force annihilated, as if there were one too many for the good! We shall see a new Europe formed, on bases that are so unjust, so brutal, so bloody, so soiled with a monstrous blotch, that it cannot help but be worse than that of to-day, — more iniquitous, more barbarous, more violent.

"One feels oneself oppressed by a terrible discouragement. We are tossing about in a blind alley, with guns trained on us from all the roofs. Our work is that of sailors going through their last exercise before the ship goes down. Our pleasures are those of the condemned criminal, who fifteen minutes before his execution is offered a choice morsel. Anguish paralyzes our thought, and the best effort of which it is capable is to calculate — by spelling out the vague discourses of ministers, by twisting the sense of the words uttered by sovereigns, by contorting the words ascribed to diplomats and reported by the newspapers at the uncertain risk of their information — whether it is to-morrow or the day after, this year or next year, that we shall be crushed. We should, indeed, seek in vain in history for a more uncertain epoch, one which is so full of anxieties" (E. Rod, *Le Sens de la Vie*, pp. 208–213).

It is pointed out that the power is in the hands of those who are ruining themselves, in the hands of the separate individuals forming the mass; it is pointed out that the source of evil is in the state. It would seem clear that the contradiction of the consciousness and of life has reached the limit beyond which it is impossible to go and after which its solution must ensue.

But the author does not think so. He sees in this the tragedy of human life, and, having pointed out all the terror of the situation, concludes that human life must take place in this terror.

Such is the second relation to war of those men who see something fatal and tragical in it.

The third relation is that of men who have lost their conscience, and so their common sense and human feeling.

To this class belong Moltke, whose opinion is quoted by Maupassant, and the majority of military men, who are educated in this cruel superstition, who live by it, and so are often naïvely convinced that war is not only an inevitable, but even a useful matter. Thus, judge also non-military, so-called learned, cultured, refined people.

Here is what the famous Academician, Dousset, writes in the number of the *Revue des Revues* in which the letters about war are collected, in reply to the editor's inquiry as to his views on war:

"Dear Sir: — When you ask the most peaceable of Academicians whether he is an advocate of war, his answer is ready in advance: unfortunately, dear sir, you yourself regard as a dream the peaceful thoughts which at the present time inspire our magnanimous countrymen.

"Ever since I have been living in the world, I have heard many private people express their indignation against this terrifying habit of international slaughter. All men recognize and deplore this evil; but how is it to be mended? People have very often tried to abolish duels, — this seemed so easy! But no! All the efforts made for the attainment of this end have done no good and never will do any good.

"No matter how much may be said against war and against duelling at all the congresses of the world, above all arbitrations, above all treaties, above all legislations, will eternally stand man's honour, which has ever demanded duelling, and the national advantages, which will eternally demand war.

"I none the less with all my heart hope that the Congress of Universal Peace will succeed in its very grave and very honourable problem.

"Receive the assurance, etc.

"K. Dousset."

The meaning is this, that men's honour demands that people should fight, and the advantages of the nations demand that they should ruin and destroy one another, and that the attempts at stopping war are only worthy of smiles.

Similar is the opinion of another famous man, Jules Claretie:

"Dear Sir," he writes: "For an intelligent man there can exist but one opinion in respect to the question of peace and war.

"Humanity was created that it should live, being free

to perfect and better (its face) its condition by means of peaceful labour. The universal agreement, for which the Universal Congress of Peace is asking and which it preaches, may present but a beautiful dream, but it is in any case the most beautiful dream of all. Man has always before him the promised land of the future, — the harvest will mature, without fear of harm from grenades and cannon-wheels.

"But . . . Yes, but! Since the world is not ruled by philosophers and benefactors, it is fortunate that our soldiers protect our borders and our hearths, and that their arms, correctly aimed, appear to us, perhaps, as the very best guarantee of this peace, which is so fervently loved by all of us.

"Peace is given only to the strong and the determined.

"Receive the assurance, etc.

"J. CLARETIE."

The meaning of this is, that it does no harm to talk of what no one intends to do, and what ought not to be done at all. But when it comes to business, we must fight.

Here is another recent expression of opinion concerning war, by the most popular novelist of Europe, E. Zola:

"I consider war a fatal necessity, which appears inevitable to us in view of its close connection with human nature and the whole world-structure. I wish war could be removed for the longest possible time; none the less the moment will arrive when we shall be compelled to fight. I, at the present moment, am placing myself on the universal point of view, and in no way have any reference to our difference with Germany, which presents itself only as an insignificant incident in the history of humanity. I say that war is indispensable and useful, because it appears to humanity as one of the conditions of its existence. We everywhere meet with war, not only among various tribes and nations, but also in domestic and private life. It appears as one of the chief elements of progress, and every step forward, which humanity has taken, has been accompanied by bloodshed.

"People used to speak, and even now speak, of disarmament, but disarmament is something impossible, and even if it were possible, we should be obliged to reject it. Only an armed nation appears powerful and great. I am convinced that a universal disarmament would bring with it something like a moral fall, which would find its expression in universal impotence, and would be in the way of a progressive advancement of humanity. A martial nation has always enjoyed virile strength. Military art has brought with it the development of all the other arts. History testifies to that. Thus, in Athens and in Rome, commerce, industry, and literature never reached such development as at the time when these cities ruled over the then known world by force of arms. To take an example from times nearer to us, let us recall the age of Louis XIV. The wars of the great king not only did not retard the progress of the arts and sciences, but, on the contrary, seemed to aid and foster their development."

War is a useful thing!

But best of all in this sense is the opinion of the most talented writer of this camp, the opinion of the Academician Vogüé. Here is what he writes in an article about the exhibition, in visiting the military department:

"In the Esplanade des Invalides, amidst exotic and colonial buildings, one structure of a more severe style rises in the picturesque bazaar; all these representatives of the terrestrial globe adjoin the Palace of War. A superb subject of antitheses for humanitarian rhetorics! Indeed, it does not let pass an occasion for deploring such juxtaposition and for asserting that this will kill that (*ceci tuera cela*),[1] that the union of the nations through

[1] Words from Victor Hugo's novel, *Notre Dame*, in regard to printing, which will kill architecture. — *Author's Note.*

science and labour will conquer the martial instincts. We shall not keep it from fondling the hope of the chimera of a golden age, which, if it should be realized, would soon become an age of mire. All history teaches us that blood is needed to speed and confirm the union of the nations. The natural sciences have in our time confirmed the mysterious law which was revealed to Joseph de Maistre by the inspiration of his genius and the consideration of primitive dogmas; he saw how the world redeems its hereditary falls by a sacrifice; the sciences show us how the world is perfected by struggle and by compulsory selection; this is the assertion from two sides of the same decree, written out in different expressions. The assertion is naturally not a pleasant one; but the laws of the world are not established for our pleasure,— they are established for our perfection. Let us, then, enter into this unavoidable, indispensable Palace of War; and we shall have occasion to observe in what manner the most stubborn of our instincts, without losing anything of its force, is transformed, in submitting to the different demands of historic moments."

This idea, that the proof of the necessity of war is to be found in two expressions of Maistre and Darwin, two great thinkers according to his opinion, pleases Vogüé so much that he repeats it.

"Dear Sir," he writes to the editor of the *Revue des Revues*: "You ask for my opinion in regard to the success of the Universal Congress of Peace. I believe, with Darwin, that a violent struggle is a law of Nature, by which all beings are ruled.

"Like Joseph de Maistre, I believe that it is a divine law,— two different appellations for one and the same thing. If, past all expectation, some particle of humanity, say the whole civilized West, succeeded in arresting the action of this law, other, more primitive nations would apply it against us. In these nations the voice of Nature would vanquish the voice of human reason, and they would act with success, because the assurance of peace — I do not say 'peace' itself, but the 'full assurance of peace' — would evoke in men corruption and fall, which act more destructively than the most terrible war. I find that for that criminal law, war, it is necessary to do the same as for all the other criminal laws, — to mitigate them, to try to make them unnecessary, and to apply them as rarely as possible. But the whole of history teaches us that it is impossible to abolish these laws, so long as there are left in the world two men, money, and a woman between them.

"I should be very happy, if the Congress could prove the contrary to me. But I doubt whether it will be able to overthrow history, the law of Nature, and the law of God.

"Accept the assurance, etc.

"E. M. VOGÜÉ."

The idea is this, that history, man's nature, and God show us that, so long as there shall be two men and between them bread, money, and a woman, there will be war; that is, that no progress will bring men to get away from the one conception of life, where it is impossible without quarrelling to divide the bread, the money (the money is very good here), and the woman.

How strange the people are that assemble in congresses, to talk about how to catch birds by throwing salt on their tails, though they cannot help but know that it is impossible to do so; queer are those who, like Maupassant, Rod, and many others, see clearly the whole horror of war, the whole contradiction which arises from this, that men do not do what they ought to do, what is advantageous and necessary for them to do, deplore the tragedy of life, and do not see that all this tragedy will stop as soon as men will cease to discuss what they ought not to discuss, and will begin not to do what is painful for them to do, what displeases and disgusts them. These people are queer, but those who, like Vogüé and others, professing the law of evolution, recognize war not only as unavoidable, but even as useful, and so as desirable, are strange and terrible with their moral perversion. The others at least say that they hate the evil and love the good, but these simply recognize that there is no good and no evil.

All the talk about establishing peace, in the place of eternal war, is a harmful sentimental rodomontade of babblers. There is a law of evolution, from which it follows that I must live and act badly. What is to be done? I am an educated man, and I know the law of evolution, and so I will act badly.

"*Entrons au palais de la guerre.*" There is a law of evolution, and so there is nothing bad, nor good, and we must live for nothing but our personal life, leaving everything else to the law of evolution. This is the last expression of refined culture, and at the same time of that obscuration of consciousness with which all the cultured classes of our time are occupied.

The desire of the cultured classes in one way or another to maintain their favourite ideas and their life, which is based upon them, has reached its utmost limits. They lie, deceive themselves and others in the most refined way, if only they can in some way obscure and drown their consciences.

Instead of changing the life in accord with the consciousness, they try in every manner possible to obscure and drown their consciousness. But the light shines even in the dark, and so it is beginning to shine in our time.

VII.

THE cultured people of the higher classes try to drown the consciousness of the necessity of changing the present order of things, which is becoming all the time clearer and clearer; but life, continuing to develop and to become more complex in the former direction and intensifying the contradictions and sufferings of men, brings them to that last limit, beyond which it is impossible to go. Such a last limit, beyond which it is impossible to go, is the universal military service.

People generally think that universal military service and the ever increased arming, which is connected with it, and the consequent increase of taxation and of state debts among all the nations, are an accidental phenomenon, due to some political condition of Europe, and may also be removed by some political considerations, without an internal change of life.

This is quite erroneous. Universal military service is nothing but an inner contradiction which, having been carried to its utmost limits and having at a certain stage of material development become obvious, has stolen its way into the social concept of life.

The social concept of life consists in this very fact, that the meaning of life is transferred from the individual to the aggregate, and its consequence is transferred to the tribe, the family, the race, or the state.

From the social concept of life it follows that, in so far as the meaning of life is contained in the aggregate of individuals, the individuals themselves voluntarily sacrifice their interests for the interests of the aggregate.

Thus it has always been in reality in the case of certain forms of the aggregate, in the family or the tribe, independently of which preceded, or in the race, or even in the patriarchal state. In consequence of the habit, which is transmitted by education and confirmed by religious influences, the individuals have without compulsion blended their interests with the interests of the aggregate and have sacrificed their own interests for the common interest.

But the more societies became complex, the greater they grew, especially the more frequently conquests were the causes why men united into societies, the more frequently did individuals strive after attaining their ends to the disadvantage of the common good, and the more frequently was there felt the need of the exercise of power, that is, of violence, for the sake of curbing these insubmissive individuals.

The defenders of the social concept of life generally try to mix up the concept of power, that is, of violence, with that of spiritual influence, but this admixture is quite impossible.

A spiritual influence is an action upon a man, such that in consequence of it the very desires of a man are changed and coincide with what is demanded of him. A man who submits to a spiritual influence acts in accordance with his desires. But power, as this word is generally understood, is a means for compelling a man to act contrary to his wishes. A man who submits to power does not act as he would wish, but as the power compels him to act. Now what can compel a man to do, not what he wishes, but what he does not wish, is physical violence, or a threat of using such, that is, the deprivation of liberty, beating, maiming, or executable menaces that such actions will be carried out. In this has power always consisted.

In spite of the unceasing efforts made by men in power

to conceal this and to ascribe a different meaning to power, power is the application of a rope, a chain, by which a man will be bound and dragged along, or of a whip, with which he will be flogged, or of a knife, an axe, with which they will cut off his hands, feet, ears, head,—an application of these means, or a threat that they will be used. Thus it was in the time of Nero and of Dzhingis-Khan, and thus it is even now, in the most liberal of governments, in the republic of America and in that of France. If men submit to power, they do so only because they are afraid that in case they do not submit these actions will be applied to them. All governmental demands, the payment of taxes, the execution of public works, the submission to punishments imposed upon one, exile, penalties, and so forth, to which men seem voluntarily to submit, have always had bodily violence, or a threat that such will be used, for their base.

The basis of power is bodily violence.

The possibility of exerting bodily violence against people is first of all given by an organization of armed men in which all the armed men act in agreement, submitting to one will. Such assemblies of armed men, who submit to one will, are formed by the army. The army has always stood at the base of power. Power is always found in the hands of those who command an army, and all potentates — from the Roman Cæsars to the Russian and German emperors — are more than anything else concerned about the army, knowing that if the army is with them, the power will remain in their hands.

It is this formation and increase of the army, which is necessary for the support of power, that has introduced a decomposing principle into the social concept of life.

The end of power and its justification consists in the limitation of those men who might wish to attain their interests to the disadvantage of the interests of the aggregate. But whether the power has been acquired by the formation of a new power, by inheritance, or by election, men who possess power by means of an army have in no way differed from other men, and so have, like other men, been prone not to subordinate their interests to those of the aggregate, but, on the contrary, having in their hands the possibility of doing so, have been more prone than any one else to subordinate the common interests to their own. No matter how much men have devised means for depriving men in power of the possibility of subordinating the common interests to their own, or for entrusting the power only into the hands of infallible men, there have so far been discovered no means for doing either.

All methods employed, either of divine sanction, or of election, or of heredity, or of suffrage, or of assemblies, or of parliaments, or of senates, have proved ineffective. All men know that not one of these methods attains the aim of entrusting the power into none but infallible hands, or of preventing its being misused. All know that, on the contrary, men in power, be they emperors, ministers, chiefs of police, policemen, become, by the very fact of having power, more prone to commit immoralities, that is, to subordinate the common interests to their own, than men who have no power, as indeed it could not be otherwise.

The social concept of life justified itself only so long as all men voluntarily sacrificed their interests to the common interests; but the moment there appeared men who did not voluntarily sacrifice their interests, and power was needed, that is, violence, for the purpose of limiting these individuals, the decomposing principle of power, that is, violence exerted by one set of people against another, entered into the social concept of life and the structure which is based upon it.

For the power of one set of men over another to attain its end of limiting men who strove after their individual interests to the disadvantage of those of the aggregate, it was necessary to have the power vested in the hands of infallible men, as is assumed to be the case by the Chinese, and as has been assumed in the Middle Ages and at the present time by men who believe in the sanctity of anointment. It was only under this condition that the social structure received its justification.

But since this does not exist, and men in power, on the contrary, by the very fact of their possession of power, are never saintly, the social structure, which is based on power, should not have any justification.

Even if there was a time when, with a certain low level of morality and with the universal tendency of men to exert violence against each other, the existence of the power which limited this violence was advantageous, that is, when the violence of the state was not so great as that exerted by individuals against each other, it is impossible to overlook the fact that such a superiority of the state over its absence could not be permanent. The more the tendency of individuals to exert violence was diminished, the more the manners were softened, and the more the power was corrupted in consequence of its unrestraint, the more did this superiority grow less and less.

In this change of the relation between the moral development of the masses and the corruption of the governments does the whole history of the last two thousand years consist.

In the simplest form the case was like this: men lived by tribes, families, races, and waged war, committed acts of violence, and destroyed and killed one another. These cases of violence took place on a small and on a large scale: individual struggled with individual, tribe with tribe, family with family, race with race, nation with nation. Larger, more powerful aggregates conquered the weaker, and the larger and the more powerful the aggregate of people became, the less internal violence took place in it, and the more secure did the continuance of the life of the aggregate seem to be.

The members of the tribe or of the family, uniting into one aggregate, war less among themselves, and the tribe and the family do not die, like one man, but continue their existence; between the members of one state, who are subject to one power, the struggle seems even weaker, and the life of the state seems even more secure.

These unions into greater and ever greater aggregates did not take place because men consciously recognized such unions as more advantageous to themselves, as is described in the story about the calling of the Varangians, but in consequence, on the one hand, of natural growth, and on the other, of struggle and conquests.

When the conquest is accomplished, the power of the conqueror actually puts an end to internecine strife, and the social concept of life receives its justification. But this confirmation is only temporary. Internal strifes cease only in proportion as the pressure of the power is exerted upon individuals who heretofore have been warring against one another. The violence of internal struggle, which is destroyed by the power, is conceived in the power itself. The power is in the hands of just such people as all men are, that is, of such as are always or frequently prepared to sacrifice the common good for the sake of their personal good, with this one difference, that these men do not have the tempering force of the counteraction of the violated, and are subjected to the full corrupting influence of power. Thus the evil of violence, passing over into the hands of power, keeps growing more and more, and in time comes to be greater than the one which it is supposed to destroy, whereas in the members of society the proneness to violence keeps weakening more and more, and the violence of power grows less and less necessary.

The governmental power, even if it destroys inner violence, invariably introduces new forms of violence into the lives of men, and this grows greater and greater in proportion with its continuance and intensification.

Thus, although the violence is less perceptible in the state than the violence of the members of society against one another, since it is not expressed by struggle, but by submission, the violence none the less exists and for the most part in a much more powerful degree than before.

This cannot be otherwise, because the possession of power not only corrupts men, but the purpose or even unconscious tendency of the violators will consist in bringing the violated to the greatest degree of weakening, since, the weaker the violated man is, the less effort will it take to suppress him.

For this reason the violence which is exerted against him who is violated keeps growing to the farthest limit which it can attain without killing the hen that is laying the golden eggs. But if this hen does not lay, as in the case of the American Indians, the Fijians, the Negroes, it is killed, in spite of the sincere protestations of the philanthropists against such a mode of action.

The best confirmation of this is found in the condition of the labouring classes of our time, who in reality are nothing but subjugated people.

In spite of all the hypocritical endeavours of the higher classes to alleviate the condition of the working people, all the working people of our world are subject to an invariable iron law, according to which they have only as much as they need to be always incited by necessity to work and to have the strength for working for their masters, that is, for the conquerors.

Thus it has always been. In proportion with the duration and increase of power, its advantages have always been lost for those who subjected themselves to it, and its disadvantages have been increased.

Thus it has been independently of those forms of government under which the nations have lived. The only difference is this, that in a despotic form of government the power is concentrated in a small number of violators, and the form of the violence is more pronounced; in the constitutional monarchies and republics, as in France and in America, the power is distributed among a larger number of violators, and its forms are less pronounced; but the matter of violence, with which the disadvantages of the power are greater than its advantages, and its process, which brings the violated to the extreme limit of weakening to which they can be brought for the advantage of the violators, are always one and the same.

Such has been the condition of all the violated, but before this they did not know it, and in the majority of cases they believed naïvely that governments existed for their good; that without government they would perish; that the thought that men could live without governments was a blasphemy which ought not even be uttered; that this was for some reason a terrible doctrine of anarchism, with which is connected the conception of everything terrible.

Men believed, as in something absolutely proved and so needing no further proofs, that, since until now all the nations have developed in a governmental form, this form was for ever an indispensable condition of the development of humanity.

Thus it went on for hundreds and for thousands of years, and the governments, that is, men in power, have tried, and now try more and more, to keep the nations in this error.

Thus it was in the time of the Roman emperors, and thus it is at present. In spite of the fact that the idea of the uselessness and even harm of the governmental violence more and more enters into the consciousness of men, this would last for ever, if the governments were not obliged to increase the armies for the purpose of maintaining their power.

People generally think that the armies are increased by the governments for the purpose of defending the states against other states, forgetting the fact that armies are needed by the governments for the purpose of protecting themselves against their own crushed and enslaved subjects.

This has always been indispensable, and has become more and more necessary in proportion as culture has been developed among the nations, in proportion as the intercourse among the men of the same and of different nations has been increased, and it has become particularly indispensable now in connection with the communistic, socialistic, anarchistic, and universal movements among the labouring classes. The governments feel this, and so increase their main force of the disciplined army.[1]

Answering lately to a question why money was needed for the increase of the wages of under-officers, the German chancellor declared frankly in the German Reichstag that there was a need of reliable under-officers, in order to fight against socialism. Caprivi only said in the hearing of all what everybody knows, though it is carefully concealed from the nations; he explained why guards of Swiss and Scotchmen were hired out to French kings and Popes, and why in Russia they carefully shuffle up the recruits

[1] The fact that in America there exist abuses of power, in spite of the small number of troops, not only does not contradict, but even supports this proposition. In America there is a smaller army than in other countries, and so there is nowhere a lesser oppression of the oppressed classes, and nowhere can we foresee so soon the abolition of the abuses of power and of the power itself. But in America itself there have of late, in proportion as the labouring classes become more unified, been heard voices asking more and more frequently for an increase of the army, although America is not threatened by any external attack. The higher ruling classes know that fifty thousand soldiers will soon be insufficient, and, no longer depending on Pinkerton's army, they feel that the security of their position lies only in an increase of the army. — *Author's Note.*

in such a way that the regiments which are located in the centre are made up of recruits from the outlying districts, while the regiments in the outlying districts are completed by soldiers from the centre of Russia. The meaning of Caprivi's speech, translated into simple language, is this, that money was not needed for counteracting the foreign enemies, but for bribing the under-officers, so as to make them willing to act against the oppressed labouring masses.

Caprivi accidentally gave utterance to what everybody knows, or feels, if he does not know, namely, that the existing structure of life is such as it is, not because it naturally must be such, because the nation wants it to be such, but because it is maintained as such by the violence of the governments, by the army with its bribed under-officers, officers, and generals.

If a labouring man has no land, no chance of making use of the right, so natural for every man, to obtain from the land his own means of support and those of his family, this is not so because the nation wants it to be so, but because certain men, the owners of land, are granted the right to admit, or not to admit, the labouring people to it. And this unnatural order of things is maintained by means of the army. If the immense wealth, accumulated by the labouring people, is not considered as belonging to all men, but to an exclusive number of men; if the power to collect taxes from labour and to use the money for anything they may see fit is entrusted to a few men; if a few men are permitted to select the method of the religious and civil instruction and education of the children; if strikes of the labourers are opposed and strikes of the capitalists are encouraged; if a few men are granted the right to compose laws, which all must obey, and to dispose of men's property and life, — all this does not take place because the nation wants it so, but because the governments and the ruling classes want it so, and by means of bodily violence establish it so.

Every person who does not know this will find it out in every attempt at not conforming or at changing this order of things. Therefore armies are first of all indispensable to the governments and the ruling classes, in order to maintain the order of things which not only does not result from the necessity of the nation, but is frequently opposed to it and is advantageous only to the government and to the ruling classes.

Every government needs armies, first of all, in order to keep its subjects in submission, and to exploit their labours. But the government is not alone; side by side with it there is another government, which exploits its subjects by means of the same violence, and which is always ready to take away from another government the labours of its already enslaved subjects. And so every government needs an army, not only for internal use, but also for the protection of its booty against neighbouring ravishers. Every government is in consequence of this involuntarily led to the necessity of increasing its army in emulation with the other governments; but the increasing of armies is contagious, as Montesquieu remarked 150 years ago.

Every increase of an army in a state, directed against its subjects, becomes dangerous even for its neighbours, and evokes an increase in the neighbouring states.

The armies have reached their present millions not merely because the neighbours threatened the states; this resulted above all from the necessity of crushing all attempts at revolt on the part of the subjects. The increase of armies arises simultaneously from two causes, which provoke one another: armies are needed against domestic enemies and for the purpose of defending one's position against one's neighbours. One conditions the other. The despotism of a government always increases with the increase and strengthening of armies and external successes, and the aggressiveness of governments is increased with the intensification of the internal despotism.

In consequence of this, the European governments, in emulating one another in the greater and ever greater increase of the army, arrived at the inevitable necessity of the universal military service, since the universal military service was a means for obtaining in time of war the greatest quantity of soldiers at the least expense. Germany was the first to hit upon this plan, and the moment one government did it, all the others were obliged to do the same. The moment this happened, it happened that all the citizens were put under arms for the purpose of maintaining all that injustice which was committed against them; what happened was that all the citizens became oppressors of themselves.

The universal military service was an inevitable logical necessity, at which it was impossible not to arrive; at the same time it is the last expression of the inner contradiction of the social concept of life, which arose at a time when violence was needed in order to maintain it. In the universal military service this contradiction became obvious. Indeed, the meaning of the social concept of life consists in this, that a man, recognizing the cruelty of the struggle of individuals among themselves and the perishableness of the individual himself, transfers the meaning of his life to the aggregate of individuals; but in the universal military service it turns out that men, having brought all the sacrifices demanded of them, in order to free themselves from the cruelty of the struggle and the insecurity of life, are, after all the sacrifices which they have made, again called to bear all those dangers from which they thought they had freed themselves, and, besides, that aggregate, the state, in the name of which the individuals renounced their advantages, is again subjected to the same danger of destruction to which the individual himself was subjected before.

The governments were to have freed men from the cruelty of the struggle of individuals and to have given them the assurance of the inviolability of the order of the state life; but, instead, they impose upon the individuals the necessity of the same struggle, except that the struggle with the nearest individuals is transferred to the struggle with the individuals of other states, and they leave the same danger of the destruction of the individual and of the state.

The establishment of the universal military service is like what would happen if a man were to brace up a dilapidated house: the walls bend inwards — supports are put up; the ceiling is sagging down — other supports are put up; boards hang down between the supports — some more supports are put up. A point is finally reached when the supports indeed hold the house together, but it is impossible to live in the house because there are so many supports.

The same is true of the universal military service. It destroys all those advantages of the social life which it is called to preserve.

The advantages of the social life consist in the security of property and labour and in the coöperation in the aggregate perfection of life, — the universal military service destroys all that.

The taxes which are collected from the masses for war preparations swallow the greater share of the production of labour which the army is supposed to protect.

The tearing away of the men from the habitual course of life impairs the possibility of the work itself.

The menaces of a war that is likely to break out at any time make all the perfections of the social life useless and in vain.

If a man was formerly told that if he did not submit to the power of the state he would be subjected to the attacks of evil men, of external and internal enemies;

that he would be compelled himself to struggle with them and to subject himself to being killed; that therefore it would be advantageous for him to bear certain privations, in order to free himself from these calamities, — he was able to believe it all, because the sacrifices which he made for the state were only private sacrifices and gave him the hope for a peaceful life in an imperishable state, in the name of which he made these sacrifices. But now, when these sacrifices have not only increased tenfold, but the advantages promised to him are absent, it is natural for any one to imagine that his submission to power is quite useless.

But not in this alone lies the fatal significance of the universal military service, as a manifestation of that contradiction which is contained in the social concept of life. The main manifestation of this contradiction consists in the fact that with the universal military service every citizen, upon becoming a soldier, becomes a supporter of the state structure, and a participant in everything which the government does and the legality of which he does not recognize.

The governments assert that the armies are needed mainly for the purpose of external defence; but that is not true. They are needed first of all against their subjects, and every man who does military service involuntarily becomes a participant in all the violence which the state exerts over its own subjects.

To convince himself that every man who does his military service becomes a participant in such deeds of the government as he does not acknowledge and cannot acknowledge, let a man only remember what is being done in every state in the name of order and of the good of the nation, things which the army appears as the executor of. All the struggles of dynasties and of the various parties, all the executions, which are connected with these disturbances, all the suppressions of revolts, all the employment of military force for the dispersion of popular crowds, the suppression of strikes, all the extortions of taxes, all the injustice of the distribution of the ownership of land, all the oppressions of labour, — all this is produced, if not directly by the armies, at least by the police, which is supported by the armies. He who does military service becomes a participant in all these matters, which in some cases are doubtful to him and in many cases are directly opposed to his conscience. Some people do not wish to leave the land which they have been working for generations; people do not wish to disperse, as they are commanded to do by the government; people do not want to pay the taxes which are exacted of them; people do not wish to recognize the obligatoriness for them of laws which they have not made; people do not wish to be deprived of their nationality, — and I, by doing military service, am obliged to come and beat these people. Being a participant in these deeds, I cannot help but ask myself whether these deeds are good, and whether I ought to contribute to their execution.

Universal military service is for the government the last degree of violence, which is necessary for the support of the whole structure; and for the subjects it is the extreme limit of the possibility of their obedience. It is that keystone which holds the walls and the extraction of which causes the building to cave in.

The time came when the growing abuses of the governments and their strifes among themselves had this effect, that from every subject there were demanded, not only material, but also moral sacrifices, when every man had to stop and ask himself, "Can I make these sacrifices? And in the name of what must I make these sacrifices? These sacrifices are demanded in the name of the state. In the name of the state they demand of me the renunciation of everything which may be dear to man, of peace, of family, of security, of human dignity.

What is that state in the name of which such terrible sacrifices are demanded of me? And why is it so indispensably necessary?"

"The state," we are told, "is indispensably necessary, in the first place, because without the state, I and all of us would not be protected against violence and the attack of evil men; in the second place, without the state all of us would be savages, and would have no religious, nor educational, nor mercantile institutions, nor roads of communication, nor any other public establishments; and, in the third place, because without the state we should be subject to enslavement by neighbouring nations."

"Without the state," we are told, "we should be subject to violence and to the attacks of evil men in our own country."

But who among us are these evil men, from the violence and attacks of whom the state and its army save us? If three, four centuries ago, when men boasted of their military art and their accoutrements, when it was considered a virtue to kill men, there existed such men, there are none now, for no men of the present time use or carry weapons, and all, professing the rules of philanthropy and of compassion for their neighbours, wish the same as we,— the possibility of a calm and peaceful life. There now are no longer those particular violators against whom the state should defend us. But if, by the people, from whose attack the state saves us, we are to understand those men who commit crimes, we know that they are not some especial beings, like rapacious animals among the sheep, but just such people as we are, who are just as disinclined to commit crimes as those against whom they commit them. We know now that threats and punishments cannot diminish the number of such men, and that it is only the change of surroundings and the moral influence upon people that diminish it. Thus the explanation of the necessity of governmental violence for the purpose of defending men against violators may have had a basis three or four centuries ago, but has none at the present time. Now the contrary would be more correct, namely, that the activity of the governments, with their morality which has fallen behind the common level, with their cruel methods of punishments, of prisons, of hard labour, of gallows, of guillotines, rather contributes to the brutalization of the masses than to the softening of their manners, and so rather to the increase than to the diminution of the number of violators.

"Without the state," they also say, "there would not be all those institutions of education, of learning, of religion, of roads of communication, and others. Without the state men would not be able to establish the public things which are indispensable for all men." But this argument, too, could have a basis only several centuries ago.

If there was a time when men were so disunited among themselves and the means for a closer union and for the transmission of thought were so little worked out that they could not come to any understanding nor agree upon any common mercantile, or economical, or cultural matter without the medium of the state, there now no longer exists such a disunion. The widely developed means for communion and for the transmission of thought have had this effect, that, for the formation of societies, assemblies, corporations, congresses, learned, economic, or political institutions, the men of our time can get along without any government, and the governments in the majority of cases are more likely to interfere with the attainment of these ends than to coöperate with it.

Beginning with the end of the last century, almost every forward step of humanity has not only not been encouraged by the government, but has always been retarded by it. Thus it was with the abolition of corporal punishment, of torture, of slavery, and with the establishment of the freedom of the press and of assemblies. In our time the power of the state and the governments not only fail to coöperate with, but are distinctly opposed to, all that activity by means of which men work out new forms of life. The solutions of labouring, agronomic, political, religious questions are not only not encouraged, but directly interfered with by the power of the state.

"Without the state and the government, the nations would be enslaved by their neighbours."

It is hardly necessary to retort to this last argument. The retort is found in itself.

The governments, so we are told, are necessary with their armies for the purpose of defending us against our neighbours, who might enslave us. But this is what all the governments say of one another, and at the same time we know that all the European nations profess the same principles of freedom and of brotherhood, and so are in no need of defending themselves against one another. But if protection against barbarians is meant, then one-thousandth of all the armies now under arms would suffice. Thus the contrary to what is asserted is what actually happens: the power of the state, far from saving us from the attacks of our neighbours, on the contrary causes the danger of the attacks.

Thus a man, who by means of his military service is placed under the necessity of thinking about the significance of the state, in the name of which the sacrifice of his peace, his security, and his life is demanded of him, cannot help but see clearly that for these sacrifices there no longer exists any basis in our time.

But it is not only by theoretical reflections that any man may see that the sacrifices demanded of him by the state have no foundation whatever; even by reflecting practically, that is, by weighing all those hard conditions in which a man is placed by the state, no one can fail to see that for him personally the fulfilment of the demands of the state and his submission to military service is in the majority of cases more disadvantageous than a refusal to do military service.

If the majority of men prefer submission to insubmission, this is not due to any sober weighing of the advantages and disadvantages, but because the men are attracted to submission by means of the hypnotization to which they are subjected in the matter. In submitting, men only surrender themselves to those demands which are made upon them, without reflection, and without making any effort of the will; for insubmission there is a need of independent reflection and of effort, of which not every man is capable. But if, excluding the moral significance of submission and insubmission, we should consider nothing but the advantages, insubmission would in general always be more advantageous to us than submission.

No matter who I may be, whether I belong to the well-to-do, oppressing classes, or to the oppressed labouring classes, the disadvantages of insubmission are less than the disadvantages of submission, and the advantages of insubmission are greater than the advantages of submission.

If I belong to the minority of oppressors, the disadvantages of insubmission to the demands of the government will consist in this, that I, refusing to comply with the demands of the government, shall be tried and at best shall be discharged or, as they do with the Mennonites, shall be compelled to serve out my time at some unmilitary work; in the worst case I shall be condemned to deportation or imprisonment for two or three years (I speak from examples that have happened in Russia), or, perhaps, to a longer term of incarceration, or to death, though the probability of such a penalty is very small.

Such are the disadvantages of insubmission; but the disadvantages of submission will consist in this: at best I shall not be sent out to kill men, and I myself shall not be subjected to any great probability of crippling or death, but shall only be enlisted as a military slave, — I shall be dressed up in a fool's garments; I shall be at the mercy of every man above me in rank, from a corporal to a field-marshal; I shall be compelled to contort my body according to their desire, and, after being kept from one to five years, I shall be left for ten years in a condition of readiness to appear at any moment for the purpose of going through all these things again. In the worst case I shall, in addition to all those previous conditions of slavery, be sent to war, where I shall be compelled to kill men of other nations, who have done me no harm, where I may be crippled and killed, and where I may get into a place, as happened at Sevastopol and as happens in every war, where men are sent to certain death; and, what is most agonizing, I may be sent out against my own countrymen, when I shall be compelled to kill my brothers for dynastic or other reasons, which are entirely alien to me. Such are the comparative disadvantages.

The comparative advantages of submission and of insubmission are these:

For him who has not refused, the advantages will consist in this, that, having submitted to all the humiliations and having executed all the cruelties demanded of him, he may, if he is not killed, receive red, golden, tin-foil decorations over his fool's garments, and he may at best command hundreds of thousands of just such bestialized men as himself, and be called a field-marshal, and receive a lot of money.

But the advantages of him who refuses will consist in this, that he will retain his human dignity, will earn the respect of good men, and, above all else, will know without fail that he is doing God's work, and so an incontestable good to men.

Such are the advantages and the disadvantages on both sides for a man from the wealthy classes, for an oppressor;

for a man of the poor, working classes the advantages and disadvantages will be the same, but with an important addition of disadvantages. The disadvantages for a man of the labouring classes, who has not refused to do military service, will also consist in this, that, by entering upon military service, he by his participation and seeming consent confirms the very oppression under which he is suffering.

But it is not the reflections as to how much the state which men are called upon to support by their participation in the military service is necessary and useful to men, much less the reflections as to the advantages or disadvantages accruing to each man from his submission or insubmission to the demands of the government, that decide the question as to the necessity of the existence or the abolition of the state. What irrevocably and without appeal decides this question is the religious consciousness or conscience of every individual man, before whom, in connection with the universal military service, involuntarily rises the question as to the existence or non-existence of the state.

VIII.

PEOPLE frequently say that if Christianity is a truth, it ought to have been accepted by all men at its very appearance, and ought at that very moment to have changed the lives of men and made them better. But to say this is the same as saying that if the seed is fertile, it must immediately produce a sprout, a flower, and a fruit.

The Christian teaching is no legislation which, being introduced by violence, can at once change the lives of men. Christianity is another, newer, higher concept of life, which is different from the previous one. But the new concept of life cannot be prescribed; it can only be freely adopted.

Now the new life-conception can be acquired only in two ways: in a spiritual (internal) and an experimental (external) way.

Some people — the minority — immediately, at once, by a prophetic feeling divine the truth of the teaching, abandon themselves to it, and execute it. Others — the majority — are led only through a long path of errors, experiences, and sufferings to the recognition of the truth of the teaching and the necessity of acquiring it.

It is to this necessity of acquiring the teaching in an experimental external way that the whole mass of the men of the Christian world have now been brought.

Sometimes we think: what need was there for that corruption of Christianity which even now more than anything else interferes with its adoption in its real sense? And yet this corruption of Christianity, having brought men to the condition in which they now are, was a necessary condition for the majority of men to be able to receive it in its real significance.

If Christianity had been offered to men in its real, and not its corrupted, form, it would not have been accepted by the majority of men, and the majority of men would have remained alien to it, as the nations of Asia are alien to it at the present time. But, having received it in its corrupted form, the nations who received it were subjected to its certain, though slow, action, and by a long experimental road of errors and of sufferings resulting therefrom are now brought to the necessity of acquiring it in its true sense.

The corruption of Christianity and its acceptance in its corrupted form by the majority of men was as indispensable as that a seed, to sprout, should be for a time concealed by the earth.

The Christian teaching is a teaching of the truth and at the same time a prophecy.

Eighteen hundred years ago the Christian teaching revealed to men the truth of how they should live, and at the same time predicted what human life would be if men would not live thus, but would continue to live by those principles by which they had lived heretofore, and what it would be if they should accept the Christian teaching and should carry it out in life.

In imparting in the Sermon on the Mount the teaching which was to guide the lives of men, Christ said:

"Therefore, whosoever heareth these sayings of mine, and doeth them, I will liken him unto a wise man, which built his house upon a rock: and the rain descended, and the floods came, and the winds blew, and beat upon that house; and it fell not: for it was founded upon a rock. And every one that heareth these sayings of mine, and doeth them not, shall be likened unto a foolish man, which built his house upon the sand: and the rain descended, and the floods came, and the winds blew, and beat upon that house; and it fell: and great was the fall of it" (Matt. vii. 24–27).

Now, after eighteen hundred years, the prophecy has been fulfilled. By not following Christ's teaching in general and its manifestation in public life as non-resistance to evil, men involuntarily came to that position of inevitable ruin which was promised by Christ to those who would not follow His teaching.

People frequently think that the question of non-resistance to evil is an invented question, a question which it is possible to circumvent. It is, however, a question which life itself puts before all men and before every thinking man, and which invariably demands a solution. For men in their public life this question has, ever since the Christian teaching has been preached, been the same as the question for a traveller which road to take, when he comes to a fork on the highway on which he has been walking. He must go on, and he cannot say, "I will not think, and I will continue to walk as before." Before this there was one road, and now there are two of them, and it is impossible to walk as before, and one of the two roads must inevitably be chosen.

Even so it has been impossible to say, ever since Christ's teaching was made known to men, "I will continue to live as I lived before, without solving the question as to resisting or not resisting evil by means of violence." It is inevitably necessary at the appearance of every struggle to solve the question, "Shall I with violence resist that which I consider to be an evil and violence, or not?"

The question as to resisting or not resisting evil by means of violence appeared when there arose the first struggle among men, since every struggle is nothing but a resistance by means of violence to what each of the contending parties considers to be an evil. But the men before Christ did not see that the resistance by means of violence to what each considers to be an evil, only because he regards as an evil what another regards as a good, is only one of the means of solving the struggle, and that another means consists in not at all resisting evil by means of violence.

Previous to Christ's teaching it appeared to men that there was but one way of solving a struggle, and that was by resisting evil with violence, and so they did, each of the contending parties trying to convince himself and others that what each of them considered to be an evil was a real, absolute evil.

And so since most remote times men have endeavoured to discover such definitions of evil as would be obligatory for all men, and as such were given out the statutes of law which, it was assumed, were received in a supernatural manner, or the injunctions of men or of assemblies of men, to whom is ascribed the quality of infallibility. Men have employed violence against other men and have assured themselves and others that they have employed this violence against the evil which was acknowledged by all men.

This means has been employed since remote antiquity, especially by those men who usurped the power, and men for a long time did not see the irrationality of this means.

But the longer men lived, the more complex their relations became, the more obvious did it become that it was irrational by means of violence to resist that which is by every one regarded as an evil, that the struggle was not diminished by doing so, and that no human definitions could succeed in making that which was considered to be evil by one set of men considered such by others.

Even at the time of the appearance of Christianity, in the place where it made its appearance, in the Roman Empire, it was clear for the majority of men that what by Nero and Caligula was considered to be an evil which ought to be resisted with violence could not be considered an evil by other men. Even then men began to understand that human laws which were given out as being divine had been written by men, that men could not be infallible, no matter with what external grandeur they might be vested, and that erring men could not become infallible simply because they came together and called themselves a senate or some such name. This was even then felt and understood by many, and it was then that Christ preached His teaching, which did not consist simply in this, that evil ought not to be resisted by means of violence, but in the teaching of the new comprehension of life, a part, or rather an application of which to public life was the teaching about the means for abolishing the struggle among all men, not by obliging only one part of men without a struggle to submit to what would be prescribed to them by certain authorities, but by having no one, consequently even not those (and preëminently not those) who rule, employ violence against any one, and under no consideration.

The teaching was at that time accepted by but a small number of disciples; but the majority of men, especially all those who ruled over men, continued after the nominal acceptance of Christianity to hold to the rule of violently resisting that which they considered to be evil. Thus it was in the time of the Roman and the Byzantine emperors, and so it continued even afterward.

The inadequacy of the principle of defining with authority what is evil and resisting it with violence, which was already obvious in the first centuries of Christianity, became even more obvious during the decomposition of the Roman Empire into many states of equal right, with their mutual hostilities and the inner struggles which took place in the separate states.

But men were not prepared to receive the solution which was given by Christ, and the former means for the definition of the evil, which had to be resisted by establishing laws which, being obligatory for all, were carried out by the use of force, continued to be applied. The arbiter of what was to be considered an evil and what was to be resisted by means of force was now the Pope, now the emperor, now the king, now an assembly of the elect, now the whole nation. But both inside and outside the state there always existed some men who did not recognize the obligatoriness for themselves either of the injunctions which were given out to be the commands of the divinity, or of the decrees of men who were vested with sanctity, or of the institutions which purported to represent the will of the people, and these men, who considered to be good what the existing powers regarded as evil, fought against the powers, using the same violence which was directed against themselves.

Men who were vested with sanctity regarded as evil what men and institutions that were vested with civil power considered to be good, and vice versa, and the struggle became ever more acute. And the more such people held to this method for solving their struggle, the more obvious did it become that this method was useless, because there is and there can be no such external authority for the definition of evil as would be recognized by all men.

Thus it lasted for eighteen hundred years, and it reached the present point, — the complete obviousness of the fact that there is and there can be no external definition of evil which would be obligatory for all men. It reached such a point that men ceased to believe in the possibility of finding this common definition which would be obligatory for all men, and even in the necessity of putting forward such a definition. It came to such a pass that the men in power stopped proving that that which they considered to be an evil was an evil, and said outright that they considered that an evil which did not please them; and the men who obeyed the power began to obey it, not because they believed that the definitions of evil given by this power were correct, but only because they could not help but obey. Nice is added to France, Lorraine to Germany, Bohemia to Austria; Poland is divided; Ireland and India are subjected to English rule; war is waged against China and the Africans; the Americans expel the Chinese, and the Russians oppress the Jews; the landowners use the land which they do not work, and the capitalists make use of the labours of others, not because this is good, useful, and needful to men and because the contrary is evil, but because those who are in power want it to be so. What has happened is what happens now: one set of men commit acts of violence, no longer in the name of resisting evil, but in the name of their advantage or whim, while another set submit to violence, not because they assume, as was the case formerly, that violence is exerted against them in the name of freeing them from evil and for their good, but only because they cannot free themselves from this violence.

If a Roman, a man of the Middle Ages, a Russian, as I remember him to have been fifty years ago, was incontestably convinced that the existing violence of the power was necessary in order to free him from evil, that taxes, levies, serf law, prisons, whips, knouts, hard labour, capital punishment, militarism, wars, must exist, — it will be hard now to find a man who either believes that all acts of violence free any one from anything, or even does not see clearly that the majority of all those cases of violence to which he is subject and in which he partly shares are in themselves a great and useless evil.

There is now no such a man who does not see, not only the uselessness, but even the insipidity, of collecting taxes from the labouring classes for the purpose of enriching idle officials; or the senselessness of imposing punishments upon corrupt and weak people in the shape of deportation from one place to another, or in the form of imprisonment in jails, where they live in security and idleness and become more corrupted and weakened; or, not the uselessness and insipidity, but simply the madness and cruelty of military preparations and wars, which ruin and destroy the masses and have no explanation and justification, — and yet these cases of violence are continued and even maintained by the very men who see their uselessness, insipidity, and cruelty, and suffer from them.

If fifty years ago a rich idle man and an ignorant labouring man were both equally convinced that their condition of an eternal holiday for the one and of eternal labour for the other was ordained by God Himself, it is now, not only in Europe, but even in Russia, thanks to the migration of the populace, and the dissemination of culture and printing, hard to find either a rich or a poor man who, from one side or another, has not been assailed by doubts of the justice of such an order of things. Not only do the rich know that they are guilty even because they are rich, and try to redeem their guilt by offering contributions to art and science, as formerly they redeemed their sins by means of contributions to the churches, but even the greater half of the working people recognize the present order as being false and subject to destruction or change. One set of religious people, of whom there are millions in Russia, the so-called sectarians, recognize this order as false and subject to destruction on the basis of the Gospel teaching as taken in its real meaning; others consider it to be false on the basis of socialistic, communistic, anarchistic theories, which now have penetrated into the lower strata of the working people.

Violence is now no longer maintained on the ground that it is necessary, but only that it has existed for a long time, and has been so organized by men to whom it is advantageous, that is, by governments and the ruling classes, that the men who are in their power cannot tear themselves away from it.

The governments in our time — all governments, the most despotic and the most liberal — have become what Herzen so aptly called Dzhingis-Khans with telegraphs, that is, organizations of violence, which have nothing at their base but the coarsest arbitrary will, and yet use all those means which science has worked out for the aggregate social peaceful activity of free and equal men, and which they now employ for the enslavement and oppression of men.

The governments and the ruling classes do not now lean on the right, not even on the semblance of justice, but on an artificial organization which, with the aid of the perfections of science, encloses all men in the circle of violence, from which there is no possibility of tearing themselves away. This circle is now composed of four means of influencing men. All those means are connected and sustain one another, as the links in the ring of a united chain.

The first, the oldest, means is the means of intimidation. This means consists in representing the existing state structure (no matter what it may be, — whether a free republic or the wildest despotism) as something sacred and invariable, and so in inflicting the severest penalties for any attempt at changing it. This means, having been used before, is even now used in an unchanged form wherever there are governments: in Russia — against the so-called nihilists; in America — against the anarchists; in France — against the imperialists, monarchists, communists, and anarchists. The railways, telegraphs, photographs, and the perfected method of removing people, without killing them, into eternal solitary confinement, where, hidden from men, they perish and are forgotten, and many other modern inventions, which governments employ more freely than any one else, give them such strength that as soon as the power has fallen into certain hands, and the visible and the secret police.

and the administration, and all kinds of prosecutors, and jailers, and executioners are earnestly at work, there is no possibility of overthrowing the government, no matter how senseless or cruel it may be.

The second means is that of bribery. It consists in taking the wealth away from the labouring classes in the shape of monetary taxes, and distributing this wealth among the officials, who for this remuneration are obliged to maintain and strengthen the enslavement of the masses.

These bribed officials, from the highest ministers to the lowest scribes, who, forming one continuous chain of men, are united by the same interest of supporting themselves by the labours of the masses, and grow wealthier in proportion as they more humbly do the will of their governments, always and everywhere, stopping short before no means, in all branches of activity, in word and deed, defend the governmental violence, upon which their very well-being is based.

The third means is what I cannot call by any other name than the hypnotization of the people. This means consists in retarding the spiritual development of men and maintaining them with all kinds of suggestions in a concept of life which humanity has already outlived, and on which the power of the governments is based. This hypnotization is at the present time organized in the most complex manner, and, beginning its action in childhood, continues over men to their death. This hypnotization begins at early youth in compulsory schools which are established for the purpose, and in which the children are instilled with world-conceptions which were peculiar to their ancestors and are directly opposed to the modern consciousness of humanity. In countries in which there is a state religion, the children are taught the senseless blasphemies of ecclesiastical catechisms, in which the necessity of obeying the powers is pointed out; in republican governments they are taught the savage superstision of patriotism, and the same imaginary obligation of obeying the authorities. At a more advanced age, this hypnotization is continued by encouraging the religious and the patriotic superstitions.

The religious superstition is encouraged by means of the institution of churches, processions, monuments, festivities, from the money collected from the masses, and these, with the aid of painting, architecture, music, incense, but chiefly by the maintenance of the so-called clergy, stupefy the masses: their duty consists in this, that with their representations, the pathos of the services, their sermons, their interference in the private lives of the people, — at births, marriages, deaths, — they bedim the people and keep them in an eternal condition of stupefaction. The patriotic superstition is encouraged by means of public celebrations, spectacles, monuments, festivities, which are arranged by the governments and the ruling classes on the money collected from the masses, and which make people prone to recognize the exclusive importance of their own nation and the grandeur of their own state and rulers, and to be ill inclined toward all other nations and even hate them. In connection with this, the despotic governments directly prohibit the printing and dissemination of books and the utterance of speeches which enlighten the masses, and deport or incarcerate all men who are likely to rouse the masses from their lethargy; besides, all governments without exception conceal from the masses everything which could free them, and encourage everything which could corrupt them, such as the authorship of books which maintain the masses in the savagery of their religious and patriotic superstitions, all kinds of sensuous amusements, spectacles, circuses, theatres, and even all kinds of physical intoxications, such as tobacco, and brandy, which furnish the chief income of states; they even encourage prostitution, which is not only acknowledged, but even organized by the majority of governments. Such is the third means.

The fourth means consists in this, that with the aid of the three preceding means there is segregated, from the men so fettered and stupefied, a certain small number of men, who are subjected to intensified methods of stupefaction and brutalization, and are turned into involuntary tools of all those cruelties and bestialities which the governments may need. This stupefaction and brutalization is accomplished by taking the men at that youthful age when they have not yet had time to form any firm convictions in regard to morality, and, having removed them from all natural conditions of human life, from home, family, native district, rational labour, locking them all up together in narrow barracks, dressing them up in peculiar garments, and making them, under the influence of shouts, drums, music, glittering objects, perform daily exercises specially invented for the purpose, and thus inducing such a state of hypnosis in them that they cease to be men, and become unthinking machines, which are obedient to the command of the hypnotizer. These hypnotized, physically strong young men (all young men, on account of the present universal military service), who are provided with instruments of murder, and who are always obedient to the power of the governments and are prepared to commit any act of violence at their command, form the fourth and chief means for the enslavement of men.

With this means the circle of violence is closed.

Intimidation, bribery, hypnotization, make men desirous to become soldiers; but it is the soldiers who give the power and the possibility for punishing people, and picking them clean (and bribing the officials with the money thus obtained), and for hypnotizing and enlisting them again as soldiers, who in turn afford the possibility for doing all this.

The circle is closed, and there is no way of tearing oneself away from it by means of force.

If some men affirm that the liberation from violence, or even its weakening, may be effected, should the oppressed people overthrow the oppressing government by force and substitute a new one for it, a government in which such violence and enslavement would not be necessary, and if some men actually try to do so, they only deceive themselves and others by it, and thus fail to improve men's condition, and even make it worse. The activity of these men only intensifies the despotism of the governments. The attempts of these men at freeing themselves only give the governments a convenient excuse for strengthening their power, and actually provoke its strengthening.

Even if we admit that, in consequence of an unfortunate concurrence of events in the government, as, for example, in France in the year 1870, some governments may be overthrown by force and the power pass into other hands, this power would in no case be less oppressive than the former one, and, defending itself against the infuriated deposed enemies, would always be more despotic and cruel than the former, as indeed has been the case in every revolution.

If the socialists and communists consider the individualistic, capitalistic structure of society to be an evil, and the anarchists consider the government itself to be an evil, there are also monarchists, conservatives, capitalists, who consider the socialistic, communistic, and anarchistic order to be evil; and all these parties have no other means than force for the purpose of uniting men. No matter which of these parties may triumph, it will be compelled, for the materialization of its tenets, as well as for the maintenance of its power, not only to make use of all the existing means of violence, but also to invent new ones. Other men will be enslaved, and men will be compelled to do something else; but there will be, not only the same, but even a more cruel form of violence and enslavement, because, in consequence of the struggle, the hatred of men toward one another will be intensified, and at the same time new means of enslavement will be worked out and confirmed.

Thus it has always been after every revolution, every attempt at a revolution, every plot, every violent change of government. Every struggle only strengthens the means of the enslavement of those who at a given time are in power.

The condition of the men of our Christian world, and especially the current ideals themselves prove this in a striking manner.

There is left but one sphere of human activity which is not usurped by the governmental power, — the domestic, economic sphere, the sphere of the private life and of labour. But even this sphere, thanks to the struggle of the communists and socialists, is slowly being usurped by the governments, so that labour and rest, the domicile, the attire, the food of men will by degrees be determined and directed by the governments, if the wishes of the reformers are to be fulfilled.

The whole long, eighteen-centuries-old course of the life of the Christian nations has inevitably brought them back to the necessity of solving the question, so long evaded by them, as to the acceptance or non-acceptance of Christ's teaching, and the solution of the question resulting from it as regards the social life, whether to resist or not to resist evil with violence, but with this difference, that formerly men could accept the solution which Christianity offered, or not accept it, while now the solution has become imperative, because it alone frees them from that condition of slavery in which they have become entangled as in a snare.

But it is not merely the wretchedness of men's condition that brings them to this necessity.

Side by side with the negative proof of the falseness of

the pagan structure, there went the positive proof of the truth of the Christian teaching.

There was a good reason why, in the course of eighteen centuries, the best men of the whole Christian world, having recognized the truths of the teaching by means of an inner, spiritual method, should have borne witness to them before men, in spite of all threats, privations, calamities, and torments. With this their martyrdom these best men have put the stamp of truthfulness upon the teaching and have transmitted it to the masses.

Christianity penetrated into the consciousness of humanity, not merely by the one negative way of proving the impossibility of continuing the pagan life, but also by its simplification, elucidation, liberation from the dross of superstitions, and dissemination among all the classes of people.

Eighteen hundred years of the profession of Christianity did not pass in vain for the men who accepted it, even though only in an external manner. These eighteen centuries have had this effect that, continuing to live a pagan life, which does not correspond to the age of humanity, men have not only come to see clearly the whole wretchedness of the condition in which they are, but believe in the depth of their hearts (they live only because they believe) in this, that the salvation from this condition is only in the fulfilment of the Christian teaching in its true significance. As to when and how this salvation will take place, all men think differently, in accordance with their mental development and the current prejudices of their circle; but every man of our world recognizes the fact that our salvation lies in the fulfilment of the Christian teaching. Some believers, recognizing the Christian teaching as divine, think that the salvation will come when all men shall believe in Christ, and the second advent shall approach; others, who also recognize the divinity of Christ's teaching, think that this salvation will come through the church, which, subjecting all men to itself, will educate in them Christian virtues and will change their lives. Others again, who do not recognize Christ as God, think that the salvation of men will come through a slow, gradual progress, when the foundations of the pagan life will slowly give way to the foundations of liberty, equality, fraternity, that is, to Christian principles; others again, who preach a social transformation, think that the salvation will come when men by a violent revolution shall be compelled to adopt community of possession, absence of government, and collective, not individual, labour, that is, the materialization of one of the sides of the Christian teaching.

In one way or another, all men of our time in their consciousness not only reject the present obsolete pagan order of life, but recognize, frequently not knowing it themselves and regarding themselves as enemies of Christianity, that our salvation lies only in the application of the Christian teaching, or of a part of it, in its true meaning, to life.

For the majority of men, as its teacher has said, Christianity could not be realized at once, but had to grow, like an immense tree, from a small seed. And so it grew and has spread, if not in reality, at least in the consciousness of the men of our time.

Now it is not merely the minority of men, who always comprehended Christianity internally, that recognizes it in its true meaning, but also that vast majority of men which on account of its social life seems to be so far removed from Christianity.

Look at the private life of separate individuals; listen to those valuations of acts, which men make in judging one another; listen, not only to the public sermons and lectures, but also to those instructions which parents and educators give to their charges, and you will see that no matter how far the political, social life of men, which is united through violence, is from the realization of

Christian truths in private life, it is only the Christian virtues that are by all and for all, without exception and indubitably, considered to be good, and that the anti-Christian vices are by all and for all, without exception and indubitably, considered to be bad. Those are considered to be the best of men who renounce and sacrifice their lives in the service of humanity and who sacrifice themselves for others; those are considered to be the worst who are selfish, who exploit the misery of their neighbours for their own personal advantage.

If by some, who have not yet been touched by Christianity, are recognized the non-Christian ideals, force, valour, wealth, these are ideals which are not experienced and shared by all men, and certainly not by men who are considered to be the best.

The condition of our Christian humanity, if viewed from without, with its cruelty and its slavery, is really terrible. But if we look upon it from the side of its consciousness, an entirely different spectacle is presented to us.

The whole evil of our life seems to exist for no other reason than that it was done long ago, and the men who have done it have not yet had time to learn how not to do it, though none of them wish to do it.

All this evil seems to exist for some other reason, which is independent of the consciousness of men.

No matter how strange and contradictory this may seem, all the men of our time despise the very order of things which they help to maintain.

I think it is Max Müller who tells of the surprise of an Indian converted to Christianity, who, having grasped the essence of the Christian teaching, arrived in Europe and saw the life of the Christians. He could not recover from his astonishment in the presence of the reality, which was the very opposite of what he had expected to find among the Christian nations.

If we are not surprised at the contradiction between

our beliefs, convictions, and acts, this is due only to the fact that the influences which conceal this contradiction from men act also upon us. We need only look upon our life from the standpoint of the Indian, who understood Christianity in its real significance, without any compromises and adaptations, and upon those savage bestialities, with which our life is filled, in order that we may be frightened at the contradictions amidst which we live, frequently without noticing them.

We need but think of warlike preparations, mitrailleuses, silver-plated bullets, torpedoes, — and the Red Cross; of the construction of prisons with solitary cells, of the experiments at electrocution, — and of the benevolent cares for the imprisoned; of the philanthropic activity of rich men, — and of their lives, which are productive of those very poor whom they benefit. And these contradictions do not result, as may appear, because people pretend to be Christians, when in reality they are pagans, but, on the contrary, because people lack something, or because there is some force which keeps them from being what they already feel themselves to be in their consciousness and what they actually wish to be. The men of our time do not pretend to hate oppression, inequality, the division of men, and all kinds of cruelty, not only toward men, but also toward animals, — they actually do hate all this, but they do not know how to destroy it all, and they have not the courage to part with what maintains all this and seems to them to be indispensable.

Indeed, ask any man of our time privately, whether he considers it laudable or even worthy of a man of our time to busy himself with collecting taxes from the masses, who frequently are poverty-stricken, receiving for this work a salary which is entirely out of proportion with his labour, this money to be used for the construction of cannon, torpedoes, and implements for murdering men, with whom we wish to be at peace, and who wish to be at peace with us; or for a salary to devote all his life to the construction of these implements of murder; or to prepare himself and others to commit murder. And ask him whether it is laudable and worthy of a man, and proper for a Christian, to busy himself, again for money, with catching unfortunate, erring, frequently ignorant, drunken men for appropriating to themselves other people's possessions in much smaller quantities than we appropriate things to ourselves, and for killing men differently from what we are accustomed to kill men, and for this to put them in prisons, and torment, and kill them, and whether it is laudable and worthy of a man and a Christian, again for money, to preach to the masses, instead of Christianity, what is well known to be insipid and harmful superstitions; and whether it is laudable and worthy of a man to take from his neighbour, for the sake of his own lust, what his neighbour needs for the gratification of his prime necessities, as is done by the large landowners; or to compel him to perform labour above his strength, which ruins his life, in order to increase his own wealth, as is done by manufacturers, by owners of factories; or to exploit men's want for the purpose of increasing his wealth, as is done by merchants. And each of them taken privately, especially in speaking of another, will tell you that it is not. And yet this same man, who sees all the execrableness of these acts, who is himself not urged by any one, will himself voluntarily, and frequently without the monetary advantage of a salary, for the sake of childish vanity, for the sake of a porcelain trinket, a ribbon, a piece of lace, which he is permitted to put on, go into military service, become an examining magistrate, a justice of the peace, a minister, a rural officer, a bishop, a sexton, that is, he will take an office in which he is obliged to do things the disgrace and execrableness of which he cannot help but know.

I know many of these men will self-conceitedly prove that they consider their positions not only legitimate, but even indispensable; they will say in their defence that the power is from God, that political offices are necessary for the good of humanity, that wealth is not contrary to Christianity, that the rich young man was told to give up his wealth only if he wished to be perfect, that the now existing distribution of wealth and commerce must be so and is advantageous for everybody, and so forth. But, no matter how they may try to deceive themselves and others, all these men know that what they do is contrary to everything they believe in, and in the name of which they live, and in the depth of their hearts, when they are left alone with their consciences, they think with shame and pain of what they are doing, especially if the execrableness of their activity has been pointed out to them. A man of our time, whether he professes the divinity of Christ or not, cannot help but know that to take part, whether as a king, a minister, a governor, or a rural officer, in the sale of a poor family's last cow for taxes, with which to pay for cannon or the salaries and pensions of luxuriating, idle, and harmful officials; or to have a share in putting the provider of a family into prison, because we ourselves have corrupted him, and let his family go a-begging; or to take part in the plunders and murders of war; or to help substitute savage and idolatrous superstitions for Christ's law; or to detain a trespassing cow of a man who has no land of his own; or to deduct a sum from the wages of a factory hand for an article which he accidentally ruined; or to extort a double price from a poor fellow, only because he is in need, — a man of our time cannot help but know that all these things are disgraceful and execrable, and that they should not be done. They all know it: they know that what they do is bad, and they would not be doing it under any consideration, if they were able to withstand those forces which, closing their eyes to the criminality of their acts, draw them on to committing them.

In nothing is the degree of the contradiction which the lives of the men of our time have reached so striking, as in that phenomenon which forms the last means and expression of violence, — in the universal military service.

Only because this condition of universal arming and military service has come step by step and imperceptibly, and because for its maintenance the governments employ all means in their power for intimidating, bribing, stupefying, and ravishing men, we do not see the crying contradiction between this condition and those Christian feelings and thoughts, with which all the men of our time are really permeated.

This contradiction has become so habitual to us that we do not even see all the terrifying senselessness and immorality of the acts, not only of the men who voluntarily choose the profession of killing as something honourable, but even of those unfortunate men who agree to perform military duty, or even of those who in countries where military service is not introduced, voluntarily give up their labours to hire soldiers and prepare them to commit murder. All these men, be they Christians or men who profess humanity and liberalism, certainly know that, in committing these crimes, they become the participants, and, in personal military service, the actors, in the most senseless, aimless, cruel of murders, and yet they commit them.

But more than this: in Germany, whence comes the universal military service, Caprivi said openly, what before was carefully concealed, that the men who had to be killed were not merely the foreigners, but the working people, from whom come the majority of the soldiers. And this confession did not open men's eyes, did not frighten them. Even after this, as before, they continue to go like sheep to the enlistment and to submit to everything demanded of them.

And this is not enough: lately the German Emperor stated more definitely the significance and the calling of a soldier, when distinguishing, thanking, and rewarding a soldier for having shot a defenceless prisoner, who had attempted to run away. In thanking and rewarding the man for an act which has always been regarded as the lowest and basest by men who stand on the lowest stage of morality, William showed that the chief duty of a soldier, the one most valued by the authorities, consisted in being an executioner, not one like the professional executioners, who kill only condemned criminals, but one who kills all those innocent men whom he is ordered by his superiors to kill.

But more than this: in 1891 this same William, the *enfant terrible* of the political power, who expresses what others think, in speaking with some soldiers, said the following in public, and the next day thousands of newspapers reprinted these words:

"Recruits! In the sight of the altar and the servant of God you swore allegiance to me. You are still too young to understand the true meaning of everything which is said here, but see to this, that you first of all follow the commands and instructions given you. You have sworn allegiance to me; this, children of my guard, means that you are now my soldiers, that you have surrendered your souls and bodies to me. For you there now exists but one enemy, namely, the one who is my enemy. With the present socialistic propaganda it may happen that I will command you to shoot at your own relatives, your brothers, even parents, — which God forfend, — and then you are obliged without murmuring to do my commands."

This man expresses what all wise men know, but carefully conceal. He says frankly that men who serve in the army serve him and his advantage, and must be prepared for his advantage to kill their brothers and fathers.

He expresses frankly and with the coarsest of words all the horror of the crime for which the men who enter into military service are prepared, all that abyss of degradation which they reach, when they promise obedience. Like a bold hypnotizer, he tests the degree of the hypnotized man's sleep: he puts the glowing iron to his body, the body sizzles and smokes, but the hypnotized man does not wake.

This miserable, ill man, who has lost his mind from the exercise of power, with these words offends everything which can be holy for a man of our time, and men, — Christians, liberals, cultured men of our time, — all of them, are not only not provoked by this insult, but even do not notice it. The last, extreme trial, in its coarsest, most glaring form, is offered to men, and men do not even seem to notice that this is a trial, that they have a choice. It looks as though it seemed to them that there was not even any choice, and that there was but the one path of slavish obedience. One would think that these senseless words, which offend everything which a man of our time considers to be sacred, ought to have provoked people, but nothing of the kind took place. All the young men of all Europe are year after year subjected to this trial, and with the rarest exceptions they all renounce everything which is and can be sacred to a man, they all express their readiness to kill their brothers, even their fathers, at the command of the first erring man who is clad in a red livery embroidered with gold, and all they ask is when and whom to kill. And they are ready.

Every savage has something sacred for which he is prepared to suffer and for which he will make no concessions. But where is this sacredness for a man of our time? He is told, "Go into slavery to me, into a slavery in which you have to kill your own father," and he, who very frequently is a learned man, who has studied all the sciences in a university, submissively puts his neck into the yoke. He is dressed up in a fool's attire, is commanded to jump, to contort his body, to bow, to kill, — and he does everything submissively. And when he is let out, he returns briskly to his former life and continues to talk of man's dignity, liberty, equality, and fraternity.

"Yes, but what is to be done?" people frequently ask, in sincere perplexity. "If all should refuse, it would be well; otherwise I alone shall suffer, and no one will be helped by it."

And, indeed, a man of the social concept of life cannot refuse. The meaning of his life is the good of his personality. For the sake of his personality it is better for him to submit, and he submits.

No matter what may be done to him, no matter how he may be tortured and degraded, he will submit, because he can do nothing himself, because he has not that foundation in the name of which he could by himself withstand the violence; but those who govern men will never give them a chance to unite. It is frequently said that the invention of terrible implements of murder will abolish war and that war will abolish itself. That is not true. As it is possible to increase the means for the slaughter of men, so it is possible to increase the means for subjugating the men of the social concept of life. Let them be killed by the thousand, by the million, and be torn to pieces, — they will none the less go to the slaughter like senseless cattle, because they are driven with a goad; others will go, because for this they will be permitted to put on ribbons and galloons, and they will even be proud of it.

And it is in connection with such a contingent of men, who are so stupefied that they promise to kill their parents, that the public leaders — the conservatives, liberals, socialists, anarchists — talk of building up a rational and moral society. What rational and moral society can be built up with such men? Just as it is impossible to build a house with rotten and crooked logs, no matter how one may transpose them, so it is impossible with such people to construct a rational and moral society. Such people can only form a herd of animals which is directed by the shouts and goads of the shepherds. And so it is.

And so, on the one hand, Christians by name, who profess liberty, equality, and fraternity, are side by side with that prepared in the name of liberty for the most slavish and degraded submission, in the name of equality for the most glaring and senseless divisions of men by external signs alone into superiors and inferiors, their allies and their enemies, and in the name of fraternity for the murder of these brothers.[1]

The contradictions of consciousness and the resulting wretchedness of life have reached the extremest point, beyond which it is impossible to go. The life which is built up on the principles of violence has reached the negation of those very principles in the name of which it was built up. The establishment of society on the principles of violence, which had for its aim the security of the personal, domestic, and social good, has led men to a complete negation and destruction of this good.

The first part of the prophecy has been fulfilled in respect to men and their generations, who did not accept the teaching, and their descendants have now been brought to the necessity of experiencing the justice of its second part.

[1] The fact that some nations, the English and the Americans, have not yet any universal military service (though voices in its favour are already heard), but only the enlistment and hire of soldiers, does in no way change the condition of slavery in which the citizens stand relative to the governments. Here everybody has to go himself to kill and be killed; there everybody has to give his labours for the hire and preparation of murderers. — *Author's Note.*

IX.

The condition of the Christian nations in our time has remained as cruel as it was in the times of paganism. In many relations, especially in the enslavement of men, it has become even more cruel than in the times of paganism.

But between the condition of the men of that time and of our time there is the same difference that there is for the plants between the last days of autumn and the first days of spring. There, in the autumnal Nature, the external lifelessness corresponds to the internal condition of decay; but here, in the spring, the external lifelessness is in the sharpest contradiction to the condition of the internal restoration and the change to a new form of life.

The same is true of the external resemblance between the previous pagan life and the present one: the external condition of men in the times of paganism and in our time is quite different.

There the external condition of cruelty and slavery was in full agreement with the internal consciousness of men, and every forward movement increased this agreement; but here the external condition of cruelty and slavery is in complete disagreement with the Christian consciousness of men, and every forward step only increases this disagreement.

What is taking place is, as it were, useless sufferings, — something resembling childbirth. Everything is prepared for the new life, but the life itself has not made its appearance.

The situation seems to be without an issue, and it

would be so, if the individual man, and so all men, were not given the possibility of another, higher conception of life, which at once frees him from all those fetters which, it seemed, bound him indissolubly.

Such is the Christian concept of life, which was pointed out to humanity eighteen hundred years ago.

A man need only make this life-concept his own, in order that the chains which seemed to have fettered him so indissolubly may fall off of themselves, and that he may feel himself quite free, something the way a bird would feel free when it expanded its wings in a place which is fenced in all around.

People speak of the liberation of the Christian church from the state, of granting or not granting liberty to Christians. In these thoughts and expressions there is some terrible misconception. Liberty cannot be granted to a Christian or to Christians, or taken from them. Liberty is a Christian's inalienable property.

When people speak of granting liberty to Christians, or taking it from them, it is evident that they are not speaking of real Christians, but of men who call themselves Christians. A Christian cannot be anything else but free, because the attainment of the end which he has set before himself cannot be retarded or detained by any one or anything.

A man need but understand his life as Christianity teaches him to understand it, that is, understand that life does not belong to him, his personality, or the family, or the state, but to Him who sent him into this life; that, therefore, he must not fulfil the law of his personality, his family, or the state, but the unlimited law of Him from whom he has come, in order that he may feel himself quite free from every human power and may even stop seeing this power as something which may be oppressive for any one.

A man need but understand that the aim of his life is

the fulfilment of God's law, in order that this law, taking for him the place of all other laws and subjugating him to itself, by this very subjugation may deprive all the human laws in his eyes of all their obligatoriness and oppression.

A Christian is freed from every human power in that he considers for his life and for the lives of others the divine law of love, which is implanted in the soul of every man and is brought into consciousness by Christ, as the only guide of his life and of that of other men.

A Christian may submit to external violence, may be deprived of his bodily freedom, may not be free from his passions (he who commits a sin is a slave of sin), but he cannot help but be free, in the sense of not being compelled by some danger or external threat to commit an act which is contrary to his consciousness.

He cannot be compelled to do this, because the privations and sufferings which are produced by violence, and which form a mighty tool against the men of the social concept of life, have no compulsory force with him. The privations and sufferings which take from the men of the social concept of life the good for which they live, cannot impair the Christian's good, which consists in the fulfilment of God's will; they can only strengthen him, when they assail him in the performance of this will.

And so a Christian, in submitting to the internal, divine law, cannot only not perform the prescription of the external law, when it is not in accord with the divine law of love as recognized by him, as is the case in the demands set forth by the government, but cannot even recognize the obligation of obeying any one or anything, — he cannot recognize what is called the subject's allegiance. For a Christian the promise of allegiance to any government — that very act which is regarded as the foundation of the political life — is a direct renunciation of Christianity, because a man who unconditionally promises in advance to submit to laws which are made and will be made by men, by this very promise in a very definite manner renounces Christianity, which consists in this, that in all problems of life he is to submit only to the divine law of love, of which he is conscious in himself.

It was possible with the pagan world-conception to promise to do the will of the civil authorities, without violating the will of God, which consisted in circumcision, the Sabbath, praying at set times, abstaining from a certain kind of food, and so forth. One did not contradict the other. But the Christian profession differs in this very thing from the pagan, in that it does not demand of a man certain external negative acts, but places him in another relation to man from what he was in before, a relation from which may result the most varied acts, which cannot be ascertained in advance, and so a Christian cannot promise to do another person's will, without knowing in what the demands of this will may consist, and cannot obey the variable human laws; he cannot even promise to do anything definite at a certain time or to abstain from anything at a certain time, because he cannot know what at any time that Christian law of love, the submission to which forms the meaning of his life, may demand of him. In promising in advance unconditionally to fulfil the laws of men, a Christian would by this very promise indicate that the inner law of God does not form for him the only law of his life.

For a Christian to promise that he will obey men or human laws is the same as for a labourer who has hired out to a master to promise at the same time that he will do everything which other men may command him to do. It is impossible to serve two masters.

A Christian frees himself from human power by recognizing over himself nothing but God's power, the law of which, revealed to him by Christ, he recognizes in himself, and to which alone he submits.

And this liberation is not accomplished by means of a struggle, not by the destruction of existing forms of life, but only by means of the changed comprehension of life. The liberation takes place in consequence of this, in the first place, that a Christian recognizes the law of love, which was revealed to him by his teacher, as quite sufficient for human relations, and so regards all violence as superfluous and illegal, and, in the second place, that those privations, sufferings, threats of sufferings and privations, with which the public man is brought to the necessity of obeying, present themselves to a Christian, with his different concept of life, only as inevitable conditions of existence, which he, without struggling against them by exercising violence, bears patiently, like diseases, hunger, and all other calamities, but which by no means can serve as a guide for his acts. What serves as a guide for a Christian's acts is only the divine principle that lives within him and that cannot be oppressed or directed by anything.

A Christian acts according to the word of the prophecy applied to his teacher, "He shall not strive, nor cry; neither shall any man hear His voice in the streets; a bruised reed shall He not break, and smoking flax shall He not quench, till He send forth judgment unto victory" (Matt. xii. 19–20).

A Christian does not quarrel with any one, does not attack any one, nor use violence against one; on the contrary, he himself without murmuring bears violence; but by this very relation to violence he not only frees himself, but also the world from external power.

"And ye shall know the truth, and the truth shall make you free" (John viii. 32). If there were any doubt as to Christianity being truth, that complete freedom, which cannot be oppressed by anything, and which a man experiences the moment he makes the Christian life-conception his own, would be an undoubted proof of its truth.

In their present condition men are like bees which have just swarmed and are hanging down a limb in a cluster. The position of the bees on the limb is temporary, and must inevitably be changed. They must rise and find a new home for themselves. Every one of the bees knows that and wishes to change its position and that of the others, but not one is able to do so before the others are going to do so. They cannot rise all at once, because one hangs down from the other, keeping it from separating itself from the swarm, and so all continue to hang. It would seem that the bees could not get out of this state, just as it seems to worldly men who are entangled in the snare of the social world-conception. But there would be no way out for the bees, if each of the bees were not separately a living being, endowed with wings. So there would also be no way out for men, if each of them were not a separate living being, endowed with the ability of acquiring the Christian concept of life.

If every bee which can fly did not fly, the rest, too, would not move, and the swarm would never change its position. And as one bee need but open its wings, rise up, and fly away, and after it a second, third, tenth, hundredth, in order that the immovable cluster may become a freely flying swarm of bees, so one man need but understand life as Christianity teaches him to understand it, and begin to live accordingly, and a second, third, hundredth, to do so after him, in order that the magic circle of the social life, from which there seemed to be no way out, be destroyed.

But people think that the liberation of all men in this manner is too slow, and that it is necessary to find and use another such a means, so as to free all at once; something like what the bees would do, if, wishing to rise and fly away, they should find that it was too long for them to wait for the whole swarm to rise one after another, and should try to find a way where every individual bee would not have to unfold its wings and fly away, but the whole swarm could fly at once wherever it wanted. But that is impossible: so long as the first, second, third, hundredth bee does not unfold its wings and fly, the swarm, too, will not fly away or find the new life. So long as every individual man does not make the Christian life-conception his own, and does not live in accordance with it, the contradiction of the human life will not be solved and the new form of life will not be established.

One of the striking phenomena of our time is that preaching of slavery which is disseminated among the masses, not only by the governments, which need it, but also by those men who, preaching socialistic theories, imagine that they are the champions of liberty.

These people preach that the improvement of life, the bringing of reality in agreement with consciousness, will not take place in consequence of personal efforts of separate men, but of itself, in consequence of a certain violent transformation of society, which will be inaugurated by somebody. What is preached is that men do not have to go with their own feet whither they want and have to go, but that some kind of a floor will be put under their feet, so that, without walking, they will get whither they have to go. And so all their efforts must not be directed toward going according to one's strength whither one has to go, but toward constructing this imaginary floor while standing in one spot.

In the economic relation they preach a theory, the essence of which consists in this, that the worse it is, the better it is, that the more there shall be an accumulation of capital, and so an oppression of the labourer, the nearer will the liberation be, and so every personal effort of a man to free himself from the oppression of capital is useless; in the relation of the state, they preach that the greater the power of the state, which according to this theory has to take in the still unoccupied field of the private life, the better it will be, and that, therefore, the interference of the governments in the private life has to be invoked; in the political and international relations they preach that the increase of the means of destruction, the increase of the armies, will lead to the necessity of disarmament by means of congresses, arbitrations, and so forth. And, strange to say, the obstinacy of men is so great that they believe in these theories, although the whole course of life, every step in advance, betrays its incorrectness.

Men suffer from oppression, and to save themselves from this oppression, they are advised to invent common means for the improvement of their situation, to be applied by the authorities, while they themselves continue to submit to them. Obviously, nothing results from it but a strengthening of the power, and consequently the intensification of the oppression.

Not one of the errors of men removes them so much from the end which they have set for themselves as this one. In order to attain the end which they have set before themselves, men do all kinds of things, only not the one, simple thing which all have to do. They invent the most cunning of ways for changing the situation which oppresses them, except the one, simple one that none of them should do that which produces this situation.

I was told of an incident which happened with a brave rural judge who, upon arriving at a village where the peasants had been riotous and whither the army had been called out, undertook to settle the riot in the spirit of Nicholas I., all by himself, through his personal influence. He sent for several wagon-loads of switches, and, collecting all the peasants in the corn-kiln, locked himself up with them, and so intimidated the peasants with his shouts, that they, obeying him, began at his command to flog one another. They continued flogging one another until there was found a little fool who did not submit and shouted to his companions to stop flogging one another. It was only then that the flogging stopped, and the rural judge ran away from the kiln. It is this advice of the fool that the men of the social order do not know how to follow, for they flog one another without cessation, and men teach this mutual flogging as the last word of human wisdom.

Indeed, can we imagine a more striking example of how men flog themselves than the humbleness with which the men of our time carry out the very obligations which are imposed upon them and which lead them into servitude, especially the military service? Men obviously enslave themselves, suffer from this slavery, and believe that it must be so, that it is all right and does not interfere with the liberation of men, which is being prepared somewhere and somehow, in spite of the ever increasing and increasing slavery.

Indeed, let us take a man of our time, whoever he be (I am not speaking of a true Christian, but of a man of the rank and file of our time), cultured or uncultured, a believer or unbeliever, rich or poor, a man of a family or a single man. Such a man of our time lives, doing his work or enjoying himself, employing the fruits of his own labour or those of others for his own sake or for the sake of those who are near to him, like any other man, despising all kinds of oppressions and privations, hostility, and sufferings. The man lives peacefully; suddenly people come to him, who say: "In the first place, promise and swear to us that you will slavishly obey us in everything which we shall prescribe to you, and that everything we shall invent, determine, and call a law you will consider an indubitable truth and will submit to; in the second place, give part of your earnings into our keeping: we shall use this money for keeping you in slavery and preventing you from forcibly opposing our decrees; in the third place, choose yourself and others as imaginary participants in the government, knowing full well that the government will take place entirely independently of those stupid speeches which you will utter to your like, and that it will take place according to our will, in whose hands is the army; in the fourth place, appear at a set time in court and take part in all those senseless cruelties which we commit against the erring men, whom we ourselves have corrupted, in the shape of imprisonments, exiles, solitary confinements, and capital punishments. And finally, in the fifth place, besides all this, though you may be in the most friendly relations with people belonging to other nations, be prepared at once, when we command you, to consider such of these men as we shall point out to you your enemies, and to coöperate personally or by hiring others in the ruin, pillage, and murder of their men, women, children, old people, and, perhaps, your own countrymen, even your parents, if we want it."

What could any man of our time who is not stupefied answer to such demands?

"Why should I do all this?" every spiritually healthy man, we should think, ought to say. "Why should I promise to do all that which I am commanded to do, to-day by Salisbury, to-morrow by Gladstone, to-day by Boulanger, to-morrow by a Chamber of just such Boulangers, to-day by Peter III., to-morrow by Catherine, day after to-morrow by Pugachév, to-day by the crazy King of Bavaria, to-morrow by William? Why should I promise to obey them, since I know them to be bad or trifling men, or do not know them at all? Why should I in the shape of taxes give them the fruits of my labours, knowing that the money will be used for bribing the officials, for prisons, churches, armies, for bad things and my own enslavement? Why should I flog myself? Why should I go, losing my time and pulling the wool over my eyes, and ascribing to the violators a semblance of legality, and take part in the government, when I know full well that the government of the state is in the hands of those in whose hands is the army? Why should I go into courts and take part in the torture and punishments of men for having erred, since I know, if I am a Christian, that the law of revenge has given way to the law of love, and, if I am a cultured man, that punishments do not make men who are subjected to them better, but worse? And why should I, above all, simply because the keys of the temple at Jerusalem will be in the hands of this bishop and not of that, because in Bulgaria this and not that German will be prince, and because English and not American merchants will catch seals, recognize as enemies the men of a neighbouring nation, with whom I have heretofore lived at peace and wish to live in love and concord, and why should I hire soldiers or myself go and kill and destroy them, and myself be subjected to their attack? And why, above all else, should I coöperate personally or by the hiring of a military force in the enslavement and murder of my own brothers and fathers? Why should I flog myself? All this I do not need, and all this is harmful for me, and all this on all sides of me is immoral, abominable. So why should I do it all? If you tell me that without it I shall fare ill at somebody's hands, I, in the first place, do not foresee anything so bad as that which you cause me if I listen to you; in the second place, it is quite clear to me that, if you do not flog yourself, nobody is going to flog us. The government is the kings, the ministers, the officials with their pens, who cannot compel me to do anything like what the rural judge compelled the peasants to do: those who will take me forcibly to court, to prison, to the execution are not the kings and the officials with their pens, but those very people who are in the same condition in which I am. It is just as useless and harmful and disagreeable for them to be flogged as it is for me, and so in all probability, if I open their eyes, they not only must do me no violence, but must even do as I do.

"In the third place, even if it should happen that I must suffer for it, it still is more advantageous for me to be exiled or shut up in a prison, while defending common sense and the good, which shall triumph, if not to-day, certainly to-morrow, or in a very short time, than to suffer for a foolish thing and an evil, which sooner or later must come to an end. And so it is even in this case more advantageous for me to risk being deported, locked up in a prison, or even executed, than through my own fault to pass my whole life as a slave to other bad men, than to be ruined by an enemy making an incursion and stupidly to be maimed or killed by him, while defending a cannon, or a useless piece of land, or a stupid rag which they call a flag.

"I do not want to flog myself, and I won't. There is no reason why I should. Do it yourselves, if you are so minded, but I won't."

It would seem that not only the religious or moral feeling, but the simplest reflection and calculation would make a man of our time answer and act in this manner. But no: the men of the social life-conception find that it is not right to act in this manner, and that it is even harmful to act thus if we wish to obtain the end of the liberation of men from slavery, and that it is necessary for us, as in the case of the rural judge and the peasants, to continue to flog one another, consoling ourselves with the thought that the fact that we prattle in Chambers and assemblies, form labour-unions, parade the streets on the first of May, form plots, and secretly tease the government which flogs us, — that all this will have the effect of freeing us very soon, though we are enslaving ourselves more and more.

Nothing so much impedes the liberation of men as this remarkable delusion. Instead of directing all his forces to the liberation of himself, to the change of his world-conception, every man seeks for an external aggregate means for freeing himself, and thus fetters himself more and more.

It is as though men should affirm that, in order to fan a fire, it is not necessary to make every coal catch fire, but to place the coals in a certain order.

In the meantime it has been getting more and more obvious of late that the liberation of all men will take place only through the liberation of the individual men. The liberation of individual persons in the name of the Christian life-conception from the enslavement of the state, which used to be an exclusive and imperceptible phenomenon, has of late received a significance which is menacing to the power of state.

If formerly, in the days of Rome, in the Middle Ages, it happened that a Christian, professing his teaching, refused to take part in sacrifices, to worship the emperors and gods, or in the Middle Ages refused to worship the images, to recognize the papal power, these refusals were, in the first place, accidental; a man might have been put to the necessity of professing his faith, and he might have lived a life without being placed in this necessity. But now all men without exception are subject to these trials. Every man of our time is put to the necessity of recognizing his participation in the cruelties of the pagan life, or rejecting it. And, in the second place, in those days the refusals to worship the gods, the images, the Pope, did not present any essential phenomena for the state: no matter how many men worshipped the gods, the images, or the Pope, the state remained as strong as ever. But now the refusal to comply with the non-Christian demands of governments undermines the power of state to the root, because all the power of the state is based on these non-Christian demands.

The worldly powers were led by the course of life to the proposition that for their own preservation they had to demand from all men such acts as could not be performed by those who professed true Christianity.

And so in our time every profession of true Christianity by a separate individual most materially undermines the power of the government and inevitably leads to the emancipation of all men.

What importance can there be in such phenomena as the refusals of a few dozens of madmen, as they are called, who do not wish to swear to the government, or pay taxes, or take part in courts and military service? These men are punished and removed, and life continues as of old. It would seem that there is nothing important in these phenomena, and yet it is these very phenomena that more than anything else undermine the power of the state and prepare the emancipation of men. They are those individual bees which begin to separate from the swarm and fly about, awaiting what cannot be delayed, — the rising of the whole swarm after them. The governments know this, and are afraid of these phenomena more than of all socialists, communists, anarchists, and their plots with their dynamite bombs.

A new reign begins: according to the general rule and customary order all the subjects are ordered to swear allegiance to the new government. A general order is sent out, and everybody is called to the cathedral to swear. Suddenly one man in Perm, another in Túla, a third in Moscow, a fourth in Kalúga declare that they will not swear, and they base their refusal, every one of them, without having plotted together, on one and the same reason, which is, that the oath is prohibited by the Christian law, and that, even if it were not prohibited, they could not, according to the spirit of the Christian law, promise to commit the evil acts which are demanded of them in the oath, such as denouncing all those who will violate the interests of the government, defending their government with weapons in their hands, or attacking its enemies. They are summoned before the rural judges or chiefs, priests, or governors, are admonished, implored, threatened, and punished, but they stick to their determination and do not swear. Among millions of those who swear, there are a few dozens who do not. And they are asked:

"So you have not sworn?"

"We have not."

"Well, nothing happened?"

"Nothing."

All the subjects of a state are obliged to pay taxes. And all pay; but one man in Khárkov, another in Tver, a third in Samára, refuse to pay their taxes, all of them repeating, as though by agreement, one and the same thing. One says that he will pay only when he is told what the money taken from him will be used for: if for good things, he says, he will himself give more than is asked of him; but if for bad things, he will not give anything voluntarily, because, according to Christ's teaching, which he follows, he cannot contribute to evil deeds. The same, though with different words, is said by the others, who do not voluntarily pay their taxes. From those who possess anything, the property is taken by force, but those who have nothing to give are left alone.

"Well, you did not pay the taxes?"

"I did not."

"Well, and nothing happened to you?"

"Nothing."

Passports are established. All who remove themselves from their place of abode are obliged to take them and pay a revenue for them. Suddenly on all sides appear men who say that it is not necessary to take passports and that it is not right to recognize one's dependence on a government which lives by violence, and they take no passports and pay no revenue. Again it is impossible to make these people carry out what is demanded of them.

They are locked up in prisons and let out again, and they continue to live without passports.

All the peasants are obliged to serve as hundred-men, ten-men, and so forth. Suddenly a peasant refuses in Khárkov to perform this office, explaining his refusal by this, that, according to the Christian law which he professes, he cannot bind, lock up, and lead a man from one place to another. The same is asserted by a peasant in Tver, in Támbov. The peasants are cursed, beaten, locked up, but they stick to their determination and do not do what is contrary to their faith. And they are no longer chosen as hundred-men, and that is the end of it.

All the citizens must take part in court proceedings in the capacity of jurymen. Suddenly the greatest variety of men, wheelwrights, professors, merchants, peasants, gentlemen, as though by agreement, all refuse to serve, not for causes which are recognized by the law, but because the court itself, according to their conviction, is an illegal, non-Christian thing, which ought not to exist. These men are fined, without being allowed publicly to express the motives of their refusal, and others are put in their places. The same is done to those who on the same grounds refuse to be witnesses at court. And nothing more happens.

All men of twenty-one years of age are obliged to draw lots. Suddenly one young man in Moscow, another in Tver, a third in Khárkov, a fourth in Kiev, appear, as though by previous agreement, in court, and declare that they will neither swear nor serve, because they are Christians. Here are the details of one of the first cases (since then these refusals have become more and more frequent), with which I am acquainted.[1] In all the other cases approximately the same was done. A young man of

[1] All the details of this and the preceding cases are authentic. — *Author's Note.*

medium culture refuses in the Moscow Council to serve. No attention is paid to his words, and he is ordered to pronounce the words of the oath, just like the rest. He refuses, pointing out the definite place in the Gospel where taking an oath is prohibited. No attention is paid to his arguments, and they demand that he fulfil their command, but he does not do so. Then it is assumed that he is a sectarian and so understands Christianity incorrectly, that is, not in the way the clergy in the government pay understand it, and so the young man is sent under convoy to the priests, to be admonished. The priests begin to admonish the young man, but their admonitions in the name of Christ to renounce Christ have apparently no effect upon the young man, and he is sent back to the army, having been declared incorrigible. The young man still refuses to take the oath and openly declines to fulfil his military duties. This case is not provided for in the laws. It is impossible to admit a refusal to do the will of the authorities, and it is equally impossible to rate this as a case of simple disobedience. In a consultation the military authorities determine to get rid of the troublesome young man by declaring him to be a revolutionist, and send him under guard into the office of the secret police. The police and the gendarmes examine the young man, but nothing of what he says fits in with the crimes dealt with in their departments, and there is absolutely no way of accusing him of revolutionary acts, or of plotting, since he declares that he does not wish to destroy anything, but, on the contrary, rejects all violence, and conceals nothing, but seeks an opportunity for saying and doing in a most open manner what he says and does. And the gendarmes, though no laws are binding on them, like the clergy, find no cause for an accusation and return the young man to the army. Again the chiefs confer and decide to enlist the young man in the army, though he refuses to take the oath. He is dressed up, entered on the lists, and sent under guard to the place where the troops are distributed. Here the chief of the section into which he enters again demands of the young man the fulfilment of military duties, and he again refuses to obey, and in the presence of other soldiers gives the cause for his refusal, saying that, as a Christian, he cannot voluntarily prepare himself to commit murder, which was prohibited even by the laws of Moses.

The case takes place in a provincial city. It evokes interest and even sympathy, not only among outsiders, but also among officers, and so the superiors do not dare to apply the usual disciplinary measures for a refusal to serve. However, for decency's sake the young man is locked up in prison, and an inquiry is sent to the higher military authority, requesting it to say what is to be done. From the official point of view a refusal to take part in military service, in which the Tsar himself serves and which is blessed by the church, presents itself as madness, and so they write from St. Petersburg that, since the young man is, no doubt, out of his mind, no severe measures are to be used against him, but he is to be sent to an insane asylum, where his mental health is to be investigated and he is to be cured. He is sent there in the hope that he will stay there, just as happened ten years before with another young man, who in Tver refused to do military service and who was tortured in an insane asylum until he gave in. But even this measure does not save the military authorities from the inconvenient young man. The doctors examine him, are very much interested in him, and, finding in him no symptoms whatever of any mental trouble, naturally return him to the army. He is received, and, pretending that his refusal and motives are forgotten, they again propose to him that he go to the exercises; but he again, in the presence of other soldiers, refuses, and gives the cause for his refusal. This case more and more attracts the attention of the soldiers and the inhabitants of the town. Again they write to St. Petersburg, and from there comes the decision that the young man be transferred to the army at the frontier, where it is in a state of siege, and where he may be shot for refusing to serve, and where the matter may pass unnoticed, since in that distant country there are few Russians and Christians, and mostly natives and Mohammedans. And so they do. The young man is attached to the troops located in the Transcaspian Territory, and with criminals he is despatched to a chief who is known for his determination and severity.

During all this time, with all these transportations from one place to another, the young man is treated rudely: he is kept cold, hungry, and dirty, and his life in general is made a burden for him. But all these tortures do not make him change his determination. In the Transcaspian Territory, when told to stand sentry with his gun, he again refuses to obey. He does not refuse to go and stand near some haystacks, whither he is sent, but he refuses to take his gun, declaring that under no condition would he use violence against any one. All this takes place in the presence of other soldiers. It is impossible to let such a case go unpunished, and the young man is tried for violation of discipline. The trial takes place, and the young man is sentenced to incarceration in a military prison for two years. He is again sent by étapes with other criminals to the Caucasus and is shut up in a prison, where he falls a prey to the uncontrolled power of the jailer. There he is tormented for one year and six months, but he still refuses to change his decision about taking up arms, and he explains to all those with whom he comes in contact why he does not do so, and at the end of his second year he is discharged before the expiration of his term, by counting, contrary to the law, his time in prison as part of his service, only to get rid of him as quickly as possible.

Just like this man, as though having plotted together, act other men in various parts of Russia, and in all those cases the mode of the government's action is as timid, indefinite, and secretive. Some of these men are sent to insane asylums, others are enlisted as scribes and are transferred to service in Siberia, others are made to serve in the forestry department, others are locked up in prisons, and others are fined. Even now a few such men who have refused are sitting in prisons, not for the essential point in the case, the rejection of the legality of the government's action, but for the non-fulfilment of the private demands of the government. Thus an officer of the reserve, who did not keep the authorities informed of his residence and who declared that he would not again serve as a military man, was lately, for not fulfilling the commands of the authorities, fined thirty roubles, which, too, he refused to pay voluntarily. Thus several peasants and soldiers, who lately refused to take part in military exercises and take up arms, were locked up for disobedience and contempt.

And such cases of refusing to comply with the government demands which are contrary to Christianity, especially refusals to do military service, have of late occurred not in Russia alone, but even elsewhere. Thus, I know that in Servia men of the so-called sect of Nazarenes constantly refuse to do military service, and the Austrian government has for several years been vainly struggling with them, subjecting them to imprisonment. In the year 1885 there were 130 such refusals. In Switzerland, I know men were incarcerated in the Chillon Fortress in the year 1890 for refusing to do military service, and they did not change their determination in consequence of their imprisonment. Such refusals have also happened in Prussia. I know of an under-officer of the Guard, who in 1891 declared to the authorities in Berlin that as a Christian he would not continue to serve, and, in spite of all admonitions, threats, and punishments, he stuck to his decision. In France there has of late arisen in the south a community of men, who bear the name of Hinschists (this information is received from the *Peace Herald*, July, 1891), the members of which on the basis of the Christian profession refuse to do military service, and at first were inscribed in hospitals, but now, having increased in numbers, are subjected to punishments for disobedience, but still refuse to take up arms.

The socialists, communists, anarchists, with their bombs, riots, and revolutions, are by no means so terrible to the governments as these scattered people, who from various sides refuse to do military service, — all of them on the basis of the same well-known teaching. Every government knows how and why to defend itself against revolutionists, and they have means for it, and so are not afraid of these external enemies. But what are the governments to do against those men who point out the uselessness, superfluity, and harmfulness of all governments, and do not struggle with them, but only have no use for them, get along without them, and do not wish to take part in them?

The revolutionists say, "The governmental structure is bad for this and that reason, — it is necessary to put this or that in its place." But a Christian says, "I know nothing of the governmental structure, about its being good or bad, and do not wish to destroy it for the very reason that I do not know whether it is good or bad, but for the same reason I do not wish to sustain it. I not only do not wish to, but even cannot do so, because what is demanded of me is contrary to my conscience."

What is contrary to a Christian's conscience is all obligations of state, — the oath, the taxes, the courts, the army. But on all these obligations the state is founded.

The revolutionary enemies struggle with the state from

without; but Christianity does not struggle at all, — it inwardly destroys all the foundations of government.

Among the Russian people, where, especially since the time of Peter I., the protest of Christianity against the government has never ceased, where the structure of life is such that men have gone away by whole communities to Turkey, to China, to uninhabitable lands, and not only are in no need of the government, but always look upon it as an unnecessary burden, and only bear it as a calamity, be it Turkish, Russian, or Chinese, — among the Russian people there have of late been occurring more and more frequently cases of the Christian conscious emancipation of separate individuals from submission to the government. And now especially these manifestations are very terrible to the government, because those who refuse frequently do not belong to the so-called lower uncultured classes, but to the people with a medium or higher education, and because these men no longer base their refusals on some mystical exclusive beliefs, as was the case formerly, nor connect them with some superstition or savage practices, as is the case with the Self-Consumers and Runners, but put forth the simplest and clearest truths, which are accessible to all men and recognized by them all.

Thus they refuse to pay their taxes voluntarily, because the taxes are used for acts of violence, for salaries to violators and military men, for the construction of prisons, fortresses, cannon, while they, as Christians, consider it sinful and immoral to take part in these things. Those who refuse to take the common oath do so because to promise to obey the authorities, that is, men who are given to acts of violence, is contrary to the Christian teaching; they refuse to take their oath in courts, because the oath is directly forbidden in the Gospel. They decline to serve in the police, because in connection with these duties they have to use force against their own brothers and torment them, whereas a Christian may not do so. They decline to take part in court proceedings, because they consider every court proceeding a fulfilment of the law of revenge, which is incompatible with the Christian law of forgiveness and love. They decline to take part in all military preparations and in the army, because they do not wish to be and cannot be executioners, and do not want to prepare themselves for the office of executioner.

All the motives of these refusals are such that, no matter how despotic a government may be, it cannot punish them openly. To punish them for such refusals, a government must itself irretrievably renounce reason and the good; whereas it assures men that it serves only in the name of reason and of the good.

What are the governments to do against these men?

Indeed, the governments can kill off, for ever shut up in prisons and at hard labour their enemies, who wish by the exercise of violence to overthrow them; they can bury in gold half of the men, such as they may need, and bribe them; they can subject to themselves millions of armed men, who will be ready to destroy all the enemies of the governments. But what can they do with men who, not wishing to destroy anything, nor to establish anything, wish only for their own sakes, for the sake of their lives, to do nothing which is contrary to the Christian law, and so refuse to fulfil the most common obligations, which are most indispensable to the governments?

If they were revolutionists, who preach violence and murder, and who practise all these things, it would be easy to oppose them: part of them would be bribed, part deceived, part frightened into subjection; and those who could not be bribed, or deceived, or frightened, would be declared malefactors and enemies of society, would be executed or locked up, and the crowd would applaud the action of the government. If they were some horrible sectarians who preached a peculiar faith, it would be possible, thanks to those superstitions of falsehood, which by them are mixed in with their doctrine, to overthrow whatever truth there is in their faith. But what is to be done with men who preach neither revolution, nor any special religious dogmas, but only, because they do not wish to harm any one, refuse to take the oath of allegiance, to pay taxes, to take part in court proceedings, in military service, and in duties on which the whole structure of the government is based? What is to be done with such men? It is impossible to bribe them: the very risk which they take shows their unselfishness. Nor can they be deceived by claiming that God wants it so, because their refusal is based on the explicit, undoubted law of God, which is professed by the very men who wish to make them act contrary to it. Still less is it possible to intimidate them with threats, because the privations and sufferings to which they are subjected for their faith only strengthen their desire, and because it says distinctly in their law that God must be obeyed more than men, and that they should not fear those who may ruin their bodies, but that which may ruin both their bodies and their souls. Nor can they be executed or locked up for ever. These men have a past, and friends, and their manner of thinking and acting is known; all know them as meek, good, peaceful men, and it is impossible to declare them to be malefactors who ought to be removed for the safety of society. The execution of men who by all men are recognized to be good will only call forth defenders of the refusal and commentators on it; and the causes of the refusal need but be made clear, in order that it may become clear to all men that the causes which make these Christians refuse to comply with the demands of the state are the same for all other men, and that all men ought to have done so long ago.

In the presence of the refusals of the Christians the

governments are in a desperate plight. They see that the prophecy of Christianity is being fulfilled, — it tears asunder the fetters of the fettered and sets free the men who lived in slavery, and they see that this liberation will inevitably destroy those who keep others in slavery. The governments see this; they know that their hours are numbered, and are unable to do anything. All they can do for their salvation is to defer the hour of their ruin. This they do, but their situation is none the less desperate.

The situation of the governments is like the situation of a conqueror who wants to save the city that is fired by its own inhabitants. He no sooner puts out the fire in one place than it begins to burn in two other places; he no sooner gives way to the fire and breaks off what is burning in a large building, than even this building begins to burn from two sides. These individual fires are still rare, but having started with a spark, they will not stop until everything is consumed.

And just as the governments find themselves in such unprotected straits in the presence of men who profess Christianity, and when but very little is wanting for this force, which seems so powerful and which was reared through so many centuries, to fall to pieces, the public leaders preach that it is not only unnecessary, but even harmful and immoral, for every individual to try and free himself from slavery. It is as though some people, to free a dammed up river, should have all but cut through a ditch, when nothing but an opening is necessary for the water to flow into this ditch and do the rest, and there should appear some people who would persuade them that, rather than let off the water, they should construct above the river a machine with buckets, which, drawing the water up on one side, would drop it into the same river from the other side.

But the matter has gone too far: the governments feel their indefensibleness and weakness, and the men of the

Christian consciousness are awakening from their lethargy and are beginning to feel their strength.

"I brought the fire upon earth," said Christ, "and how I long for it to burn up!"

And this fire is beginning to burn up.

X.

CHRISTIANITY in its true meaning destroys the state. Thus it was understood from the very beginning, and Christ was crucified for this very reason, and thus it has always been understood by men who are not fettered by the necessity of proving the justification of the Christian state. Only when the heads of the states accepted the external nominal Christianity did they begin to invent all those impossible finely spun theories, according to which Christianity was compatible with the state. But for every sincere and serious man of our time it is quite obvious that true Christianity — the teaching of humility, of forgiveness of offences, of love — is incompatible with the state, with its magnificence, its violence, its executions, and its wars. The profession of true Christianity not only excludes the possibility of recognizing the state, but even destroys its very foundations.

But if this is so, and it is true that Christianity is incompatible with the state, there naturally arises the question: "What is more necessary for the good of humanity, what more permanently secures the good of men, the political form of life, or its destruction and the substitution of Christianity in its place?"

Some men say that the state is most necessary for humanity, that the destruction of the political form would lead to the destruction of everything worked out by humanity, that the state has been and continues to be the only form of the development of humanity, and that all that evil which we see among the nations who live in the political form is not due to this form, but to the abuses, which can be mended without destruction, and that humanity, without impairing the political form, can develop and reach a high degree of well-being. And the men who think so adduce in confirmation of their opinion philosophic, historic, and even religious arguments, which to them seem incontrovertible. But there are men who assume the opposite, namely, that, as there was a time when humanity lived without a political form, this form is only temporary, and the time must arrive when men shall need a new form, and that this time has arrived even now. And the men who think so also adduce in confirmation of their opinion philosophic, and historic, and religious arguments, which also seem incontrovertible to them.

It is possible to write volumes in the defence of the first opinion (they have been written long ago, and there is still no end to them), and there can be written much against it (though but lately begun, many a brilliant thing has been written against it).

It is impossible to prove, as the defenders of the state claim, that the destruction of the state will lead to a social chaos, mutual rapine, murder, and the destruction of all public institutions, and the return of humanity to barbarism; nor can it be proved, as the opponents of the state claim, that men have already become so wise and good that they do not rob or kill one another, that they prefer peace to hostility, that they will themselves without the aid of the state arrange everything they need, and that therefore the state not only does not contribute to all this, but, on the contrary, under the guise of defending men, exerts a harmful and bestializing influence upon them. It is impossible to prove either the one or the other by means of abstract reflections. Still less can it be proved by experience, since the question consists in this, whether the experiment is to be made or not. The question as to whether the time has come for abolishing the state, or not, would be insoluble, if there did not exist another vital method for an incontestable solution of the same.

Quite independently of anybody's reflections as to whether the chicks are sufficiently matured for him to drive the hen away from the nest and let the chicks out of their eggs, or whether they are not yet sufficiently matured, the incontestable judges of the case will be the chicks themselves, when, unable to find enough room in their eggs, they will begin to pick them with their bills, and will themselves come out of them.

The same is true of the question whether the time for destroying the political form and for substituting another form has come, or not. If a man, in consequence of the higher consciousness matured in him, is no longer able to comply with the demands of the state, no longer finds room in it, and at the same time no longer is in need of the preservation of the political form, the question as to whether men have matured for the change of the political form, or not, is decided from an entirely different side, and just as incontestably as for the chick that has picked its shell, into which no power in the world can again return it, by the men themselves who have outgrown the state and who cannot be returned to it by any power in the world.

"It is very likely that the state was necessary and even now is necessary for all those purposes which you ascribe to it," says the man who has made the Christian life-conception his own, "but all I know is that, on the one hand, I no longer need the state, and, on the other, I can no longer perform those acts which are necessary for the existence of the state. Arrange for yourselves what you need for your lives: I cannot prove either the common necessity, or the common harm of the state; all I know is what I need and what not, what I may do and what not. I know for myself that I do not need any separation from the other nations, and so I cannot recognize my exclusive belonging to some one nation or state, and my subjection to any government; I know in my own case that I do not need all those government offices and courts, which are the product of violence, and so I cannot take part in any of them; I know in my own case that I do not need to attack other nations and kill them, nor defend myself by taking up arms, and so I cannot take part in wars and in preparations for them. It is very likely that there are some people who cannot regard all that as necessary and indispensable. I cannot dispute with them, — all I know concerning myself, but that I know incontestably, is that I do not need it all and am not able to do it. I do not need it, and I cannot do it, not because I, my personality, do not want it, but because He who has sent me into life, and has given me the incontestable law for guidance in my life, does not want it."

No matter what arguments men may adduce in proof of the danger of abolishing the power of the state and that this abolition may beget calamities, the men who have outgrown the political form can no longer find their place in it. And, no matter what arguments may be adduced to a man who has outgrown the political form, about its indispensableness, he cannot return to it, cannot take part in the affairs which are denied by his consciousness, just as the full-grown chicks can no longer return into the shell which they have outgrown.

"But even if this is so," say the defenders of the existing order, "the abolition of the violence of state would be possible and desirable only if all men became Christians So long as this is not the case, so long as among men who only call themselves Christians there are men who are no Christians, evil men, who for the sake of their personal lust are prepared to do harm to others, the abolition of the power of state would not only fail to be a good for all the rest, but would even increase their wretchedness. The abolition of the political form of life is undesirable, not only when there is a small proportion of true Christians, but even when all shall be Christians, while in their midst or all about them, among other nations, there shall remain non-Christians, because the non-Christians will with impunity rob, violate, kill the Christians and make their life miserable. What will happen will be that the evil men will with impunity rule the good and do violence to them. And so the power of state must not be abolished until all the bad, rapacious men in the world are destroyed. And as this will not happen for a long time to come, if at all, this power, in spite of the attempts of individual Christians at emancipating themselves from the power of state, must be maintained for the sake of the majority of men." Thus speak the defenders of the state. "Without the state the evil men do violence to the good and rule over them, but the power of state makes it possible for the good to keep the evil in check," they say.

But, in asserting this, the defenders of the existing order of things decide in advance the justice of the position which it is for them to prove. In saying that without the power of state the evil men would rule over the good, they take it for granted that the good are precisely those who at the present time have power, and the bad the same who are now subjugated. But it is precisely this that has to be proved. This would be true only if in our world took place what really does not take place, but is supposed to take place, in China, namely, that the good are always in power, and that, as soon as at the helm of the government stand men who are not better than those over whom they rule, the citizens are obliged to depose them. Thus it is supposed to be in China, but in reality this is not so, and cannot be so, because, in order to overthrow the power of the violating government, it is not enough to have the right to do so,—one must also have the force. Consequently this is only assumed to be so even in China; but in our Christian world this has never even been assumed. In our world there is not even any foundation for assuming that better men or the best should rule, and not those who have seized the power and retain it for themselves and for their descendants. Better men are absolutely unable to seize the power and to retain it.

In order to get the power and retain it, it is necessary to love power; but love of power is not connected with goodness, but with qualities which are the opposite of goodness, such as pride, cunning, cruelty.

Without self-aggrandizement and debasement of others, without hypocrisy, deceit, prisons, fortresses, executions, murders, a power can neither arise nor maintain itself.

"If the power of state be abolished, the more evil men will rule over the less evil ones," say the defenders of the state. But if the Egyptians subjugated the Jews, the Persians the Egyptians, the Macedonians the Persians, the Romans the Greeks, the barbarians the Romans, is it possible that all those who have subjugated were better than those whom they subjugated?

And similarly, in the transference of the power in one state from one set of persons to another, has the power always passed into the hands of those who were better? When Louis XVI. was deposed, and Robespierre and later Napoleon ruled, who did rule? Better or worse men? And when did better men rule, when men from Versailles or from the Commune were in power? or when Charles I. or Cromwell was at the head of the government? or when Peter III. was Tsar or when he was killed, and the sovereign was Catherine for one part of Russia and Pugachév for the other? Who was then evil and who good?

All men in power assert that their power is necessary in order that the evil men may not do violence to the good, meaning by this that they are those same good men, who protect others against the evil men.

But to rule means to do violence, and to do violence means to do what the other man, on whom the violence is exerted, does not wish to have done to him, and what, no doubt, he who exerts the violence would not wish to have done to himself; consequently, to rule means to do to another what we do not wish to have done to ourselves, that is, to do evil.

To submit means to prefer suffering to violence. But to prefer suffering to violence means to be good, or at least less evil than those who do to another what they do not wish to have done to themselves.

And so all the probabilities are in favour of the fact that not those who are better than those over whom they rule, but, on the contrary, those who are worse, have always been and even now are in power. There may also be worse men among those who submit to the power, but it cannot be that better men should rule over worse men.

This was impossible to assume in case of the pagan inexact definition of goodness; but with the Christian lucid and exact definition of goodness and evil, it is impossible to think so. If more or less good men, more or less bad men, cannot be distinguished in the pagan world, the Christian conception of good and evil has so clearly defined the symptoms of the good and the evil, that they can no longer be mistaken. According to Christ's teaching the good are those who humble themselves, suffer, do not resist evil with force, forgive offences, love their enemies; the evil are those who exalt themselves, rule, struggle, and do violence to people, and so, according to Christ's teaching, there is no doubt as to where the good are among the ruling and the subjugated. It even sounds ridiculous to speak of ruling Christians.

The non-Christians, that is, those who base their lives on the worldly good, must always rule over Christians, over those who assume that their lives consist in the renunciation of this good.

Thus it has always been and it has become more and more definite, in proportion as the Christian teaching has been disseminated and elucidated.

The more the true Christianity spread and entered into the consciousness of men, the less it was possible for Christians to be among the rulers, and the easier it grew for non-Christians to rule over Christians.

"The abolition of the violence of state at a time when not all men in society have become true Christians would have this effect, that the bad would rule over the good and would with impunity do violence to them," say the defenders of the existing order of life.

"The bad will rule over the good and will do violence to them."

But it has never been different, and it never can be. Thus it has always been since the beginning of the world, and thus it is now. The bad always rule over the good and always do violence to them. Cain did violence to Abel, cunning Jacob to trustful Esau, deceitful Laban to Jacob; Caiaphas and Pilate ruled over Christ, the Roman emperors ruled over a Seneca, an Epictetus, and good Romans who lived in their time. John IV. with his opríchniks, the drunken syphilitic Peter with his fools, the harlot Catherine with her lovers, ruled over the industrious religious Russians of their time and did violence to them. William rules over the Germans, Stambulov over the Bulgarians, Russian officials over the Russian people. The Germans ruled over the Italians, now they rule over Hungarians and Slavs; the Turks have ruled over Greeks and Slavs; the English rule over Hindoos; the Mongolians rule over the Chinese.

Thus, whether the political violence be abolished or not, the condition of the good men who are violated by the bad will not be changed thereby.

It is absolutely impossible to frighten men with this, that the bad will rule over the good, because what they are frightened with is precisely what has always been and cannot be otherwise.

The whole pagan history of humanity consists of only those cases when the worse seized the power over the less bad, and, having seized it, maintained it by cruelties and cunning, and, proclaiming themselves as guardians of justice and defenders of the good against the bad, ruled over the good. As to the rulers' saying that, if it were not for their power, the worse would do violence to the good, it means only this, that the violators in power do not wish to cede this power to other violators, who may wish to take it from them. But, in saying this, the rulers only give themselves away. They say that their power, that is, violence, is necessary for the defence of men against some other violators, or such as may still appear.[1]

The exercise of violence is dangerous for the very reason that, as soon as it is exercised, all the arguments adduced by the violators can, not only with the same, but even with greater force, be applied against them. They speak of the past, and more frequently of the imaginary future of violence, but themselves without cessation commit acts of violence. "You say that men used to rob and kill others, and you are afraid that men will rob and kill one another, if your power does not exist. That may be so or not, but your ruining thousands of men in prisons, at hard labour, in fortresses, in exile; your ruining

[1] Comically striking in this respect is the naïve assertion of the Russian authorities in doing violence to other nationalities, the Poles, Baltic Germans, Jews. The Russian government practises extortion on its subjects, for centuries has not troubled itself about the Little Russians in Poland, nor about the Letts in the Baltic provinces, not about the Russian peasants who have been exploited by all manner of men, and suddenly it becomes a defender of the oppressed against the oppressors, those very oppressors whom it oppresses. — *Author's Note.*

millions of families with your militarism, and destroying millions of people physically and morally, is not imaginary, but real violence, against which, according to your own statement, people ought to fight by exercising violence. Consequently, those evil men, against whom, according to your own reflection, it is absolutely necessary to exercise violence, are you yourselves," is what the violated ought to say to the violators, and the non-Christians have always spoken and thought and acted in this manner. If the violated are worse than those who exercise violence, they attack them and try to overthrow them, and, under favourable conditions, do overthrow them, or, what is most usual, enter the ranks of the violators and take part in their acts of violence.

Thus the very thing with which the defenders of the state frighten men, that, if there did not exist a violating power, the bad would be ruling over the good, is what without cessation has been accomplished in the life of humanity, and so the abolition of political violence can in no case be the cause of the increase of the violence of the bad over the good.

When the violence of the government is destroyed, acts of violence will, probably, be committed by other men than before; but the sum of the violence will in no case be increased, simply because the power will pass from the hands of one set of men into those of another.

"The violence of state will be stopped only when the bad men in society shall be destroyed," say the defenders of the existing order, meaning by this that, since there will always be bad men, violence will never come to a stop. That would be true only if what they assume actually existed, namely, that the violators are better, and that the only means for the emancipation of men from evil is violence. In that case violence could, indeed, never be stopped. But as this is not the case, and the very opposite is true, namely, that it is not the better men who exercise violence against the bad, but the bad who do violence to the good, and that outside of violence, which never puts a stop to evil, there is another means for the abolition of violence, the assertion that violence will never stop is not correct. Violence grows less and less, and must evidently stop, but not, as the defenders of the existing order imagine, because men who are subject to violence will in consequence of the influence exerted upon them by the governments become better and better (in consequence of this they will, on the contrary, always become worse), but because, since all men are constantly growing better and better, even the worst men in power, growing less and less evil, will become sufficiently good to be incapable of exercising violence.

The forward movement of humanity takes place, not in this way, that the best elements of society, seizing the power and using violence against those men who are in their power, make them better, as the conservatives and revolutionists think, but, in the first and chief place, in that all men in general unswervingly and without cessation more and more consciously acquire the Christian life-conception, and in the second place, in that, even independently of the conscious spiritual activity of men, men unconsciously, in consequence of the very process of seizure of power by one set of men and transference to another set, and involuntarily are brought to a more Christian relation to life. This process takes place in the following manner: the worst elements of society, having seized the power and being in possession of it, under the influence of the sobering quality which always accompanies it, become less and less cruel and less able to make use of the cruel forms of violence, and, in consequence of this, give place to others, in whom again goes on the process of softening and, so to speak, unconscious Christianization.

What takes place in men is something like the process of

boiling. All the men of the majority of the non-Christian life-conception strive after power and struggle to obtain it. In this struggle the most cruel and coarse, and the least Christian elements of society, by doing violence to the meeker, more Christian people, who are more sensible to the good, rise to the higher strata of society. And here with the men in this condition there takes place what Christ predicted, saying: "Woe unto you that are rich, that are full now, and when all are glorified." What happens is that men in power, who are in possession of the consequences of power, — of glory and wealth, — having reached certain different aims, which they have set to themselves in their desires, recognize their vanity and return to the position which they left. Charles V., John IV., Alexander I., having recognized all the vanity and evil of power, renounced it, because they saw all its evil and were no longer able calmly to make use of violence as of a good deed, as they had done before.

But it is not only a Charles and an Alexander who travel on this road and recognize the vanity and evil of power: through this unconscious process of softening of manners passes every man who has acquired the power toward which he has been striving, not only every minister, general, millionaire, merchant, but also every head of an office, who has obtained the place he has been ten years waiting for, every well-to-do peasant, who has laid by a hundred or two hundred roubles.

Through this process pass not only separate individuals, but also aggregates of men, whole nations.

The temptations of power and of everything which it gives, of wealth, honours, luxurious life, present themselves as a worthy aim for the activity of men only so long as the power is not attained; but the moment a man attains it, they reveal their emptiness and slowly lose their force of attraction, like clouds, which have form and beauty only from a distance: one needs but enter them, in order that that which seemed beautiful in them should disappear.

Men who have attained power and wealth, frequently the very men who have gained them, more frequently their descendants, stop being so anxious for power and so cruel in attaining it.

Having through experience, under the influence of Christianity, learned the vanity of the fruits of violence, men, at times in one, at others in a few generations, lose those vices which are evoked by the passion for power and wealth, and, becoming less cruel, do not hold their position, and are pushed out of power by other, less Christian, more evil men, and return to strata of society lower in position, but higher in morality, increasing the average of the Christian consciousness of all men. But immediately after them other, worse, coarser, less Christian elements of society rise to the top, again are subjected to the same process as their predecessors, and again in one or a few generations, having experienced the vanity of the fruits of violence and being permeated by Christianity, descend to the level of the violated, and again make place for new, less coarse violators than the preceding ones, but coarser than those whom they oppress. Thus, despite the fact that the power remains externally the same that it was, there is with every change of men in power a greater increase in the number of men who by experience are brought to the necessity of accepting the Christian life-conception, and with every change the coarsest, most cruel, and least Christian of all enter into the possession of the power, but they are such as are constantly less coarse and cruel and more Christian than their predecessors.

Violence selects and attracts the worst elements of society, works them over, and, improving and softening them, returns them to society.

Such is the process by means of which Christianity, in

spite of the violence which is exercised by the power of the state and which impedes the forward movement of humanity, takes possession of men more and more. Christianity is penetrating into the consciousness of men, not only despite the violence exerted by the power, but even by means of it.

And thus the assertion of the defenders of the political structure that, if the violence of the state be abolished, the evil men will rule over the good, not only does not prove that this (the ruling of the bad over the good) is dangerous, for it is precisely what is taking place now, but, on the contrary, proves that the violence of the state, which gives the bad a chance to rule over the good, is the very evil which it is desirable to destroy, and which is continuously destroyed by life itself.

"But even if it were true that the violence of the state will come to an end when those who are in power shall become Christian enough to renounce the power of their own choice, and there shall no longer be found any men who are prepared to take their places, and if it is true that this process is taking place," say the defenders of the existing order, "when will that be? If eighteen hundred years have passed and there are still so many volunteers who are ready to rule, and so few who are ready to submit, there is no probability that this will happen very soon, or ever at all.

"If there are, as there have been among all men, such as prefer to refuse power rather than to use it, the supply of men who prefer ruling to submitting is so great that it is hard to imagine the time when it shall be exhausted.

"For this process of the Christianization of all men to take place, for all men one after another to pass over from the pagan concept of life to the Christian, and voluntarily renounce power and wealth, and for no one to desire to make use of them, it is necessary that not only all those rude, semisavage men, who are entirely incapable of adopting Christianity and following it, and of whom there are always such a great number amidst every Christian society, but also all savage and non-Christian nations in general, of whom there are so many outside the Christian society, should be made Christian. And so, even if we admit that the process of Christianization will some day be accomplished in the case of all men, we must assume, judging from how much the matter has advanced in eighteen hundred years, that this will happen in several times eighteen hundred years, — and so it is impossible and useless to think now of the impossible abolition of power, and all we should think of is that the power should be vested in the best of hands."

Thus retort the defenders of the existing order. And this reflection would be quite correct if the transition of men from one concept of life to another took place only by force of the one process where every man learns individually and one after another by experience the vanity of power, and by an inner way reaches the Christian truths.

This process takes place without cessation, and by this way men one after another pass over to the side of Christianity.

But men pass over to the side of Christianity not by this inner path alone; there is also an external method, with which the gradualness of this transition is destroyed.

The transition of men from one structure of life to another does not always take place in the manner in which the sand is poured out from an hour-glass, — one kernel of sand after another, from the first to the last, — but rather like water pouring into a vessel that is immerged in the water, when it at first admits the water evenly and slowly at one side, and then, from the weight of the water already taken in, suddenly dips down fast and almost all at once receives all the water which it can hold.

The same occurs with societies of men at the transition

from one concept, and so from one structure of life, to another. It is only at first that one after another slowly and gradually receives the new truth by an inner way and follows it through life; but after a certain diffusion it is no longer received in an internal manner, nor gradually, but all at once, almost involuntarily.

And so there is no truth in the reflection of the defenders of the existing order that, if in the course of eighteen hundred years only a small part of mankind has passed over to the side of Christianity, it will take several times eighteen hundred years before the rest of humanity will pass over to its side; there is no truth in it, because with this reflection no attention is paid to any other than the internal attainment of the truth, and the transition from one form of life to another.

This other method of attaining a newly revealed truth and transition to a new structure of life consists in this, that men do not attain the truth simply because they perceive it with a prophetic feeling or experience of life, but also because at a certain stage of the dissemination of the truth all men who stand on a lower stage of development accept it all at once, out of confidence in those who have accepted it in an internal way, and apply it to life.

Every new truth, which changes the composition of human life and moves humanity forward, is at first accepted by only a very small number of men, who understand it in an internal way. The rest, who out of confidence had accepted the previous truth, on which the existing order is based, always oppose the dissemination of the new truth.

But since, in the first place, men do not stand still, but incessantly move forward, comprehending the truth more and more, and approaching it with their lives, and, in the second place, all of them, through their age, education, and race, are predisposed to a gradation of men, from those who are most capable to comprehend newly revealed truths in an internal way to those who are least capable to do so, the men who stand nearest to those who have attained the truth in an internal way one after another, at first after long periods of time, and then more and more frequently, pass over to the side of the new truth, and the number of men who recognize the new truth grows larger and larger, and the truth grows all the time more and more comprehensible.

The greater the number of men who attain the truth and the more the truth is comprehensible, the more confidence is evoked in the rest of the men, who in their ability to comprehend stand on a lower stage, and the easier does the attainment of the truth grow for them, and the greater is the number who make the truth their own. Thus the movement keeps accelerating and accelerating, expanding and expanding, like a snowball, until there germinates a public opinion which is in accord with the new truth, and the remaining mass of men no longer singly, but in a body, under the pressure of this force, passes over to the side of the new truth, and a new structure of life is established, which is in agreement with this truth.

Men who pass over to the side of a new truth which has reached a certain degree of dissemination always do so all at once, in a mass, and they are like that ballast with which every vessel is laden all at once for its stable equilibrium and regular course. If there were no ballast, the vessel would not stay in the water, and would be changing its course with the least change in conditions. This ballast, though at first it seems to be superfluous and even to retard the ship's motion, is a necessary condition of its regular motion.

The same is true of that mass of men who, not one by one, but always all together, under the influence of a new public opinion, pass over from one concept of life to another. By its inertia this mass always retards the rapid, frequent transitions, unverified by human wisdom, from one structure of life to another, and for a long time retains every truth which, verified by a long experience of a struggle, has entered into the consciousness of humanity.

And so there is no truth in the reflection that, if only a small, a very small, part of humanity has attained the Christian truth in the course of eighteen centuries, the whole of humanity will attain it only in many, many times eighteen hundred years, that is, that it is so far away that we of the present time need not even think of it. It is untrue, because the men who stand on a lower stage of development, those very nations and people whom the defenders of the existing order represent as a hindrance for the realization of the Christian structure of life, are the same people who always at once, in a mass, pass over to the side of a truth which is accepted by public opinion.

Therefore the change in the life of humanity, the one in consequence of which men in power will renounce the power and among the men who submit to power there will not be found such as are desirous of seizing it, will not arrive when all men one after another to the very last shall have consciously attained the Christian life-conception, but when there arises a definite, easily comprehensible Christian public opinion which will conquer all that inert mass that is unable by an internal way to attain the truths and so is always subject to the effect of public opinion.

But public opinion to arise and be diffused does not need hundreds and thousands of years, and has the property of acting infectiously upon people and with great rapidity embracing large numbers of men.

"But if it is even true," the defenders of the existing order will say, "that public opinion, at a certain stage of its definiteness and lucidity, is able to make the inert mass of men outside the Christian societies, — the non-

Christian nations, — and corrupt and coarse men, who live within the societies, submit to it, what are the symptoms that this Christian public opinion has arisen and may take the place of violence?

"It is not right for us to take the risk and reject violence, by which the existing order is maintained, and to depend on the impalpable and indefinite force of public opinion, leaving it to the savage men outside and inside the societies with impunity to rob, kill, and in every way violate the Christians.

"If with the aid of the power we with difficulty eddy away from the non-Christian elements, which are ever ready to inundate us and destroy all the progress of the Christian civilization, is there, in the first place, a probability that public opinion can take the part of this force and make us secure, and, in the second, how are we to find that moment when public opinion has become so strong that it can take the place of the power? To remove the power and to depend for our self-defence on nothing but public opinion means to act as senselessly as would a man who in a menagerie would throw away his weapons and let out all the lions and tigers from their cages, depending on the fact that the animals in the cages and in the presence of heated rods appeared tame.

"And so the men who have the power, who by fate or by God are placed in the position of the ruling, have no right to risk the ruin of all the progress of civilization, only because they would like to make an experiment as to whether public opinion can take the place of the protection of power, and so must not give up their power."

The French writer, Alphonse Karr, now forgotten, has said somewhere, when speaking of the impossibility of abolishing capital punishment, "*Que Messieurs les assassins commencent par nous donner l'exemple*," and many times after that have I heard the repetition of this joke by men who thought that with these words they gave a conclusive and clever argument against the abolition of capital punishment. And yet it is impossible more lucidly to express all that falseness of the argument of those who think that the governments cannot give up their power so long as men are capable of it, than by this very joke.

"Let the assassins," say the defenders of the violence of state, "set us the example, by abolishing murder, and then we shall abolish it." But the assassins say the same, only with greater right. The assassins say, "Let those who have undertaken to teach and guide us set us the example of abolishing murder, and then we will follow them." And they do not say so for a joke, but in all seriousness, because such indeed is the state of affairs.

"We cannot desist from violence, because we are on all sides surrounded by violators."

Nothing in our day interferes more than this false consideration with the forward motion of humanity and the establishment among it of that structure of life which is already proper for its present consciousness.

The men in power are convinced that it is only violence that moves and guides men, and so they boldly use violence for the maintenance of the present order of things. But the existing order is not maintained through violence, but through public opinion, the effect of which is impaired by violence.

Thus the activity of violence weakens and impairs precisely what it intends to maintain.

Violence, in the best case, if it does not pursue only the personal ends of men in power, always denies and condemns by the one immovable form of the law what for the most part has been denied and condemned before by public opinion, but with this difference, that, while public opinion denies and condemns all acts which are contrary to the moral law, embracing in its condemnation the most varied propositions, the law which is supported by violence condemns and persecutes only a certain, very narrow order of acts, thus, as it were, justifying all the acts of the same order which have not entered into its definition. Public opinion has ever since the time of Moses considered avarice, debauchery, and cruelty to be evil, and has condemned them; and this public opinion denies and condemns every kind of a manifestation of avarice, — not only the acquisition of another man's property by means of violence, deceit, and cunning, but also a cruel usufruct of the same; it condemns every kind of debauchery, be it fornication with a concubine, or a slave, a divorced wife, or even one's own wife; it condemns every cruelty which is expressed in assaults, in bad treatment, in the murder, not only of men, but also of animals. But the law, which is based on violence, prosecutes only certain forms of avarice, such as theft, rascality, and certain forms of debauchery and cruelty, such as the violation of marital fidelity, murders, crippling, — therefore, as it were, permitting all those phases of avarice, debauchery, and cruelty which do not fit in with the narrow definition, which is subject to misinterpretations.

But not only does violence distort public opinion, — it also produces in men that pernicious conviction that men are not moved by spiritual force, which is the source of every forward movement of humanity, but by violence, — that very action which not only does not bring people nearer to truth, but always removes them from it. This delusion is pernicious in that it compels men to neglect the fundamental force of their life, — their spiritual activity, — and to transfer all their attention and energy to the superficial, idle, and for the most part harmful, activity of violence.

This delusion is like the one men would be in if they wished to make a locomotive move by turning its wheels with their hands, forgetting entirely that the prime cause of its motion is the expansion of steam and not the motion of the wheels. Men who would turn the wheels with their hands and with levers would produce nothing but a semblance of motion, in the meantime bending the wheels and interfering with the possibility of the locomotive's real motion.

It is this that men do when they want to move men by means of external violence.

Men say that a Christian life without violence cannot be established, because there are savage nations outside of Christian society, — in Africa, in Asia (some people represent the Chinese as such a peril for our civilization), — and there are such savage, corrupt, and, according to the new theory of heredity, confirmed criminals amidst Christian societies; and that violence is needed for the purpose of keeping either from destroying our civilization.

But those savage men, outside and within the societies, with whom we frighten ourselves and others, have never submitted to violence, and are not even now conquered by it.

Nations have never subjugated other nations by violence alone. If a nation which subjugated another stood on a lower stage of development, there was always repeated the phenomenon that it did not introduce its structure of life by means of violence, but, on the contrary, always submitted to the structure of life which existed in the conquered nation. If a nation, crushed by force, is subjugated or close to subjugation, it is so only through public opinion, and by no means through violence, which, on the contrary, provokes the nation more and more.

If men have ever been subjugated by whole nations to a new religious confession, and by whole nations have been baptized or have passed over to Mohammedanism, these transformations did not take place because men in power compelled them to do so (violence has, on the contrary, more frequently encouraged the movements in the opposite direction), but because public opinion compelled them to do so; but the nations that were compelled by force to accept the faiths of their conquerors have never accepted them.

The same is true in respect to those savage elements which exist within the societies: it is not the increase nor the decrease of the severity of punishments, nor the change of prisons, nor the increase of the police, that diminish or increase the number of crimes, — it is changed only in consequence of the change in public opinion. No severities have eradicated duels and vendettas in some countries. No matter how much the Circassians may be punished for theft, they continue to steal out of bravado, because not one maiden will marry a man who has not shown his daring, by stealing a horse, or at least a sheep. If men shall stop fighting duels and Circassians shall stop stealing, this will not be so because they are afraid of punishment (the fear of being punished only increases the charm of the daring), but because public opinion will be changed. The same is true in all other crimes. Violence can never destroy what is accepted by public opinion. On the contrary, public opinion need only be diametrically opposed to violence to destroy its every action, as has always been the case with every martyrdom.

We do not know what would happen if no violence were exerted against hostile nations and criminal elements of society. But that the employment of violence at the present time does not subjugate either of them, that we know from protracted experience.

Indeed, how can we subjugate by force the nations whose whole education, all whose traditions, even religious teaching, leads them to see the highest virtue in a struggle with their enslavers and in striving after liberty? And how are we forcibly to eradicate crimes in the midst of our societies, when what by the governments are considered to be crimes are considered to be virtues by public opinion. It is possible by means of violence to destroy such nations and such men, as is indeed done, but it is impossible to subjugate them.

The judge of everything, the fundamental force which moves men and nations, has always been the one invisible, impalpable force, — the resultant of all the spiritual forces of a certain aggregate of men and of all humanity, which is expressed in public opinion.

Violence only weakens this force, retards, and distorts it, and puts in its place another activity, which is not only not useful, but even harmful for the forward movement of humanity.

To subjugate to Christianity all the wild people outside the Christian world, — all the Zulus, Manchurians, and Chinese, whom many consider to be wild, — and the savages within the Christian world, there is one, only one means, — the dissemination among these nations of a Christian public opinion, which is established only through a Christian life, Christian acts, Christian examples. And so in order to conquer the nations which have remained unconquered by Christianity, the men of our time, who possess one, and only one, means for this purpose, do precisely the opposite of what might attain their end.

To conquer to Christianity the wild nations, who do not touch us and who do not in any way provoke us to oppress them, we — instead of leaving them first of all alone, and, in case of necessity or of a wish to get in closer relations with them, acting upon them only through a Christian relation to them, through the Christian teaching as proved by truly Christian acts of suffering, humility, abstinence, purity, brotherhood, love —begin by this, that we open among them new markets for our commerce, with nothing but our advantage in view, seize their land, that is, rob them, sell them wine, tobacco, opium, that is, corrupt them, and establish among them our order, teach them violence and all its methods, that is, the following of nothing but the animal law of struggle, below which no man can descend, and we do everything which can be done in order to conceal from them whatever of Christianity there is in us. And after that we send to them about two dozen missionaries, who prattle some hypocritical ecclesiastic absurdities and, in the shape of incontrovertible proofs of the impossibility of applying the Christian truths to life, adduce these our experiments at the Christianization of the savages.

The same is true of the so-called criminals, who live within our societies. To subjugate these men to Christianity, there is but one, the only way, — the Christian public opinion, which can be established among these men only by means of the true Christian teaching, confirmed by a true, Christian example of life.

And so, to preach this Christian teaching and confirm it by a Christian example, we establish among these people agonizing prisons, guillotines, gallows, capital punishments, preparations for murder, for which we use all our strength; we establish for the common people idolatrous doctrines, which are to stupefy them, we establish the governmental sale of intoxicants, — wine, tobacco, opium; we establish even prostitution; we give the land to those who do not need it; we establish spectacles of senseless luxury amidst wretchedness; we destroy every possibility of every semblance of a Christian public opinion; we cautiously destroy the established Christian public opinion, — and then we quote these very men, who have carefully been corrupted by ourselves, and whom we lock up, like wild beasts, in places from which they cannot get away, and in which they grow more bestial still, or whom we kill, as examples of the impossibility of acting upon them otherwise than through violence.

What takes place is like what happens when conscientious ignorant physicians place a patient who has been cured by the force of Nature under most unhygienic conditions and stuff him full of poisonous medicines, and then claim that it was only thanks to their hygiene and care that the patient did not die, whereas the sick man would have been well long ago, if they had left him alone.

Violence, which is put forth as the instrument for maintaining the Christian structure of life, not only does not produce this effect, but, on the contrary, prevents the social structure from being what it could and should be. The social structure is such as it is, not thanks to violence, but in spite of it.

And so there is no truth in the assertion of the defenders of the existing order, that, if violence barely keeps the evil non-Christian elements of humanity from attacking us, the abolition of violence and the substitution of public opinion for it will not protect humanity. It is not true, because violence does not protect humanity, but, on the contrary, deprives humanity of the one possibility of a true protection through the establishment and diffusion of the Christian public opinion as regards the existing order of life. Only with the abolition of violence will Christian public opinion cease to be corrupt, and receive the possibility of an unimpeded diffusion, and men will not direct their strength toward what they do not need, but toward the one spiritual force which moves them.

"But how can we reject the visible, palpable protection of the policeman with his revolver, and depend on something invisible, impalpable, — the public opinion? Does it still exist, or not? Above all else, we know the order of things in which we live. Be it good or bad, we know its defects and are used to it; we know how to act, what to do under present conditions; but what will happen when we reject them and depend on something invisible, impalpable, and entirely unknown?" And the uncertainty upon which men enter, when rejecting the known order of things seems terrible to them.

It is all very well to be afraid of the uncertainty, when

our position is firm and secure; but our position is not only not secure, — we know for certain that we are standing on the brink of perdition.

If we have to be afraid of something, let us be afraid of what is really terrible, and not of what we only imagine to be terrible.

In our fear to make an effort to tear ourselves away from the conditions which ruin us, only because the future is not quite certain to us, we resemble the passengers of a sinking ship, who, for fear of stepping into a boat which is to take them to the shore, retreat to their cabins and refuse to come out from them; or those sheep which, out of fear of the fire which has enveloped the whole yard, press close under the penthouses and do not walk through the open gates.

How can we, who are standing on the threshold of a war of inner revolutions, which is terrifying by its wretchedness and destructiveness, and in comparison with which, as those who are preparing it say, the terrors of the year '93 will be play, speak of a danger which is threatened us by the Dahomeans, the Zulus, etc., who live far, far away, and do not think of attacking us, and by those few thousands of robbers, thieves, and murderers, whom we ourselves have stupefied and corrupted, and whose number is not at all diminishing as the result of all our courts, prisons, and capital punishments?

Besides, this fear of the abolition of the visible protection of the policeman is preëminently a fear of city people, that is, of people who live under abnormal and artificial conditions. Men who live under normal conditions of life, not amidst cities, but amidst Nature, struggling with it, live without this protection and know how little violence can protect them against the actual dangers with which they are surrounded. In this fear there is something morbid, which depends mainly on those false conditions under which many of us live and have grown up.

An alienist told me how one summer day he was accompanied by his insane patients as far as the gate of the hospital which he was leaving. "Come with me to the city," the doctor proposed to them. The patients agreed to it, and a small crowd followed the doctor. But the farther they proceeded along the street, where took place the free motion of sound men, the more did they feel timid, and the more did they press close to the doctor, retarding his walk. Finally, they all began to ask him to take them back to the hospital, to their senseless, but habitual mode of life, to their guards, their blows, their long sleeves, their solitary cells.

Even thus men press close and hanker after their senseless structure of life, their factories, courts, prisons, capital punishments, wars, though Christianity calls them to freedom, to the free, rational life of the future, the imminent age.

Men say, "By what shall we be made secure, when the existing order is destroyed? What will the new orders be which will take the place of those of the present time, and in what will they consist? So long as we do not know how our life will be composed, we shall not move on or budge from our place."

This demand is what the explorer of new countries might put forth, in demanding a detailed description of the country into which he is entering.

If the life of the individual man, in passing from one age to another, were fully known to him, he would have no reason for living. The same is true of the life of humanity: if it had a programme of the life which awaits it as it enters upon its new age, this would be the surest symptom that it is not living, does not move on, but is whirling about in one spot.

The conditions of the new structure of life cannot be known to us, because they have to be worked out by ourselves. In this alone does life consist, namely, in recognizing the unknown and conforming our activity to this new cognition.

In this does the life of every individual and the life of human societies and of humanity consist.

XI.

THE condition of Christian humanity, with its prisons, hard labour, gallows, with its factories, accumulations of capital, with its taxes, churches, saloons, houses of ill fame, ever growing armaments, and millions of stupefied men, who are ready, like chained dogs, to thrust themselves upon those the masters may set them on, would be terrible if it were the product of violence, whereas it is above all the product of public opinion. But what is established by public opinion not only can be, but actually is, destroyed by it.

Hundreds of millions in money, tens of millions of disciplined men, implements of destruction of wonderful power, with an organization which of late has been carried to the highest degree of perfection, with a whole army of men whose calling it is to deceive and hypnotize the masses, and all this, by means of electricity, which annihilates space, subjected to men, who not only consider such a structure of society to be advantageous for them, but even such that without it they would inevitably perish, and who, therefore, use every effort of their minds in order to maintain it, — what an invincible force, one would think!

And yet, one needs but get a conception of what it all tends to and what no one can keep back, — that among men there will be established a Christian public opinion, with the same force and universality as the pagan public opinion, and that it will take the place of the pagan one, that the majority of men will be just as ashamed of all participation in violence and its exploitation as men are now ashamed of rascality, stealing, beggary, cowardice, and immediately this complex and apparently powerful structure of life falls of its own accord, without any struggle. It is not necessary for anything new to enter into the consciousness of men, but only for the mist to disappear, which conceals from men the true meaning of some acts of violence, in order that this may happen and the growing Christian public opinion should get the better of the obsolescent pagan public opinion, which admitted and justified acts of violence. All that is needed is that men should feel as much ashamed of doing acts of violence, of taking part in them, and exploiting them, as it is now a disgrace to pass for a rascal, a thief, a coward, a beggar. And it is precisely this that is beginning to happen. We do not notice it, just as men do not notice any motion, when they move together with everything surrounding them.

It is true, the structure of life in its main features remains as violent in nature as it was one hundred years ago, and not only the same, but in some relations, especially in the preparations for war and in the wars themselves, it appears to be even more cruel; but the germinating Christian public opinion, which at a certain stage of its development is to change the whole pagan structure of life, is beginning to be active. The dried-up tree stands apparently as firm as before, — it even looks firmer, because it is rougher, — but it is already weakened at the pith and is getting ready to fall. The same is true of the present structure of life, which is based on violence. The external condition of men is the same: some are the violators, as before, and others are the violated; but the view of the violators and the violated upon the meaning and worth of the position of either has changed.

The violating people, that is, those who take part in the government, and those who make use of the violence, that is, the rich, no longer represent, as formerly, the flower of society and the ideal of human well-being and grandeur, toward which all the violated used to strive. Now very frequently it is not so much the violated who strive after the position of the violators and try to imitate them, as the violators, who frequently of their own free will renounce the advantages of their position, choose the condition of the violated, and try in simplicity of life to emulate the violated.

To say nothing of the now openly despised occupations and offices, such as those of spies, agents of secret police, usurers, saloon-keepers, a large number of occupations of violators, which formerly used to be considered respectable, such as those of policemen, courtiers, members of courts, the administration, the clergy, the military, monopolists, bankers, not only are not considered by all to be desirable, but are even condemned by a certain most respectable circle of men. There are now men who voluntarily renounce these positions, which heretofore were considered to be above reproach, and who prefer less advantageous positions, which are not connected with violence.

It is not only men of the state, but also rich men, who, not from a religious feeling, as used to be the case, but only from a peculiar sensitiveness for the germinating public opinion, refuse to receive their inherited fortunes, considering it just to use only so much as they earn by their own labour.

The conditions of the participant in the government and of the rich man no longer present themselves, as they presented themselves formerly and even now present themselves among the non-Christian nations, as unquestionably honourable and worthy of respect and as divine blessings. Very sensitive, moral men (they are for the most part the most highly cultured) avoid these conditions and prefer more modest ones, which are independent of violence.

The best young men, at an age when they are not yet

corrupted by life and when they choose a career, prefer the activities of physicians, technologists, teachers, artists, writers, even simply of agriculturists, who live by their own labour, to positions in courts, in the administration, in the church, and in the army, which are paid by the government, or the positions of men who live on their own incomes.

The majority of monuments which are now erected are no longer in commemoration of men of state, of generals, and less certainly not of the rich, but of the learned, of artists, of inventors, of men who have not only had nothing in common with the governments, or with the authorities, but who frequently have struggled against them. It is not so much men of state and rich men, as learned men and artists, who are extolled in poetry, represented in plastic art, and honoured with festive jubilees.

The best men of our time tend toward these most honoured positions, and so the circle from which the men of state and the rich come is growing smaller and smaller, so that in intellect, culture, and especially in moral qualities, the men who now stand at the head of governments, and the rich no longer represent, as in olden times, the flower of society, but, on the contrary, stand below the average.

As in Russia and in Turkey, so in America and in France, no matter how much the governments may change their officials, the majority of them are selfish and venal men, who stand on so low a level of morality that they do not satisfy even those low demands of simple integrity which the governments make upon them. We now frequently get to hear the naïve regrets of men of state, because the best men by some strange accident, as they think, are always in the hostile camp. It is as though men should complain that by a strange accident it is always men with little refinement, who are not particularly good, that become hangmen.

The majority of rich men, similarly, in our time are no longer composed of the most refined and cultured men of society, as used to be the case, but of coarse accumulators of wealth, who are interested only in their enrichment, for the most part by dishonest means, or of degenerating descendants of these accumulators, who not only do not play any prominent part in society, but in the majority of cases are subject to universal contempt.

Not only is the circle of men, from which the servants of the government and the rich men are chosen, growing all the time smaller and smaller, and more and more debased, but these men themselves no longer ascribe to the positions which they hold their former significance, and frequently, being ashamed of them, to the disadvantage of the cause which they serve, neglect to carry out what by their position they are called upon to do. Kings and emperors have the management of hardly anything, hardly ever have the courage to make internal changes and to enter into new external political conditions, but for the most part leave the solution of these questions to state institutions or to public opinion. All their duties reduce themselves to being the representatives of state unity and supremacy. But even this duty they are performing worse and worse. The majority of them not only do not keep themselves in their former inaccessible grandeur, but, on the contrary, are becoming more and more democratized, and even keep low company, throwing off their last external prestige, that is, violating precisely what they are called upon to maintain.

The same takes place among the military. The military men of the higher ranks, instead of encouraging the coarseness and cruelty of the soldiers, which are necessary for their business, themselves disseminate culture among the military, preach humanitarianism, and frequently themselves share the socialistic convictions of the masses, and reject war. In the late plots against the Russian government, many of those mixed up with them were army men. The number of these military plotters is growing larger and larger. Very frequently it happens, as was the case lately, that the soldiers, who are called upon to pacify the inhabitants, refuse to shoot at them. Military bravado is directly condemned by army men themselves, and frequently serves as a subject for ridicule.

The same is true of judges and prosecuting attorneys: judges, whose duty it is to judge and sentence criminals, manage the proceedings in such a way as to discharge them, so that the Russian government, to have men sentenced that it wants to have sentenced, never subjects them to common courts, but turns them over to so-called military courts, which represent but a semblance of courts. The same is true of prosecuting attorneys, who frequently refuse to prosecute, and, instead of prosecuting, circumvent the law, defending those whom they should prosecute. Learned jurists, who are obliged to justify the violence of power, more and more deny the right to punish, and in its place introduce theories of irresponsibility, and even not of the correction, but of the cure of those whom they call criminals.

Jailers and superintendents of hard-labour convicts for the most part become defenders of those whom they are supposed to torture. Gendarmes and spies constantly save those whom they are supposed to ruin. Clerical persons preach toleration, often also the negation of violence, and the more cultured among them try in their sermons to avoid the lie which forms the whole meaning of their position and which they are called upon to preach. Executioners refuse to carry out their duties, so that in Russia capital punishment can frequently not be carried out for want of executioners, since, in spite of the advantages held out to make hard-labour convicts become executioners, there is an ever decreasing number of such as are willing to take up the duty. Governors, rural judges and officers, collectors of taxes, publicans, pitying the people, frequently try to find excuses for not collecting the taxes from them. Rich men cannot make up their minds to use their wealth for themselves alone, but distribute it for public purposes. Landowners erect on their lands hospitals and schools, and some of them even renounce the ownership of land and transfer it to the agriculturists, or establish communes on it. Manufacturers build hospitals, schools, houses for their workmen, and establish savings-banks and pensions; some establish companies, in which they take an equal share with other shareholders. Capitalists give part of their capital for public, educational, artistic, philanthropic institutions. Unable to part from their wealth during their lifetime, many of them will it away after their death in favour of public institutions.

All these phenomena might appear accidental, if they did not all reduce themselves to one common cause, just as it might seem accidental that the buds should swell on some of the trees in spring, if we did not know that the cause of it is the common spring, and that, if the buds have begun to swell on some of the trees, the same no doubt will happen with all of the trees.

The same is true in the manifestation of the Christian public opinion as regards the significance of violence and of what is based upon it. If this public opinion is already influencing some very sensitive men, and causes them, each in his own business, to renounce the privileges which violence grants, or not to use them, it will continue to act on others, and will act until it will change the whole activity of men and will bring them in agreement with that Christian consciousness which is already living among the leading men of humanity.

And if there now are rulers who do not have the courage to undertake anything in the name of their own power, and who try as much as possible to resemble, not monarchs, but the simplest mortals, and who show their readiness to renounce their prerogatives and to become the first citizens of their republics; and if there are now army men who understand all the evil and sinfulness of war and do not wish to shoot at men belonging to another nation, or to their own; and judges and prosecuting attorneys, who do not wish to prosecute and condemn criminals; and clergymen, who renounce their lie; and publicans, who try as little as possible to perform what they are called upon to perform; and rich men, who give up their wealth, — the same will inevitably happen with other governments, other army men, other members of the court, clergymen, publicans, and rich men. And when there shall be no men to hold these positions, there will be none of these positions and no violence.

But it is not by this road alone that public opinion leads men to the abolition of the existing order and the substitution of another for it. In proportion as the positions of violence become less and less attractive, and there are fewer and fewer men willing to occupy them, their uselessness becomes more and more apparent.

In the Christian world there are the same rulers and governments, the same courts, the same publicans, the same clergy, the same rich men, landowners, manufacturers, and capitalists, as before, but there is an entirely different relation of men toward men and of the men themselves toward their positions.

It is still the same rulers, the same meetings, and chases, and feasts, and balls, and uniforms, and the same diplomats, and talks about alliances and wars; the same parliaments, in which they still discuss Eastern and African questions, and alliances, and breaches of relations, and Home Rule, and an eight-hour day. And the ministries give way to one another in the same way, and there are the same speeches, the same incidents. But men who see how one article in a newspaper changes the state of affairs more than dozens of meetings of monarchs and sessions of parliaments, see more and more clearly that it is not the meetings and rendezvous and the discussions in the parliaments that guide the affairs of men, but something independent of all this, which is not centred anywhere.

There are the same generals, and officers, and soldiers, and guns, and fortresses, and parades, and manœuvres, but there has been no war for a year, ten, twenty years, and, besides, one can depend less on the military for the suppression of riots, and it is getting clearer and clearer that, therefore, generals, and officers, and soldiers are only members of festive processions, — objects of amusement for rulers, large, rather expensive corps-de-ballet.

There are the same prosecutors and judges, and the same proceedings, but it is getting clearer and clearer that, since civil cases are decided on the basis of all kinds of considerations except that of justice, and since criminal cases have no sense, because punishments attain no purpose admitted even by the judges, these institutions have no other significance than that of serving as a means for supporting men who are not fit for anything more useful.

There are the same clergymen, and bishops, and churches, and synods, but it is becoming clearer and clearer to all men that these men have long ago ceased to believe in what they preach, and that, therefore, they cannot convince any one of the necessity of believing in what they themselves do not believe.

There are the same collectors of taxes, but they are becoming less and less capable of taking away by force people's property, and it is becoming clearer and clearer that people can without collectors of taxes collect all that is necessary by subscribing it voluntarily.

There are the same rich men, but it is becoming clearer and clearer that they can be useful only in proportion as they cease to be personal managers of their wealth and give to society all, or at least a part, of their fortunes.

When all this shall become completely clear to all, it will be natural for men to ask themselves, "But why should we feed and maintain all these kings, emperors, presidents, and members of all kinds of Chambers and ministries, if nothing results from all their meetings and discussions? Would it not be better, as some jester said, to make a queen out of rubber?"

"And what good to us are the armies, with their generals, and music, and cavalry, and drums? What good are they when there is no war and no one wants to conquer any one, and when, even if there is a war, the other nations do not let us profit from it, and the troops refuse to shoot at their own people?"

"And what good are judges and prosecutors who in civil cases do not decide according to justice and in criminal cases know themselves that all punishments are useless?"

"And of what use are collectors of taxes who unwillingly collect the taxes, while what is needed is collected without them?"

"And of what use is the clergy, which has long ago ceased to believe in what it preaches?"

"And of what use is capital in private hands, when it can be of use only by becoming the common possession?"

And having once asked themselves this, people cannot help but come to the conclusion that they ought not to support all these useless institutions.

But not only will the men who support these institutions arrive at the necessity of abolishing them, — the men themselves who occupy these positions will simultaneously or even earlier be brought to the necessity of giving up their positions.

Public opinion more and more condemns violence, and so men, more and more submitting to public opinion, are less and less desirous of holding their positions, which are maintained by violence, and those who hold these positions are less and less able to make use of violence.

But by not using violence, and yet remaining in positions which are conditioned by violence, the men who occupy these positions become more and more useless. And this uselessness, which is more and more felt by those who maintain these positions and by those who hold them, will finally be such that there will be found no men to maintain them and none who would be willing to hold them.

Once I was present in Moscow at some discussions about faith, which, as usual, took place during Quasimodo week near a church in Hunter's Row. About twenty men were gathered on the sidewalk, and a serious discussion on religion was going on. At the same time there was some kind of a concert in the adjoining building of the Assembly of Noblemen, and an officer of police, noticing a crowd of people gathered near the church, sent a mounted gendarme to order them to disperse. The officer had personally no desire that they should disperse. The crowd of twenty men were in nobody's way, but the officer had been standing there the whole morning, and he had to do something. The gendarme, a young lad, with his right arm jauntily akimbo and clattering sword, rode up to us and shouted commandingly, "Scatter! What are you doing there?" Everybody looked at the gendarme, and one of the speakers, a modest man in a long coat, said calmly and kindly: "We are talking about something important, and there is no reason why we should scatter. Young man, you had better get down and listen to what we are talking about,—it will do you good," and turning away, he continued his discourse. The gendarme made no reply, wheeled his horse around, and rode off.

The same thing must happen in all matters of violence.

The officer feels ennui, he has nothing to do; the poor fellow is placed in a position where he must command. He is deprived of all human life, and all he can do is to look and command, to command and look, though his commands and his watching are of no earthly use. In such a condition all those unfortunate rulers, ministers, members of parliaments, governors, generals, officers, bishops, clergymen, even rich men are now partly and soon will be completely. They can do nothing else but command, and they command and send their messengers, as the officer sends his gendarme, to be in people's way, and since the people whom they trouble turn to them with the request that they be left alone, they imagine that they are indispensable.

But the time is coming, and will soon be here, when it shall be quite clear for all men that they are not any good and are only in the way of people, and the people whom they bother will say to them kindly and meekly, as that man in the long overcoat, "Please, do not bother us." And all the messengers and senders will have to follow that good advice, that is, stop riding with arms akimbo among the people, bothering them, and get down from their hobbies, take off their attire, listen to what people have to say, and, joining them, take hold with them of the true human work.

The time is coming, and will inevitably come, when all the institutions of violence of our time will be destroyed in consequence of their too obvious uselessness, silliness, and even indecency.

The time must come, when with the men of our world, who hold positions that are given by violence, will happen what happened with the king in Andersen's fable, "The New Royal Garment," when a small child, seeing the naked king, naïvely called out, "Behold, he is naked!" and all those who had seen it before, but had not expressed it, could no longer conceal it.

The point of the fable is this, that to the king, a lover of new garments, there come some tailors who promise to make him an extraordinary garment. The king hires the tailors, and they begin to sew, having informed him that the peculiarity of their garment is this, that he who is useless in his office cannot see the garments.

The courtiers come to see the work of the tailors, but they see nothing, as the tailors stick their needles into empty space. But, mindful of the condition, all the courtiers say that they see the garment, and they praise it. The king does the same. The time arrives for the procession, when the king is to appear in his new garment. The king undresses himself and puts on his new garments, that is, he remains naked, and goes naked through the city. But, mindful of the condition, no one dares to say that there are no garments, until a small child calls out, "Behold, he is naked!"

The same thing must happen with all those who from inertia hold offices which have long ago become useless, when the first man who is not interested (as the proverb has it, "One hand washes the other"), in concealing the uselessness of these institutions, will point out their uselessness and will naïvely call out, "But, good people, they have long ago ceased to be good for anything."

The condition of Christian humanity, with its fortresses, guns, dynamite, cannon, torpedoes, prisons, gallows, churches, factories, custom-houses, palaces, is indeed terrible; but neither fortresses, nor cannon, nor guns shoot themselves at any one, prisons do not themselves lock any one up, the gallows does not hang any one, the churches do not of themselves deceive any one, the custom-houses hold no one back, palaces and factories do not erect and maintain themselves, but everything is done by men. But when men understand that this ought not to be done, there will be none of these things.

Men are already beginning to understand this. If not

all men understand it as yet, the leaders among men do, those after whom follow all other men. And what the leaders have once come to understand, they can never stop understanding, and what the leaders have come to understand, all other men not only can, but inevitably must understand.

Thus the prediction that the time will come when all men shall be instructed by God, shall stop warring, shall forge the swords into ploughshares and the spears into pruning-hooks, that is, translating into our language, when all the prisons, fortresses, barracks, palaces, churches, shall remain empty, and all the gallows, guns, cannon, shall remain unused, is no longer a dream, but a definite, new form of life, toward which humanity is moving with ever increasing rapidity.

But when shall this be?

Eighteen hundred years ago Christ answered this question by saying that the end of the present world, that is, of the pagan structure of the world, would come when the calamities of men should be increased to their farthest limit and at the same time the gospel of the kingdom of God, that is, the possibility of a new, violenceless structure of the world, should be preached in all the world (Matt. xxiv. 3–28).

"But of that day and hour knoweth no man, but my Father only" (Matt. xxiv. 36), is what Christ says, for it may come any time, at any moment, even when we do not expect it.

In reply to the question when this hour shall arrive, Christ says that we cannot know it; but for the very reason that we do not know the time of its coming, we should not only be at all times prepared to meet it, as must be the goodman watching the house, and the virgins with their lamps going forth to meet the bridegroom, but also we should work with all our strength for the coming of that hour, as the servants had to work for the talents given to them (Matt. xxiv. 43; xxv. 1–30). In reply to the question when this hour should come, Christ admonished all men to work with all their strength for its quicker coming.

There can be no other answer. People can nowise know when the day and the hour of the kingdom of God shall arrive, because the coming of that hour depends on no one but the men themselves.

The answer is the same as that of the sage, who in reply to the question of a passer-by, how far it was to the city, answered, "Go."

How can we know how far it is to the goal toward which humanity is moving, since we do not know how humanity, on whom it depends whether to go or not, to stop, to temper the motion, or to accelerate it, will move toward that goal?

All we can know is, what we, who compose humanity, must do, and what not, in order that the kingdom of God may come. That we all know. And every one need but begin to do what we must do, and stop doing what we must not do; every one of us need only live by all that light which is within us, in order that the promised kingdom of God, toward which the heart of every man is drawn, may come at once.

XII.

CONCLUSION

1

I HAD ended this two years' labour, when, on the ninth of September, I happened to travel on a train to a locality in the Governments of Túla and Ryazán, where the peasants had been starving the year before, and were starving still more in the present year. At one of the stations the train in which I was travelling met a special train which, under the leadership of the governor, was transporting troops with guns, cartridges, and rods for the torture and killing of those very famine-stricken peasants.

The torturing of the peasants with rods for the purpose of enforcing the decision of the authorities, although corporal punishment was abolished by law thirty years ago, has of late been applied more and more freely in Russia.

I had heard of it, had even read in newspapers of the terrible tortures of which the Governor of Nízhni-Nóvgorod, Baránov, is said to have boasted, of the tortures which had taken place in Chernígov, Tambóv, Sarátov, Astrakhán, Orél, but not once had I had a chance to see men in the process of executing these deeds.

Here I saw with my own eyes good Russians, men who are permeated with the Christian spirit, travelling with guns and rods, to kill and torture their starving brothers.

The cause that brought them out was the following:

In one of the estates of a wealthy landowner the peasants had raised a forest on a pasture which they owned in common with the proprietor (had raised, that is, had watched it during its growth), and had always made use of it, and so regarded this forest as their own, at least as a common possession; but the proprietor, appropriating to himself this forest, began to cut it down. The peasants handed in a complaint. The judge of the first instance irregularly (I say "irregularly," using the word employed by the prosecuting attorney and the governor, men who ought to know the case) decided the case in favour of the proprietor. All the higher courts, among them the senate, though they could see that the case had been decided irregularly, confirmed the decision, and the forest was adjudged to the proprietor. The proprietor began to cut down the forest, but the peasants, unable to believe that such an obvious injustice could be done them by a higher court, did not submit to the decree, and drove away the workmen who were sent to cut down the forest, declaring that the forest belonged to them, and that they would petition the Tsar, but would not allow the proprietor to cut down the forest.

The case was reported to St. Petersburg, whence the governor was ordered to enforce the decree of the court. The governor asked for troops, and now the soldiers, armed with bayonets, ball-cartridges, and, besides, a supply of rods, purposely prepared for this occasion and carried in a separate car, were travelling to enforce this decree of the higher authorities.

The enforcement of the decree of the higher authorities is accomplished by means of killing, of torturing men, or by means of a threat of doing one or the other, according as to whether any opposition is shown or not.

In the first case, if the peasants show any opposition, the following takes place in Russia (the same things happen wherever there are a state structure and property rights): the chief makes a speech and demands submission. The excited crowd, generally deceived by its leaders, does not understand a word that the representative of the power says in official book language, and continues to be agitated. Then the chief declares that if they do not submit and disperse, he will be compelled to have recourse to arms. If the crowd does not submit even then, the chief commands his men to load their guns and shoot above the heads of the crowd. If the crowd does not disperse even then, he commands the soldiers to shoot straight into the crowd, at haphazard, and the soldiers shoot, and in the street fall wounded and killed men, and then the crowd generally runs away, and the troops at the command of the chiefs seize those who present themselves to them as the main rioters, and lead them away under guard.

After that they pick up the blood-stained, dying, maimed, killed, and wounded men, frequently also women and children; the dead are buried, and the maimed are sent to the hospital. But those who are considered to be the plotters are taken to the city and tried by a special military court. If on their part there was any violence, they are sentenced to be hanged. Then they put up a gallows and with the help of ropes choke to death a few defenceless people, as has many times been done in Russia and as is being done, and must be done where the public structure is based on violence. Thus they do in case of opposition.

In the second case, when the peasants submit, there takes place something special and peculiarly Russian. What happens is this: the governor arrives at the place of action, makes a speech to the people, rebuking them for their disobedience, and either stations troops in the farms of the village, where the soldiers, quartering at times as much as a month at a time, ruin the peasants, or, satisfied with threatening them, graciously pardons the people and returns home, or, which happens more frequently than anything else, announces to them that the instigators ought to be punished, and arbitrarily, without trial, selects a certain number of men, who are declared to be the instigators and in his presence are subjected to tortures.

In order to give an idea as to how these things are done, I will describe an affair which took place at Orél and received the approval of the higher authorities.

What happened in Orél was this: just as here, in the Government of Túla, a proprietor wanted to take away some property from certain peasants, and the peasants opposed him, just as they did here. The point was that the landed proprietor wanted without the consent of the peasants to keep the water in his mill-pond at so high a level that their fields were inundated. The peasants objected. The proprietor entered a complaint before the County Council chief. The County Council chief illegally (as was later declared by the court) decided the case in favour of the proprietor, by permitting him to raise the water. The proprietor sent his workmen to raise the ditch through which the water ran down. The peasants were provoked by this irregular decision, and called out their wives, to prevent the proprietor's workmen from raising the ditch. The women went to the dam, overturned the carts, and drove off the workmen. The proprietor entered a complaint against the women for taking the law into their hands. The County Council chief ordered one woman from each peasant farm in the whole village to be locked up ("in the cold room"). The decision could not well be carried out; since there were several women on each farm, it was impossible to determine which of them was liable to arrest, and so the police did not carry out the decree. The proprietor complained to the governor of the inactivity of the police, and the governor, without looking into the matter, gave the rural chief the strict order immediately to enforce the decision of the County Council chief. Obeying the higher authorities, the rural chief arrived in the village and, with a disrespect for men which is characteristic of the Russian authorities, commanded the policemen to seize one woman from each house. But since there were was more than one woman in each house, and it was impossible to tell which one of them was subject to incarceration, there began quarrels, and opposition was shown. In spite of these quarrels and this opposition, the rural chief commanded that one woman, no matter who she be, be seized in each house and led to a place of confinement. The peasants began to defend their wives and mothers, did not give them up, and upon this occasion beat the police and the rural chief. There appeared the first terrible crime,— an assault on the authorities,—and this new crime was reported to the city. And so the governor, like the Governor of Túla, arrived on a special train with a battalion of soldiers, with guns and rods, having made use of the telegraph, of telephones, and of the railway, and brought with him a learned doctor, who was to watch the hygienic conditions of the flogging, thus fully personifying Dzhingis Khan with the telegraphs, as predicted by Herzen.

Near the township office stood the troops, a squad of policemen with red cords, to which is attached the revolver, official persons from among the peasants, and the accused. Round about stood a crowd of one thousand people or more. Upon driving up to the township office, the governor alighted from his carriage, delivered a speech previously prepared, and called for the guilty and for a bench. This command was not understood at first. But a policeman, whom the governor always took with him, and who attended to the preparation of the tortures, which had more than once been employed in the Government, explained that what was meant was a bench for flogging. A bench was brought, the rods, which had been carried on the train, were piled up, and the executioners were called, for. These had been previously chosen from among the horse-thieves of the village, because the soldiers refused to perform this duty.

When everything was ready, the governor commanded the first of the twelve men pointed out by the proprietor as the most guilty to step forward. The one that came out was the father of a family, a respected member of society of about forty years of age, who had bravely defended the rights of society and so enjoyed the respect of the inhabitants. He was led up to the bench, his body was bared, and he was ordered to lie down.

The peasant tried to beg for mercy, but when he saw that this was useless, he made the sign of the cross and lay down. Two policemen rushed forward to hold him down. The learned doctor stood near by, ready to offer learned medical aid. The prisoners, spitting into their hands, swished the rods and began to strike. However, it turned out that the bench was too narrow and that it was too difficult to keep the writhing, tortured man upon it. Then the governor ordered another bench to be brought and to be cleated to the first. Putting their hands to their visors and muttering: "Yes, your Excellency," some men hurriedly and humbly fulfilled the commands; meanwhile the half-naked, pale, tortured man, frowning and looking earthward, waited with trembling jaws and bared legs. When the second bench was attached, he was again put down, and the horse-thieves began to beat him again. The back, hips, and thighs, and even the sides of the tortured man began more and more to be covered with wales and bloody streaks, and with every blow there were heard dull sounds, which the tortured man was unable to repress. In the surrounding crowd were heard the sobs of the wives, mothers, children, relatives of the tortured man and of all those who were selected for the punishment.

The unfortunate governor, intoxicated by his power,

thought that he could not do otherwise, and, bending his fingers, counted the blows, and without stopping smoked cigarettes, to light which several officious persons hastened every time to hand him a lighted match. When fifty blows had been dealt, the peasant stopped crying and stirring, and the doctor, who had been educated in a Crown institution for the purpose of serving his Tsar and country with his scientific knowledge, walked over to the tortured man, felt his pulse, listened to the beating of his heart, and announced to the representative of power that the punished man had lost consciousness and that according to the data of science it might be dangerous to his life to continue the punishment. But the unfortunate governor, who was now completely intoxicated by the sight of blood, commanded the men to go on, and the torture lasted until they had dealt seventy blows, to which number it for some reason seemed to him necessary to carry the number of the blows. When the seventieth blow was dealt, the governor said, "Enough! The next!" And the disfigured man, with his swollen back, was lifted up and carried away in a swoon, and another was taken up. The sobs and groans of the crowd became louder; but the representative of the governmental power continued the torture.

Thus they flogged the second, third, fourth, fifth, sixth, seventh, eighth, ninth, tenth, eleventh, twelfth man,— each man receiving seventy blows. All of them begged for mercy, groaned, cried. The sobs and groans of the mass of women grew louder and more heartrending, and the faces of the men grew gloomier and gloomier; but the troops stood all about them, and the torture did not stop until the work was accomplished in the measure which for some reason appeared indispensable to the caprice of the unfortunate, half-drunken, deluded man, called a governor.

Not only were officials, officers, soldiers present, but

with their presence they took part in this matter and kept this order of the fulfilment of the state act from being impaired on the part of the crowd.

When I asked one of the governors why these tortures are committed on men, when they have already submitted and troops are stationed in the village, he replied to me, with the significant look of a man who has come to know all the intricacies of state wisdom, that this is done because experience has shown that if the peasants are not subjected to torture they will again counteract the decrees of the power, while the performance of the torture in the case of a few men for ever confirms the decrees of the authorities.

And so now the Governor of Túla was travelling with his officials, officers, and soldiers, in order to perform just such a work. In just the same manner, that is, by means of murder or torture, were to be carried out the decree of the higher authorities, which consisted in this, that a young fellow, a landed proprietor, who had an income of one hundred thousand roubles per year, was to receive another three thousand roubles, for a forest which he had in a rascally manner taken away from a whole society of hungry and cold peasants, and be able to spend this money in two or three weeks in the restaurants of Moscow, St. Petersburg, or Paris. It was to do such a deed that the men whom I met were travelling.

Fate, as though on purpose, after my two years' tension of thought in one and the same direction, for the first time in my life brought me in contact with this phenomenon, which showed me with absolute obviousness in practice what had become clear to me in theory, namely, that the whole structure of our life is not based, as men who enjoy an advantageous position in the existing order of things are fond of imagining, on any juridical principles, but on the simplest, coarsest violence, on the murder and torture of men.

Men who own large tracts of land or have large capitals, or who receive large salaries, which are collected from the working people, who are in need of the simplest necessities, as also those who, as merchants, doctors, artists, clerks, savants, coachmen, cooks, authors, lackeys, lawyers, live parasitically about these rich people, are fond of believing that those prerogatives which they enjoy are not due to violence, but to an absolutely free and regular exchange of services, and that these prerogatives are not only not the result of assault upon people, and the murder of them, like what took place this year in Orél and in many other places in Russia, and continually takes place in all of Europe and of America, but has even no connection whatsoever with these cases of violence. They are fond of believing that the privileges which they enjoy exist in themselves and take place and are due to a voluntary agreement among people, while the violence exerted against people also exists in itself and is due to some universal and higher juridical, political, and economical laws. These men try not to see that they enjoy the privileges which they enjoy only by dint of the same thing which now would force the peasants, who raised the forest and who were very much in need of it, to give it up to the rich proprietor, who took no part in the preservation of the forest and had no need of it, that is, that they would be flogged or killed if they did not give up this forest.

And yet, if it is quite clear that the Orél mill began to bring greater returns to the proprietor, and that the forest, which the peasants raised, is turned over to the proprietor, only in consequence of assaults or murders, or the threat of them, it must be just as clear that all the other exclusive rights of the rich, which deprive the poor of their prime necessities, are based on the same thing. If the peasants, who are in need of the land for the support of their families, do not plough the land which adjoins their very farms, while this land, which is capable of supporting something like one thousand families, is in the hands of one man, — a Russian, Englishman, Austrian, or some large landed proprietor, — who does not work on this land, and if the merchant, buying up the corn from the needy agriculturists, can securely keep this corn in his granaries, amidst starving people, and sell it at three times its price to the same agriculturists from whom he bought it at one-third its present worth, it is evident that this takes place from the same causes. And if one man cannot buy cheap goods, which are sold to him from beyond a conventional line called a border, without paying customs dues to people who had no share whatsoever in the production of the goods; and if people cannot help but give up their last cow for taxes, which are distributed by the government to officials and are used for the maintenance of soldiers who will kill these very taxpayers, it would seem to be obvious that even this does not take place in consequence of some abstract rights, but in consequence of the same that happened in Orél and that now may happen in the Government of Túla, and periodically in one form or another takes place in the whole world, wherever there is a state structure and there are the rich and the poor.

Because not all human relations of violence are accompanied by tortures and murders, the men who enjoy the exclusive prerogatives of the ruling classes assure themselves and others that the privileges which they enjoy are not due to any tortures or murders, but to other mysterious common causes, abstract rights, and so forth. And yet, it would seem, it is clear that, if people, though they consider this to be an injustice (all working people now do), give the main portion of their work to the capitalist, the landed proprietor, and pay taxes, though they know that bad use is made of them, they do so first of all, not because they recognize any abstract rights, of which they have never heard, but only because they know that they will be flogged and killed, if they do not do so.

But if there is no occasion to imprison, flog, and kill men, every time the rent for the land is collected by the landed proprietor, and the man in need of corn pays to the merchant who has cheated him a threefold price, and the factory hand is satisfied with a wage which represents proportionately half the master's income, and if a poor man gives up his last rouble for customs dues and taxes, this is due to the fact that so many men have been beaten and killed for their attempts to avoid doing what is demanded of them, that they keep this well in mind. As the trained tiger in the cage does not take the meat which is placed under his mouth, and does not lie quiet, but jumps over a stick, whenever he is ordered to do so, not because he wants to do so, but because he remembers the heated iron rod or the hunger to which he was subjected every time he did not obey, — even so men who submit to what is not advantageous for them, what even is ruinous to them, do so because they remember what happened to them for their disobedience.

But the men who enjoy prerogatives which are the result of old violence, frequently forget, and like to forget, how these prerogatives were obtained. We need, however, only think of history, not the history of the successes of various dynasties of rulers, but real history, the history of the oppression of the majority by a small number of men, to see that the bases of all the prerogatives of the rich over the poor have originated from nothing but switches, prisons, hard labour, murders.

We need but think of that constant, stubborn tendency of men to increase their well-being, which guides the men of our time, to become convinced that the prerogatives of the rich over the poor could not and cannot be maintained in any other way.

There may be oppressions, assaults, prisons, executions,

which have not for their purpose the preservation of the prerogatives of the wealthy classes (though this is very rare), but we may boldly say that in our society, for each well-to-do, comfortably living man, there are ten who are exhausted by labour, who are envious and greedy, and who frequently suffer with their whole families,—all the prerogatives of the rich, all their luxury, all that superfluity which the rich enjoy above the average labourer, all that is acquired and supported only by tortures, incarcerations, and executions.

2

The train which I came across the ninth of September, and which carried soldiers, with their guns, cartridges, and rods, to the starving peasants, in order to secure to the rich proprietor the small forest, which he had taken from the peasants and which the peasants were in dire need of, showed me with striking obviousness to what extent men have worked out the ability of committing acts which are most revolting to their convictions and to their conscience, without seeing that they are doing so.

The special train with which I fell in consisted of one car of the first class for the governor, the officials, and the officers, and of several freight-cars, which were cram-full of soldiers.

The dashing young soldiers, in their clean new uniforms, stood crowding or sat with dangling legs in the wide-open doors of the freight-cars. Some smoked, others jostled one another, jested, laughed, displaying their teeth; others again cracked pumpkin seeds, spitting out the shells with an air of self-confidence. Some of them were running up and down the platform, toward the water-barrel, in order to get a drink, and, upon meeting an officer, tempered their gait, went through the stupid gesture of putting their hands to their brows, and with serious faces, as though they were doing not only something sensible, but even important, walked past them, seeing them off with their eyes, and then raced more merrily, thumping with their feet on the planks of the platform, laughing, and chattering, as is characteristic of healthy, good lads, who in good company travel from one place to another.

They were travelling to slay their hungry fathers and grandfathers, as though going to some very jolly, or at least very usual, piece of work.

The same impression was conveyed by the officials and officers in gala-uniform, who were scattered on the platform and in the hall of the first class. At the table, which was covered with bottles, dressed in his semi-military uniform, sat the governor, the chief of the expedition, eating something, and speaking calmly about the weather with an acquaintance whom he had met, as though the matter which he was about to attend to were so simple and so common that it could not impair his calm and his interest in the change of the weather.

At some distance away from the table, not partaking of any food, sat a general of gendarmes, with an impenetrable, but gloomy look, as though annoyed by the tedious formality. On all sides moved and chattered officers, in their beautiful, gold-bedecked uniforms: one, sitting at the table, was finishing a bottle of beer; another, standing at the buffet, munched at an appetizing patty, shaking off the crumbs, which had lodged on the breast of his uniform, and throwing the money on the table with a self-confident gesture; a third, vibrating both legs, was walking past the cars of our train, ogling the feminine faces.

All these men, who were on their way to torture or kill hungry, defenceless men, the same that fed them, had the appearance of men who know conclusively that they are doing what is right, and even are proud, "stuck up," at what they are doing.

What is this?

All these men are one half-hour's ride away from the place where, to secure to a rich fellow some three thousand useless roubles, which he has taken away from a whole community of starving peasants, they may be compelled to perform the most terrible acts that one can imagine, may begin, just as in Orél, to kill or to torture innocent men, their brothers, and they calmly approach the place and time where and when this may happen.

It is impossible to say that these men, all these officials, officers, and soldiers, do not know what awaits them, because they prepared themselves for it. The governor had to give his orders concerning the rods, the officials had to purchase birch switches, to haggle for them, and to enter this item as an expense. The military gave and received and executed commands concerning the ball-cartridges. All of them know that they are on the way to torture and, perhaps, to kill their famished brothers, and that they will begin to do this, perhaps, within an hour.

It would be incorrect to say that they do this from conviction, — as is frequently said and as they themselves repeat, — from the conviction that they do this because it is necessary to maintain the state structure, in the first place, because all these men have hardly ever even thought of the state structure and of its necessity; in the second place, they can in no way be convinced that the business in which they take part maintains the state, instead of destroying it, and, in the third place, in reality the majority of these men, if not all, will not only never sacrifice their peace and pleasure for the purpose of supporting the state, but will even never miss a chance of making use, for their peace and pleasure, of everything they can, even though it be to the disadvantage of the state. Consequently they do not do so for the sake of the abstract principle of the state.

What is it, then?

I know all these men. If I do not know them personally, I know approximately their characters, their past, their manner of thought. All of them have mothers, and some have wives and children. They are, for the most part, good-hearted, meek, frequently tender men, who despise every cruelty, to say nothing of the murder of men, and many of them would be incapable of killing or torturing animals; besides, they are all people who profess Christianity and consider violence exerted against defenceless men a low and disgraceful matter. Not one of these men would be able for the sake of his smallest advantage to do even one-hundredth part of what the Governor of Orél did to those people; and any of them would even be offended, if it were assumed that in his private life he would be capable of doing anything like it.

And yet, here they are, within half an hour's ride from the place, where they may be led inevitably to the necessity of doing it.

What is it, then?

But, besides these people who are travelling on the train, and who are ready to commit murder and tortures, how could those people with whom the whole matter began, — the proprietor, the superintendent, the judges, and those who from St. Petersburg prescribed this matter and by their commands are taking part in it, — how could these men, the minister, the emperor, also good men, who are professing the Christian religion, have undertaken and ordered such a thing, knowing its consequences? How can even those who do not take part in this matter, the spectators, who are provoked at every special case of violence or at the torture of a horse, admit the performance of so terrible a deed? How can they help being provoked at it, standing on the road, and shouting, "No, we shall not allow hungry people to be killed and flogged for not giving up their property, which has been seized from them by force"? But not only does no one do so,

— the majority of men, even those who were the instigators of the whole thing, like the superintendent, the proprietor, the judges, and those who were the participants in it and who gave the orders, like the governor, the minister, the emperor, are calm, and do not even feel any pangs of conscience. Just as calm are apparently all those men who are travelling to commit this evil deed.

The spectators, too, it seemed, who were not in any way interested in the matter, for the most part looked with sympathy, rather than with disapproval, upon the men who were getting ready for this execrable deed. In the same car with me there was travelling a merchant, a lumber dealer from the peasant class, and he loudly proclaimed his sympathy for those tortures to which the peasants were about to be subjected: "It is not right not to obey the authorities," he said; "that's what the authorities are for. Just wait, they will have their fleas driven out of them, — they won't think of rioting after that. Serves them right."

What is it, then?

It is equally impossible to say that all these men — the instigators, participants, abettors of this matter — are such rascals that, knowing all the baseness of what they are doing, they, either for a salary, or for an advantage, or out of fear of being punished, do a thing which is contrary to their convictions. All these men know how, in certain situations, to defend their convictions. Not one of these officials would steal a purse, or read another person's letter, or bear an insult without demanding satisfaction from the insulter. Not one of these officers would have the courage to cheat at cards, not to pay his card debts, to betray a friend, to run away from the field of battle, or to abandon his flag. Not one of these soldiers would have the courage to spit out the sacrament or to eat meat on Good Friday. All these men are prepared to bear all kinds of privations, sufferings, and dangers, rather than do something which they consider to be bad. Consequently, there is in these men a counteracting force whenever they have to do something which is contrary to their convictions.

Still less is it possible to say that all these men are such beasts that it is proper and not at all painful for them to do such things. We need but have a talk with these men, to see that all of them, the proprietor, the judges, the minister, the Tsar, the governor, the officers, and the soldiers not only in the depth of their hearts do not approve of such deeds, but even suffer from the consciousness of their part in them, when they are reminded of the significance of this matter. They simply try not to think of it.

We need but have a talk with them, with all the participants in this matter, from the proprietor to the last policeman and soldier, to see that all of them in the depth of their hearts know that this is a bad thing and that it would be better not to take part in it, and that they suffer from it.

A lady of liberal tendencies, who was travelling on the same train with us, upon noticing the governor and the officers in the hall of the first class, and learning of the purpose of their journey, began on purpose in a loud voice, so as to be heard, to curse the orders of our time and to put to shame the men who were taking part in this matter. All persons present felt ill at ease. Nobody knew whither to look, but no one dared to answer her. The passengers looked as though it were not worth while to reply to such empty talk. But it was evident from the faces and fugitive eyes that all felt ashamed. This also I noticed in the case of the soldiers. They, too, knew that the business for which they were travelling was a bad one, but they did not wish to think of what awaited them.

When the lumber dealer began insincerely, as I thought, merely to show his culture, to speak of how necessary such measures were, the soldiers who heard it turned away from him, as though they did not hear him, and frowned.

All these men, both those who, like the proprietor, the superintendent, the minister, the Tsar, participated in the performance of this act, and those who are just now travelling on the train, and even those who, without taking part in this matter, look on at the accomplishment of it, know every one of them that this is a bad business, and are ashamed of the part which they are taking in it and even of their presence during its execution.

Why, then, have they been doing and tolerating it?

Ask those who, like the proprietor, started this matter, and those who, like the judges, handed down a formally legal, but obviously unjust decision, and those who ordered the enforcement of the decree, and those who, like the soldiers, the policemen, and the peasants, will with their own hands carry it into execution, — who will beat and kill their brothers, — all of them, the instigators, and the accomplices, and the executors, and the abettors of these crimes, and all will give you essentially the same answer.

The men in authority, who provoked the matter and coöperated in it and directed it, will say that they are doing what they are doing because such matters are necessary for the maintenance of the existing order; and the maintenance of the existing order is necessary for the good of the country and of humanity, for the possibility of a social life and a forward movement of progress.

The men from the lower spheres, the peasants and the soldiers, those who will be compelled with their own hands to exercise the violence, will say that they are doing what they are doing because this is prescribed by the higher authorities, and that the higher authorities know what they are doing. That the authorities consist of the very men who ought to be the authorities and that they know what they are doing, presents itself to them as an incontestable truth. If these lower executors even admit the possibility of an error or delusion, they admit it only in the case of the lower authorities; but the highest power, from whom all this proceeds, seems to them to be unquestionably infallible.

Though explaining the motives for their activities in a different manner, both the rulers and the ruled agree in this, that they do what they do because the existing order is precisely the one which is indispensable and which must exist at the present time, and which, therefore, it is the sacred duty of every person to maintain.

On this recognition of the necessity, and so of the unchangeableness of the existing order, is based the reflection, which has always been adduced by all the participants in state violence in their justification, that, since the present order is unchangeable, the refusal of a single individual to perform the duties imposed upon him will not change the essence of the matter, and will have no other effect than that in place of the person refusing there will be another man, who may perform the duty less well, that is, more cruelly, more harmfully for those men against whom the violence is practised.

This conviction that the existing order is indispensable, and so unchangeable, and that it is the sacred duty of every man to maintain it, is what gives to good people and, in private life, to moral people the possibility of participating with a more or less calm conscience in such affairs as the one which took place in Orél and the one which the people who were travelling in the Túla train were getting ready to act in.

But on what is this conviction based?

It is naturally agreeable and desirable for the proprietor to believe that the existing order is indispensable and unchangeable, because it is this very existing order which secures for him the income from his hundreds and thousands of desyatínas, thanks to which he leads his habitual idle and luxurious life.

Naturally enough, the judge, too, readily believes in the necessity of the order in consequence of which he receives fifty times as much as the most industrious labourer. This is just as comprehensible in the case of the supreme judge, who receives a salary of six or more thousand, and in the case of all the higher officials. Only with the present order can he, as a governor, prosecutor, senator, member of various councils, receive his salary of several thousands, without which he would at once perish with all his family, because, except by the position which he holds, he would not be able, with his ability, industry, and knowledge, to earn one hundredth part of what he is getting. In the same situation are the minister, the emperor, and every higher authority, but with this difference, that, the higher they are and the more exclusive their position is, the more indispensable it is for them to believe that the existing order is the only possible order, because outside of it they not only cannot get an equal position, but will have to stand much lower than the rest of mankind. A man who voluntarily hires himself out as a policeman at a salary of ten roubles, which he can easily get in any other position, has little need of the preservation of the existing order, and so can get along without believing in its unchangeableness. But a king or an emperor, who in his position receives millions; who knows that all around him there are thousands of men who are willing to depose him and take his place; who knows that in no other position will he get such an income and such honours; who in the majority of cases, with a more or less despotic rule, knows even this, that, if he should be deposed, he would be tried for everything he did while in possession of his power, cannot help but believe in the unchangeableness and sacredness of the existing order. The higher the position which a man occupies, the more advantageous and, therefore, the more unstable it is, and the more terrible and dangerous a fall from it is, the more does a man who holds that position believe in the unchangeableness of the existing order, and with so much greater peace of mind can such a man, as though not for himself, but for the support of the existing order, do bad and cruel deeds.

Thus it is in the case of all the men of the ruling classes who hold positions that are more advantageous than those which they could hold without the existing order, — beginning with the lowest police officials and ending with the highest authorities. All these men more or less believe in the unchangeableness of the existing order, because, above all else, it is advantageous for them.

But what is it that compels the peasants, the soldiers, who stand on the lowest rung of the ladder, who have no profit from the existing order, who are in a condition of the most abject submission and humiliation, to believe that the existing order, in consequence of which they are in a most disadvantageous and humble state, is the very order which must be, and which, therefore, must be maintained, even by performing the basest and most unconscionable acts for it.

What is it that compels these men to make the false reflection that the existing order is invariable and, therefore, must be maintained, whereas it is evident that, on the contrary, it is unchangeable only because it is maintained as such?

What is it that compels the men who were but yesterday taken from the plough, and who are dressed up in these monstrous, indecent garments with blue collars and gilt buttons, to travel with guns and swords, in order to kill their hungry fathers and brothers? They certainly have no advantages, and are in no danger of losing the position which they hold, because their condition is worse than the one from which they are taken.

The men of the higher ruling classes, the proprietors, ministers, kings, officers, take part in these matters, thus supporting the existing order, because it is advantageous for them. Besides, these frequently good, meek men feel themselves able to take part in these things for this other reason, that their participation is limited to instigations, decrees, and commands. None of these men in authority do themselves those things which they instigate, determine upon, and order to be done. For the most part they do not even see how all those terrible things which they provoke and prescribe are carried out.

But the unfortunate people of the lower classes, who derive no advantage from the existing order, who, on the contrary, in consequence of this order are held in the greatest contempt, why do they, who, for the maintenance of this order, with their own hands tear people away from their families, who bind them, who lock them up in prisons and at hard labour, who watch and shoot them, do all these things?

What is it that compels these men to believe that the existing order is unchangeable and that it is necessary to maintain it?

All violence is based only on them, on those men who with their own hands beat, bind, lock up, kill. If these men did not exist, — these soldiers and policemen, — the armed men in general, who are prepared on command to commit violence and to kill all those whom they are commanded to kill, not one of the men who sign the decrees for executions, life imprisonment, hard labour, would ever have the courage himself to hang, lock up, torture to death one thousandth part of those whom now, sitting quietly in their studies, they order to be hung and to be tortured in every way, only because they do not see it and it is not done by them, but somewhere far away by obedient executors.

All those injustices and cruelties which have entered into the curriculum of the existing life, have entered there only because there exist these people, who are always prepared to maintain these injustices and cruelties. If these men did not exist, there would not be any one to offer violence to all these enormous masses of violated people, and those who give orders would never even dare either to command or even to dream of what they now command with so much self-assurance. If there were no people who would be ready at the command of those whom they obey to torture or to kill him who is pointed out to them, no one would ever dare to affirm, what is with so much self-confidence asserted by the non-working landowners, that the land which surrounds the peasants, who are dying for lack of land, is the property of a man who does not work on it, and that the supply of corn, which has been garnered in a rascally manner, ought to be kept intact amidst a starving population, because the merchant needs some profit, and so forth. If there were no men who would be ready at the will of the authorities to torture and kill every person pointed out to them, it could never occur to a landed proprietor to take away from the peasants a forest which had been raised by them, nor to the officials to consider legal the payment to them of salaries, which are collected from the hungry masses, for oppressing them, to say nothing of executing men, or locking them up, or exiling them, because they overthrow the lie and preach the truth. All this is demanded and done only because these ruling people are firmly convinced that they have always at hand submissive people, who will be ready to carry any of their demands into execution by means of tortures and murders.

The only reason why they commit deeds like those committed by all the tyrants from Napoleon down to the last commander of a company, who shoots into a crowd, is because they are stupefied by the power behind them, consisting of subservient men who are ready to do anything they are commanded. The whole strength, therefore, lies in the men who with their hands do acts of violence, in the men who serve with the police, among the soldiers, more especially among the soldiers, because the police do their work only when they have an army behind them.

What is it, then, that has led these good men, who derive no advantage from it, who are compelled with their hands to do all these terrible things, men on whom the whole matter depends, into that remarkable delusion that assures them that the existing disadvantageous, pernicious, and for them painful order is the one which must be?

Who has led them into this remarkable delusion?

They have certainly not assured themselves that they must do what is not only painful, disadvantageous, and pernicious to them and their whole class, which forms nine-tenths of the whole population, and what is even contrary to their conscience.

"How are you going to kill men, when in God's law it says, 'Thou shalt not kill'?" I frequently asked soldiers, and, by reminding them of what they did not like to think about, I always made them feel awkward and embarrassed. Such a soldier knew that there was an obligatory law of God, "Thou shalt not kill," and he knew that there was an obligatory military service, but it had never occurred to him that there was any contradiction there. The sense of the timid answers that I always received to this question consisted approximately in this, that murder in war and the execution of criminals at the command of the government were not included in the common prohibition of murders. But when I told them that no such limitation was made in God's law, and reminded them of the doctrine of brotherhood, of the forgiveness of offences, of love, which are obligatory for all Christians and which could in no way be harmonized with murder, the men of the people generally agreed with me, and on their side put the question to me as to how it happened that the government, which, according to their ideas, could not err, commanded the armies, when necessary, to go to war, and ordered the execution of prisoners. When I answered them that the government acted incorrectly when it commanded these things to be done, my interlocutors became even more embarrassed, and either broke off the conversation or grew provoked at me.

"There must be such a law. I guess the bishops know better than we," I was told by a Russian soldier. And, having said this, the soldier apparently felt his conscience eased, being fully convinced that his guides had found a law, the same under which his ancestors had served, and the kings and the kings' heirs, and millions of people, and he himself served, and that what I was telling him was some piece of cunning or cleverness, like a riddle.

All the men of our Christian world know, know firmly, from tradition, and from revelation, and from the irrefutable voice of conscience, that murder is one of the most terrible crimes which a man can commit, as the Gospel says, and that this sin cannot be limited to certain men, that is, that it is a sin to kill some men, but not a sin to kill others. All know that if the sin of murder is a sin, it is always a sin, independently of what men are the victims of it, just like the sin of adultery and thieving and any other; at the same time men have seen, since childhood, since youth, that murder is not only admitted, but even blessed by all those whom they are accustomed to respect as their spiritual guides, ordained by God; they see that their worldly guides with calm assurance institute murders, bear arms of murder, of which they are proud, and demand of all, in the name of the civil and even the divine law, that they shall take part in murder. Men see that there is here some contradiction, and, being unable to solve it, they involuntarily assume that this contradiction is due only to their ignorance. The very coarseness and obviousness of the contradiction sustains them in this conviction. They cannot imagine that their enlighteners, learned men, should be able with such confidence to preach two such seemingly contradictory propositions, — the obligatoriness for every one of the law and of murder. A simple, innocent child, and later a youth, cannot imagine that men who stand so high in his opinion, whom he considers to be either holy or learned, should for any reason be deceiving him so unscrupulously. But it is precisely this that has been done to him all the time. This is accomplished, in the first place, by impressing all the labouring people, who have not themselves any time to solve moral and religious questions, from childhood, and up to old age, by example and direct teaching, with the idea that tortures and murders are compatible with Christianity, and that, for certain purposes of state, tortures and murders are not only admissible, but even peremptory; in the second place, by impressing some of them, who are chosen by enlistment or levy, with the idea that the performance of tortures and murders with their own hands forms a sacred duty and even an act which is valorous and worthy of praise and of reward.

The common deception, which is disseminated among all men, consists in this, that in all the catechisms, or the books which have taken their place and which are now the subject of obligatory instruction for the children, it says that violence, that is, tortures, imprisonments, and executions, as also murders in civil or external wars for the purpose of maintaining and defending the existing order of the state (whatever it be, autocratic, monarchical, a convention, a consulship, an empire of either Napoleon or of Boulanger, a constitutional monarchy, a commune, or a republic), is quite legitimate, and does not contradict either morality or Christianity.

This it says in all the catechisms or books used in the schools. And men are so convinced of it that they grow up, live, and die in this conviction, without doubting it even once.

This is one deception, a common deception, which is practised on all men; there is another, a private deception, which is practised on soldiers or policemen, who are chosen in one way or another and who perform the tortures and the murders which are needed for the support and the defence of the existing order.

In all the military codes it says in so many words what in the Russian military code is expressed as follows: "(Art. 87) Precisely and without discussion to carry out the commands of the authorities means to carry out precisely the command given by the authorities, without discussing whether it is good or bad, and whether it is possible to carry it out. The chief himself answers for the consequences of a command given out by him. (Art. 88) The subject may refuse to carry out the commands of his superior only when he sees clearly that by carrying out his superior's command he" — one involuntarily imagines that what will follow is "when he sees clearly that by carrying out his superior's command he violates the law of God;" but that is not at all the case: "when he sees clearly that he is violating the oath of allegiance and fidelity, and his service to the emperor."

It says that a man, being a soldier, must carry out all the commands of his chief without any exception whatever, which for a soldier mainly means murder, and so must violate all divine and human laws, except his fidelity and service to him who at the given moment happens to be in power.

Thus it says in the Russian military code, and precisely the same, though in different words, is said in all the military codes, as indeed it cannot be otherwise, because in reality upon this deception of emancipating men from their obedience to God or to their conscience, and of substituting for this obedience the obedience to the accidental superior, is all the power of the army and the state based.

So it is this on which is founded that strange conviction of the lower classes that the existing order, which is pernicious for them, is as it ought to be, and that they are, therefore, obliged to support it with tortures and murders.

This conviction is based on a conscious deception, which is practised upon them by the upper classes.

Nor can it be otherwise. To compel the lower, most numerous classes of men to oppress and torment themselves, committing with this such acts as are contrary to their conscience, it was necessary to deceive these lower, most numerous classes. And so it was done.

The other day I again saw an open practice of this shameless deceit, and I was again surprised to see with what boldness and freedom it was practised.

In the beginning of November, as I was passing through Túla, I again saw at the gate of the County Council Office the familiar dense crowd of people, from which proceeded drunken shouts and the pitiful wail of mothers and of wives. This was a levy of recruits.

As upon other occasions, I was unable to drive past this spectacle: it attracts me as by some evil charm. I again entered among the crowd, stood, looked, asked questions, and marvelled at the freedom with which this most terrible crime is perpetrated in broad daylight and in a populous city.

As in former years, the elders in all the villages of Russia, with its one hundred millions of inhabitants, on the first of November selected from lists a given number of lads, frequently their own sons, and took them to the city.

On the way the recruits went on an uninterrupted spree, in which they were not interfered with by their elders, who felt that going to such a mad business as the one to which the recruits were going, abandoning their wives and mothers and renouncing everything holy to them, in order to become somebody's senseless instruments of murder, was too painful a matter, if they did not intoxicate themselves with liquor.

And so they travelled, drinking, cursing, singing, fighting, and maiming themselves. The nights they passed in inns. In the morning they again became drunk and gathered in front of the County Council Office.

One part of them, in new short fur coats, with knitted shawls about their necks, with moist drunken eyes or with savage self-encouraging shouts, or quiet and dejected, crowd at the gate amidst weeping mothers and wives, waiting for their turns (I fell in with them on the very day of the levy, that is, when those who were sent up were to be examined); another part at this time crowds in the waiting-room of the Office.

In the Office they are busy working. The door is opened, and the janitor calls Peter Sídorov. Peter Sídorov is startled, makes the sign of the cross, and enters into a small room with a glass door. Here the prospective recruits undress themselves. A naked recruit, a companion of Peter Sídorov, just accepted, comes in from the Office, with trembling jaws, and puts on his clothes. Peter Sídorov has heard and sees by his face that he is accepted. Peter Sídorov wants to ask him something, but he is told to hurry and undress himself as quickly as possible. He throws off his fur coat, pulls off his boots with his feet, takes off his vest, draws his shirt over his head, and with protruding ribs, naked, with shivering body, and emitting an odour of liquor, tobacco, and perspiration, with bare feet, enters into the Office, without knowing what to do with his bared muscular arms.

In the Office there hangs in full sight and in a large gilt frame the portrait of the emperor in a uniform with a sash, and in the corner a small portrait of Christ in a shirt and a crown of thorns. In the middle of the room there stands a table covered with green cloth, upon which lie papers and stands a triangular thing with an eagle, which is called the Mirror of Laws. Around the table sit the chiefs, with confident, calm looks. One of them smokes, another examines some papers. The moment Sídorov has entered, a janitor comes up to him, and he is put on the measuring-scale, receives a knock under his chin, and has his legs straightened out. There walks up a man with a cigarette. It is the doctor, and he, without looking into the recruit's face, but somewhere past him, loathingly touches his body, and measures and feels, and tells the janitor to open the recruit's mouth wide, and commands him to breathe and to say something. Somebody makes some notes. Finally, without looking once into his eyes, the doctor says, "Able-bodied! Next!" and with a fatigued expression again seats himself at the table. Again soldiers push the lad and hurry him off. He somehow manages in his hurry to pull the shirt over him, after missing the sleeves, somehow puts on his trousers and leg-rags, draws on his boots, looks for his shawl and cap, grasps his fur coat, and is led into the hall, where he is placed behind a bench. Beyond this bench wait all the accepted recruits. A village lad, like him, but from a distant Government, a full-fledged soldier with a gun, with a sharp bayonet attached to it, keeps watch on him, ready to run the bayonet through him, if he should think of running away.

Meanwhile the crowd of fathers, mothers, wives, pushed by the policemen, press close to the gate, to find out who is accepted, and who not. There appears one of the rejected, and he announces that Peter has been accepted, and there is heard the wail of Peter's wife, for whom the word "accepted" means a separation of four or five years, and the life of a soldier's wife as a cook, in debauchery.

But just then a long-haired man in a special attire, which distinguishes him from all other men, drives up and, getting down from the carriage, walks up to the house of the County Council Office. The policemen clear a path for him through the crowd. "The father has come to administer the oath." And this father, who has been assured that he is a special, exclusive servant of Christ, who for the most part does not himself see the deception under which he is, enters into the room where the accepted recruits are waiting, puts on a gold-embroidered apron, draws his hair out from underneath it, opens the very Gospel in which taking an oath is prohibited, lifts up a cross, the very cross on which Christ was crucified for not doing what this His imaginary servant orders to be done, and puts it on the pulpit, and all these defenceless and deceived lads repeat after him the lie which he pronounces boldly and by habit. He reads, and they repeat after him: "I promise and swear by the Almighty God, before His holy Gospel . . . etc., to defend, that is, to kill all those whom I am commanded to kill, and to do everything I am ordered to do by those people whom I do not know, and who need me for nothing else but that I should commit the evil deeds by which they are kept in their positions, and by which they oppress my brothers." All the accepted recruits senselessly repeat these wild words, and the so-called "father" drives away with the consciousness of having correctly and scrupulously done his duty, and all these deceived lads think that all those insipid, incomprehensible words, which they have just pronounced, have now, for the whole time of their military service, freed them from their human obligations and have bound them to new, more obligatory military obligations.

And this is done publicly, and no one will shout to the deceivers and to the deceived: "Bethink yourselves and scatter, for this is the basest and meanest lie, which ruins not only our bodies, but also our souls."

No one does so; on the contrary, when all are accepted, and it becomes necessary to let them out, the military chief, as though to scorn them, enters with self-confident, majestic mien into the hall where the deceived, drunken lads are locked up, and boldly exclaims to them in military fashion, "Your health, boys! I congratulate you on your Tsar's service." And the poor fellows (somebody has instructed them what to do) babble something with an unaccustomed, half-intoxicated tongue to the effect that they are glad of it.

In the meantime, the crowd of fathers, mothers, and wives stand at the door and wait. The women look with tearful, arrested eyes through the door. And the door opens, and out come, staggering, and with a look of bravado, the accepted recruits, — Petrúkha, and Vanyúkha, and Makár, — trying not to look at their relatives. The wail of the mothers and wives is heard. Some embrace one another and weep; others try to look brave; others again console their people. Mothers and wives, knowing that now they will be orphaned for three, four, or five years, without a supporter, wail and lament at the top of their voices. The fathers do not speak much, and only pitifully smack their tongues and sigh, knowing that now they will no longer see their helpers, whom they have raised and instructed, and that there will return to them, not those peaceful, industrious agriculturists that they have been, but generally debauched, dandyish soldiers, who are no longer used to a simple life.

And now the whole crowd take up seats in their sleighs and start down the street, in the direction of inns and restaurants, and still louder are heard, interfering with one another, songs, sobs, drunken shouts, the laments of the mothers and wives, the sounds of the accordion, and curses. All make for saloons and restaurants, the revenue from which goes to the government, and they abandon themselves to intoxication, which drowns in them the percepted consciousness of the illegality of what is being done to them.

For two or three weeks they live at home, and for the

most part are having a good time, that is, are out on a spree.

On a set day they are collected, and driven like cattle to one place, and are taught military methods and exercises. They are instructed by just such deceived and bestialized men as they, who entered the service two or three years ago. The means of instruction are deception, stupefaction, kicks, vódka. And not a year passes but that spiritually sound, bright, good fellows are turned into just such wild beings as their teachers.

"Well, and if the prisoner, your father, runs away?" I asked a young soldier.

"I can run the bayonet through him," he replied, in the peculiar, senseless voice of a soldier. "And if he 'removes himself,' I must shoot," he added, apparently proud of his knowledge of what to do when his father "removes himself."

When he, the good young man, is brought to a condition lower than an animal, he is such as those who use him as an instrument of violence want him to be. He is all ready: the man is lost, and a new instrument of violence has been created.

And all this takes place every year, every autumn, everywhere, in the whole of Russia, in broad daylight, in a populous city, in the sight of all men, and the deception is so clever, so cunning, that all see it and in the depth of their hearts know all its baseness, all its terrible consequences, and are unable to free themselves from it.

3

When the eyes shall be opened to this terrible deception which is practised on men, one must marvel how preachers of the religion of Christianity and morality, educators of youth, simply good, intelligent parents, who always exist in every society, can preach any doctrine of morality amidst a society in which all the churches and governments openly acknowledge that tortures and murders form an indispensable condition of the life of all men, and that amidst all men there must always be some special men, who are prepared to kill their brothers, and that every one of us may be such.

How can children and youths be taught and men in general be enlightened, to say nothing of the enlightenment in the Christian spirit, how can they be taught any morality by the side of the doctrine that murder is indispensable for the maintenance of the common, consequently of our own, well-being, and so is legitimate, and that there are men (any of us may be these men) whose duty it is to torture and kill our neighbours and to commit all kinds of crime at the will of those who have the power in their hands? If it is possible and right to torture and kill and commit all kinds of crimes by the will of those who have the power in their hands, there is, and there can be, no moral teaching, but there is only the right of the stronger. And so it is. In reality, such a teaching, which for some men is theoretically justified by the theory of the struggle for existence, does exist in our society.

Really, what kind of a moral teaching can there be, which would admit murder for any purposes whatsoever? This is as impossible as any mathematical doctrine, which would admit that two is equal to three.

With the admission of the fact that two is equal to three there may be a semblance of mathematics, but there can be no real mathematical knowledge. With the admission of murder in the form of executions, wars, self-defence, there may be a semblance of morality, but no real morality. The recognition of the sacredness of every man's life is the first and only foundation of all morality

The doctrine of an eye for an eye, a tooth for a tooth, a life for a life was put aside by Christianity for the very reason that this doctrine is only a justification of im morality, only a semblance of justice, and is devoid of sense. Life is a quantity which has no weight and no measure and which cannot be equalized to any other, and so the destruction of one life for another can have no meaning. Besides, every social law is a law which has for its purpose the improvement of human life. But in what way can the destruction of the lives of a few individuals improve the lives of men? The destruction of life is not like its improvement, but an act of suicide.

The destruction of another man's life for the purpose of preserving justice is like what a man would do who, to mend the calamity which consists in his having lost one arm, should for the sake of justice cut off his other arm.

But, to say nothing of the sin of deception, with which the most terrible crime presents itself to men as their duty; to say nothing of the terrible crime of using Christ's name and authority for the purpose of legalizing what is most denied by this same Christ, as is done in the case of the oath; to say nothing of the offence by means of which not only the bodies, but even the souls of "these little ones" are ruined; to say nothing of all that, how can men, even in view of their personal security, men who think highly of their forms of life, their progress, admit the formation among them of that terrible, senseless, cruel, pernicious force which is established by every organized government that rests on the army? The most cruel and terrible of robber bands is not so terrible as such a state organization. Every leader of robbers is none the less limited in his power, because the men who form his band retain at least a small part of their human liberty and may oppose the performance of acts contrary to their conscience. But for men forming a part of a regularly organized government with an army, with discipline carried to the point to which it is at the present time, there are no barriers whatsoever. There are no crimes so terrible that they would not be committed by men forming a part of the government and of the army, by the will of him who accidentally (Boulanger, Pugachév, Napoleon) may stand at its head.

Frequently, when I see, not only the levies of recruits, the military exercises, the manœuvres, but also the policemen with loaded revolvers, the sentries standing with guns and adjusted bayonets; when I hear (as I do in the Khamóvniki, where I live) for whole days the whistling and the pinging of bullets striking the target; and when I see, in the very city where every attempt at self-help and violence is prohibited, where there is a prohibition against the sale of powder, medicines, fast driving, unlicensed medical practice, and so forth, when I see in this same city thousands of disciplined men, who have been taught to commit murder and who are subject to one man, — I ask myself: "How can the men who think so highly of their security bear all this?" To say nothing of the harmfulness and immorality, nothing can be more dangerous than this. How can all men, I do not say Christians, Christian pastors, but all philanthropists, moralists, all those men who value their lives, their security, their well-being, quietly look on? This organization will certainly act in the same way, no matter in whose hands it may be: to-day, let us say, this power is in the hands of an endurable ruler; to-morrow a Biron, an Elizabeth, a Catherine, a Pugachév, a Napoleon the First, a Napoleon the Third may usurp it. And again, the man in whose hands is the power, and who to-day may be endurable, may to-morrow turn into a beast, or his place may be taken by an insane or half-witted heir of his, as was the case with the King of Bavaria and Paul.

And not only these higher rulers, but also all those minor satraps, who are distributed everywhere like so many Baránovs, chiefs of police, even rural officers, commanders of companies, under-officers, may commit terrible crimes before there has been time to depose them, as happens constantly.

Involuntarily one asks himself: "How can men permit such things to happen, if not for the sake of higher considerations of state, at least for the sake of their security?"

The answer to this question is this, that it is not all men who permit this to happen (one part of them, — the great majority of men, — the deceived and the subjected, cannot help but permit anything to be done), but those who with such an organization hold an advantageous position; they permit it, because for them the risk of suffering, because at the head of the government or the army there may be a senseless or cruel man, is always less than the disadvantages to which they would be subjected in case of the destruction of the organization itself.

The judge, policeman, governor, officer will hold his position equally under Boulanger, or a republic, or Pugachév or Catherine; but he will certainly lose his position, if the existing order, which secures for him his advantageous position, falls to pieces. And so all these men are not afraid of who will stand at the head of the organization of violence, — they adapt themselves to anybody, — but only of the destruction of the organization itself, and so they always support it, often unconsciously.

One often marvels why free men, who are not urged to it by anything, the so-called flower of society, enter the army, in Russia, in England, Germany, Austria, even France, and why they seek an opportunity for becoming murderers. Why do parents, moral men, send their children to institutions which prepare them for military matters? Why do mothers buy their children helmets, guns, swords as their favourite toys? (The children of peasants never play soldier.) Why do good men, and even women, who are in no way connected with military affairs, go into ecstasies over the exploits of a Skobelévski and of others, and why do they take so much pains to praise them? Why do men, who are not urged to do so, who do not receive any salary for it, like the marshals of nobility in Russia, devote whole months of assiduous work to performing a physically hard and morally agonizing piece of business, — the reception of recruits? Why do all the emperors and kings wear military costumes, attend manœuvres and parades, distribute rewards to soldiers, erect monuments to generals and conquerors? Why do free, wealthy men consider it an honour to perform lackeys' duties to crowned heads, why do they humble themselves, and flatter them, and pretend that they believe in the special grandeur of these persons? Why do men, who have long ago stopped believing in the mediæval superstitions of the church, and who are unable to believe in them, seriously and invariably pretend that they believe, thus maintaining the offensive and blasphemous religious institution? Why is the ignorance of the masses so zealously guarded, not only by the governments, but also by the free men from the higher classes? Why do they with such fury attack every attempt at destroying the religious superstitions, and every true enlightenment of the masses? Why do men, — historians, novelists, poets, — who can certainly receive nothing for their flattery, describe as heroes long deceased emperors, kings, or generals? Why do men who call themselves learned devote their whole lives to the formation of theories, from which it follows that violence which is exerted by the power against the nation is not violence, but some especial right?

One often marvels why, for what reason a lady of the world or an artist, who, it would seem, is interested neither in social, nor in military questions, condemns labour strikes and preaches war, and always definitely attacks one side and defends the other?

But one marvels at this only so long as one does not know that this is all done so because all the men of the ruling classes feel instinctively what it is that maintains and what destroys the organization under which they can enjoy the privileges they are enjoying.

The lady of the world has not even made the reflection that, if there are no capitalists, and no armies to defend them, her husband will have no money, and she will have no salon and no costumes; and the artist has not made the reflection as to this, that he needs the capitalists, who are protected by the armies, to buy his pictures; but the instinct, which in this case takes the place of reason, guides them unerringly. It is precisely the same instinct that with few exceptions guides all those men who support all those political, religious, economic establishments, which are advantageous to them.

But can the men of the upper classes maintain this order of things, only because it is advantageous for them? These men cannot help but see that this order of things is in itself irrational, no longer corresponds to the degree of men's consciousness, not even to public opinion, and is full of dangers. The men of the ruling classes — the honest, good, clever men among them — cannot help but suffer from these internal contradictions, and cannot help but see the dangers with which this order threatens them. Is it possible the men of the lower classes, all the millions of these people, can with a calm conscience perform all these obviously bad acts, tortures, and murders, which they are compelled to perform, only because they are afraid of punishment? Indeed, that could not have been, and neither the men of the one class nor of the other could help but see the irrationality of their activity, if the peculiarity of the state structure did not conceal from them the whole unnaturalness and irrationality of the acts committed by them.

This irrationality is concealed by the fact that in the

commission of each of these acts there are so many instigators, accomplices, abettors, that not one of the men taking part in it feels himself to be morally responsible.

Murderers compel all the persons who are present at a murder to strike the dead victim, so that the responsibility may be distributed among the largest possible number of men. The same thing, having assumed definite forms, has established itself in the structure of the state in the commission of all those crimes, without the constant commission of which no state organization is thinkable. The rulers of the state always try to draw as large a number of citizens as possible into the greatest possible participation in all the crimes committed by them and indispensable for them.

Of late this has found a most lucid expression in the drafting of the citizens into the courts in the form of jurors, into the armies in the form of soldiers, and into the local government and into the legislative assembly in the form of electors and representatives.

In the structure of the state, in which, as in a basket made of rods, all the ends are so concealed that it is not possible to find them, the responsibility for crimes committed is so concealed from men that they, in committing the most awful deeds, do not see their own responsibility in them.

In olden times the tyrants were blamed for the commission of evil deeds, but in our time most awful crimes, unthinkable even in the time of a Nero, are committed, and there is no one to blame.

Some men demanded, others decreed, others again confirmed, others proposed, others reported, others prescribed, others executed. Women, old men, innocent people, are killed, hanged, flogged to death, as lately happened in Russia in the Yúzov Plant, and as happens everywhere in Europe and in America, in the struggle with anarchists and all kinds of violators of the existing order; hundreds, thousands of men will be shot to death, killed, and hanged, or, as is done in wars, millions of men will be killed or ruined, or, as is constantly done, the souls of men are ruined in solitary confinement, in the debauched condition of militarism, — and no one is to blame.

On the lowest stage of the social ladder, soldiers with guns, pistols, swords, torture and kill men, and with the same tortures and murders compel men to enter the army, and are fully convinced that the responsibility for these acts is taken from them by those authorities who prescribe these acts to them.

On the highest stage, kings, presidents, ministers, Chambers, prescribe these tortures and murders and the enlistment of soldiers, and are fully convinced that, since they are put into their places by God, or since the society which they rule over demands from them precisely what they prescribe, they cannot be blamed.

In the middle between the two are the intermediate persons, who order the tortures and murders and the enlistment of soldiers, and they are fully convinced that their responsibility has been taken from them, partly by the commands from above, and partly because the same orders are demanded of them by all those who stand on the lower stages.

The administrative and the executive powers, which lie at the two extremes of the structure of the state, meet like two ends that are united into a ring, and one conditions and maintains the other and all the intervening links.

Without the conviction that there exists such a person, or such a number of persons, who take upon themselves the responsibility for the acts committed, not one soldier would be able to raise his hands for the purpose of torturing or killing. Without the conviction that this is demanded by the whole nation, not one emperor, king, president, not one assembly would be able to prescribe these same tortures and murders. Without the conviction that there are persons who stand above him and take upon themselves the responsibility for his act, and men who stand below him and demand the fulfilment of such acts for their own good, not one of the men who stand on the stages intermediate between the ruler and the soldier would be able to commit those acts which he is committing.

The structure of the state is such that, no matter on what rung of the social ladder a man may stand, his degree of irresponsibility is always one and the same: the higher he stands, the more is he subjected to the influence of the demand for orders from below and the less he is subjected to the influence of the prescriptions from above, and vice versa.

Thus, in the case before me, every one who had taken part in the matter was the more under the influence of the demand for orders from below and the less under the influence of prescriptions from above, the higher his position was, and vice versa.

But not only do all men who are connected with the structure of the state shift their responsibility for deeds committed upon others: the peasant who is drafted into the army, upon the nobleman or merchant who has become an officer; and the officer, upon the nobleman who holds the position of governor; and the governor, upon the son of an official or nobleman who occupies the position of minister; and the minister, upon a member of the imperial house who holds the position of emperor; and the emperor again, upon all these officials, noblemen, merchants, and peasants; not only do men in this manner free themselves from the consciousness of responsibility for acts committed by them, — they even lose the moral consciousness of their responsibility for this other reason, that, uniting into a political structure, they so constantly, continuously, and tensely convince themselves and others that they are not all identical men, but men who differ from one another as does "one star from another," that they begin themselves sincerely to believe so. Thus they convince one set of men that they are not simple men, identical with others, but a special kind of men, who have to be honoured, while they impress others with the idea that they stand beneath all other men and so must unflinchingly submit to what they are commanded to do by their superiors.

On this inequality and exaltation of one class of men and the annihilation of the other is mainly based the inability of men to see the irrationality of the existing order and its cruelty and criminality, and of that deception which is practised by some and to which the others submit.

Some, those who are impressed with the idea that they are vested with some supernatural significance and grandeur, are so intoxicated by this imaginary grandeur that they stop seeing their responsibility in the acts committed by them; the other men, who, on the contrary, are impressed with the idea that they are insignificant creatures, who must in everything submit to the higher, in consequence of this constant condition of humiliation fall into a strange condition of intoxication of servility, and under the influence of their intoxication also fail to see the significance of their acts, and lose the consciousness of their responsibility for them. The intermediate people, who, partly submitting to the higher, and partly considering themselves to be superior, succumb simultaneously to the intoxication of power and that of servility, and so lose the consciousness of their responsibility.

We need but look in any country at a superior chief, intoxicated by his grandeur, accompanied by his staff, all of them on magnificently caparisoned horses, in special uniforms and signs of distinction, as he, to the sound of the harmonious and festive music produced by wind-instruments, rides past a line of soldiers stiffened up from a sense of servility and presenting arms, — we need but look at him, in order that we may understand that at these moments the highest chief and the soldier and all the intermediate persons, being in a state of intoxication, are equally capable of committing acts which they would not think of committing under other circumstances.

But the intoxication experienced by men under such phenomena as are parades, imperial receptions, church solemnities, coronations, is a temporary and acute condition; there are also other, chronic, constant conditions of intoxication, which are equally experienced by all men who have any power, from the power of the emperor to that of a policeman in the street, and by men who submit to power and who are in a condition of intoxication through servility, and who in justification of this their condition always ascribe, as has always shown itself in the case of slaves, the greatest significance and dignity to him whom they obey.

On this deception of the inequality of men and the resulting intoxication of power and of servility is preeminently based the ability of men united into a political structure to commit, without experiencing any pangs of conscience, acts which are contrary to their conscience.

Under the influence of such an intoxication, both of power and of servility, men present themselves to themselves and to others, not as what they are in reality, — men, — but as especial, conventional beings, — noblemen, merchants, governors, judges, officers, kings, ministers, soldiers, who no longer are subject to common human obligations, but, above all else, and before all human, to nobiliary, commercial, gubernatorial, judicial, military, royal, ministerial obligations.

Thus, the proprietor who litigated concerning the forest did what he did only because he did not present himself to himself as a simple man, like any of the peasants who were living by his side, but as a large landed proprietor and a member of the gentry, and so, under the influence of the intoxication of power, he felt himself insulted by the pretensions of the peasants. It was only for this reason that, without paying any attention to the consequences which might arise from his demand, he handed in the petition requesting the restitution of his imaginary right.

Similarly, the judges who irregularly adjudged the forest to the proprietor did so only because they do not imagine themselves to be simple men, just like all other men, and so under obligation in all cases to be guided only by what is the truth, but under the intoxication of power they imagine themselves to be the guardians of justice, who cannot err; but under the influence of the intoxication of servility they imagine themselves to be men who are obliged to carry out certain words which are written in a certain book and are called the law. As just such conventional persons, and not as what they are in reality, present themselves, under the influence of the intoxication of power and of servility, to themselves and to others, all the other participants in this matter, from the highest representatives of power, who sign their approval on documents, from the marshal, who drafts recruits at the levy of soldiers, and the priest, who deceives them, to the last soldier, who is now getting ready to shoot at his brothers. They all did what they did, and are preparing themselves to do what awaits them, only because they present themselves to themselves and to others, not as what they are in reality, — men who are confronted with the question as to whether they should take part in a matter which is condemned by their conscience, or not, — but as different conventional persons, — one, as an anointed king, a special being, who is called upon to care for the well-being of one hundred million men; another, as a representative of nobility; a third, as a priest, who with his ordainment has received a special grace; a fourth, as a soldier, who is obliged by his oath to fulfil without reflection what he is commanded to do.

Only under the influence of the intoxication of power and servility, which result from their imaginary positions, can all these men do what they do.

If all these men did not have a firm conviction that the callings of kings, ministers, governors, judges, noblemen, landed proprietors, marshals, officers, soldiers, are something actually in existence and very important, not one of these men would think without terror and disgust of participating in the acts which he is committing now.

The conventional positions, which were established hundreds of years ago, which have been recognized through the ages, and which are now recognized by all men about us, and which are designated by especial names and particular attires, and which, besides, are maintained by means of every kind of magnificence and effects on the outer senses, are to such a degree instilled in people that they, forgetting the habitual conditions of life, common to all, begin to look upon themselves and upon all men only from this conventional point of view, and are guided by nothing but this conventional point of view in the valuation of other men's acts.

Thus a mentally sound old man, for no other reason than that some trinket or fool's dress is put over him, some keys on his buttocks, or a blue ribbon, which is proper only for a dressed-up little girl, and that he is on that occasion impressed with the idea that he is a general, a chamberlain, a Cavalier of St. Andrews, or some such silliness, suddenly becomes self-confident, proud, and even happy; or, on the contrary, because he loses or does not receive a desired trinket or name, becomes so sad and unhappy that he even grows sick. Or, what is even more startling, an otherwise mentally sound, free, and even well-to-do young man, for no other reason than that he calls himself, and others call him, an investigating magistrate or County Council chief, seizes an unfortunate widow away from her minor children, and locks her up, or has her locked up in a prison, leaving her children without a mother, and all that because this unfortunate woman secretly trafficked in liquor and thus deprived the Crown of twenty-five roubles of revenue, and he does not feel the least compunction about it. Or, what is even more startling, an otherwise intelligent and meek man, only because a brass plate or a uniform is put on him and he is told that he is a watchman or a customs soldier, begins to shoot with bullets at men, and neither he nor those who surround him consider him blameworthy for it, and would even blame him if he did not shoot; I do not even speak of the judges and jurors, who sentence to executions, and of the military, who kill thousands without the least compunction, only because they have been impressed with the idea that they are not simply men, but jurors, judges, generals, soldiers.

Such a constant, unnatural, and strange condition of men in the life of the state is generally expressed in words as follows: "As a man I pity him, but as a watchman, judge, general, governor, king, soldier, I must kill or torture him," as though there can exist a given position, acknowledged by men, which can make void duties which are imposed upon each of us by a man's position.

Thus, for example, in the present case, men are travelling to commit murder and tortures on hungry people, and they recognize that in the dispute between the peasants and the proprietor the peasants are in the right (all men in authority told me so), and know that the peasants are unfortunate, poor, and hungry; the proprietor is rich and does not inspire sympathy, and all these men none the less are on their way to kill the peasants, in order thus to secure three thousand roubles to the proprietor, for no other reason than that these men at this moment do not consider themselves to be men, but a governor, a general of gendarmes, an officer, a soldier, and think that not the eternal demands of their consciences, but the accidental, temporary demands of their positions as officers and soldiers are binding on them.

However strange this may seem, the only explanation for this remarkable phenomenon is this, that these men are in the same position as those hypnotized persons who are commanded to imagine and feel themselves in certain conventional positions, and to act like those beings whom they represent; thus, for example, when a hypnotized person receives the suggestion that he is lame, he begins to limp, or that he is blind, he does not see, or that he is an animal, he begins to bite. In this state are not only the men who are travelling on this train, but also all men who preferably perform their social and their political duties, to the disadvantage of their human duties.

The essence of this condition is this, that the men under the influence of the one idea suggested to them are not able to reflect upon their acts, and so do, without any reflection, what is prescribed to them in correspondence with the suggested idea, and what they are led up to through example, advice, or hints.

The difference between those who are hypnotized by artificial means and those who are under the influence of the political suggestion consists in this, that to the artificially hypnotized their imaginary condition is suggested at once, by one person, and for the briefest space of time, and so the suggestion presents itself to us in a glaring form, which sets us to wondering, while to the men who act under the political suggestion their imaginary position is suggested by degrees, slowly, imperceptibly, from childhood, at times not only in a certain number of years, but through whole generations, and, besides, is not suggested by one person, but by all those who surround them.

"But," I shall be told, "in all societies the majority of men, — all the children, all the women, who are absorbed in the labour of pregnancy, child-bearing, and nursing, all the enormous masses of the working people, who are placed under the necessity of tense and assiduous physical labour, all the mentally weak by nature, all abnormal men with a weakened spiritual activity in consequence of nicotine, alcohol, and opium poisoning, or for some other reason, — all these men are always in such a condition that, not being able to reason independently, they submit either to those men who stand on a higher stage of rational consciousness, or to family and political traditions, to what is called public opinion, and in this submission there is nothing unnatural or contradictory."

And, indeed, there is nothing unnatural in it, and the ability of unthinking people to submit to the indications of men standing on a higher stage of consciousness is a constant property of men, that property in consequence of which men, submitting to the same rational principles, are able to live in societies: some, — the minority, — by consciously submitting to the same rational principles, on account of their agreement with the demands of their reason; the others, — the majority, — by submitting unconsciously to the same principles, only because these demands have become the public opinion. Such a subjection of the unthinking to public opinion presents nothing unnatural so long as the public opinion is not split up.

But there are times when the higher truth, as compared with the former degree of the consciousness of the truth, which at first is revealed to a few men, in passing by degrees from one set to another, embraces such a large number of men that the former public opinion, which is based on a lower stage of consciousness, begins to waver, and the new is ready to establish itself, but is not yet established. There are times, resembling spring, when the old public opinion has not yet been destroyed and the new is not yet established, and when men begin to criticize their own acts and those of others on the basis of the new consciousness, and yet in life, from inertia, from tradition, continue to submit to principles which only in former times formed the higher degree of rational consciousness, but which now are already in an obvious contradiction to it. And then the men, feeling, on the one hand, the necessity of submitting to the new public opinion, and not daring, on the other, to depart from the former, find themselves in an unnatural, wavering state. It is in such a condition that, in relation to the Christian truths, are not only the men on this train, but also the majority of the men of our time.

In the same condition are equally the men of the higher classes, who enjoy exclusive, advantageous positions, and the men of the lower classes, who without opposition obey what they are commanded to obey.

Some, the men of the ruling classes, who no longer possess any rational explanation for the advantageous positions held by them, are put to the necessity, for the purpose of maintaining these positions, of suppressing in themselves the higher rational faculties of love and of impressing upon themselves the necessity for their exclusive position; the others, the lower classes, who are oppressed by labour and purposely stupefied, are in a constant state of suggestion, which is unflinchingly and constantly produced on them by the men of the higher classes.

Only thus can be explained those remarkable phenomena with which our life is filled, and as a striking example of which there presented themselves to me my good, peaceful acquaintances, whom I met on September 9th, and who with peace of mind were travelling to commit a most beastly, senseless, and base crime. If the consciences of these men had not been in some way put to sleep, not one of them would be able to do one hundredth part of what they are getting ready to do, and, in all probability, will do.

It cannot be said that they do not have the conscience which forbids them to do what they are about to do, as there was no such conscience in men four hundred, three hundred, two hundred, one hundred years ago, when they burned people at the stake, tortured people, and flogged them to death; it exists in all these men, but it is put to sleep in them, — in some, the ruling men, who are in exclusive, advantageous positions, by means of auto-suggestion, as the psychiaters call it; in the others, the executors, the soldiers by a direct, conscious suggestion, hypnotization, produced by the upper classes.

The conscience is in these men put to sleep, but it exists in them, and through the auto-suggestion and suggestion, which hold sway over them, it already speaks in them and may awaken any moment.

All these men are in a condition resembling the one a hypnotized man would be in, if it were suggested to him and he were commanded to do an act which is contrary to everything which he considers rational and good, — to kill his mother or child. The hypnotized man feels himself bound by the suggestion induced in him, and it seems to him that he cannot stop; at the same time, the nearer he comes to the time and the place of the commission of the crime, the stronger does the drowned voice of the conscience rise in him, and he begins to show more and more opposition and to writhe, and wants to wake up. And it is impossible to say in advance whether he will do the suggested act, or not, and what it is that will win, the rational consciousness or the irrational suggestion. Everything depends on the relative strength of the two.

Precisely the same is now taking place in all the men on this train, and in general in all the men who in our time commit political acts of violence and exploit them.

There was a time when men, who went out for the purpose of torturing and killing people, for the purpose of setting an example, did not return otherwise than having performed the act for which they had gone out, and, having performed the act, they were not tormented by repentance and doubt, but, having flogged men to death, calmly returned home to their family, and petted their children, — jested, laughed, and abandoned themselves to quiet domestic pleasures. It did not then occur even to those who gained by these acts of violence, to the landed proprietors and the rich men, that the advantages which they enjoyed had any direct connection with these cruelties. But now it is not so: men know already, or are very near to knowing, what they are doing, and for what purpose they are doing what they are doing. They may shut their eyes and cause their consciences to be inactive, but with eyes unshut and consciences unimpaired they — both those who commit the acts and those who gain by them — no longer can fail to see the significance which these acts have. It happens that men understand the significance of what they have done only after they have performed the act; or it happens that they understand it before the very act. Thus the men who had in charge the tortures in Nízhni-Nóvgorod, Sarátov, Orél, Yúzov Plant, understood the significance of what they did only after the commission of the act, and now they are tormented with shame before public opinion and before their consciences. Both those who ordered the tortures and those who executed them are tormented. I have spoken with soldiers who have executed such acts, and they have always cautiously evaded all conversation about it; when they spoke, they did so with perplexity and terror. Cases happen when men come to their senses immediately before the commission of the act. Thus I know a case of a sergeant, who during a pacification was beaten by two peasants, and who reported accordingly, but who the next day, when he saw the tortures to which the peasants were subjected, begged the commander of the company to tear up the report and to discharge the peasants who had beaten him. I know a case when the soldiers, who were commanded to shoot some men, declined to obey; and I know many cases where the commanders refused to take charge of tortures and murders. Thus it happens that the men who establish violence and those who commit acts of violence at times come to their senses long before the commission of the act suggested to them, at others before the very act, and at others again after the act.

The men who are travelling on this train have gone out to torture and kill their brothers, but not one of them knows whether he will do what he has set out to do, or not. No matter how hidden for each of them is the responsibility in this matter, no matter how strong the suggestion may be, in all these men, that they are not men, but governors, rural judges, officers, soldiers, and that, as such beings, they may violate their human obligations, the nearer they approach the place of their destination, the stronger will the doubt rise in them whether they should do what they have started out to do, and this doubt will reach the highest degree when they reach the very moment of the execution.

The governor, in spite of all the intoxication of the surrounding circumstance, cannot help but reflect for a moment, when he has to give his last decisive command concerning the murder or the torture. He knows that the case of the Governor of Orél provoked the indignation of the best men of society, and he himself, under the influence of the public opinion of those circles to which he belongs, has more than once expressed his disapproval of it; he knows that the prosecutor, who was to have gone with them, refused outright to take part in this business, because he considered it disgraceful; he knows also that changes may take place in the government at any time, and that in consequence of them that which was a desert to-day may to-morrow be the cause of disfavour; he knows, too, that there is a press, if not in Russia, at least abroad, which may describe this matter and so disgrace him for life. He already scents that new public opinion which is making void what the former public opinion demanded. Besides, he cannot be absolutely sure that at the last moment the executors will obey him. He wavers, and it is impossible to foretell what he will do.

The same thing, in a greater or lesser measure, is experienced by all the officials and officers who are travelling with him. They all know in the depth of their hearts that the deed which is to be done is disgraceful, that participation in it lowers and defiles a man in the eyes of a few men, whose opinion they already value. They know that it is a shame to appear after the torture or murder of defenceless men in the presence of their fiancées or wives, whom they treat with a show of tenderness. Besides, like the governor, they are in doubt whether the soldiers are sure to obey them. And, no matter how unlike it is to the self-confident look with which all these ruling men now move in the station and up and down the platform, they all in the depth of their hearts suffer and even waver. It is for this very reason that they assume this confident tone, in order to conceal their inner wavering. And this sensation increases in proportion as they come nearer to the place of action.

However imperceptible this may be, and however strange it may appear, all this mass of young soldiers, who seem so subservient, is in the same state.

They are all of them no longer the soldiers of former days, men who have renounced their natural life of labour, and who have devoted their lives exclusively to dissipation, rapine, and murder, like some Roman legionaries or the warriors of the Thirty-Years War, or even the late soldiers of twenty-five years of service; they are, for the most part, men who have but lately been taken away from their families, all of them full of recollections of that good, natural, and sensible life from which they have been taken away.

All these lads, who for the most part come from the country, know what business is taking them out on the train; they know that the proprietors always offend their brothers, the peasants, and that therefore the same thing is taking place here. Besides, the greater half of these men know how to read books, and not all books are those in which the business of war is lauded, — there are also those in which its immorality is pointed out. Amidst them frequently serve freethinking companions, — volunteer soldiers, — and just such liberal young officers, and into their midst has been thrown the seed of doubt as to the unconditional legality and valour of their activity. It is true, all of them have passed through that terrible, artificial drill, worked out by ages, which kills all independence in a man, and they are so accustomed to mechanical obedience that at the words of command, "Fire by company! Company, fire!" and so forth, their guns rise mechanically and the habitual motions take place. But "Fire!" will not mean now having fun while shooting at a target, but killing their tormented, offended fathers and brothers, who — here they are — are standing in crowds, with their women and children in the street, and shouting and waving their hands. Here they are, — one of them, with a sparse beard, in a patched caftan and in bast shoes, just like their own fathers at home in the Government of Kazán or of Ryazán; another, with a gray beard and stooping shoulders, carrying a large stick, just like their father's father, their grandfather; another, a young lad in boots and red shirt, exactly as the soldier who is now to shoot at him was a year ago. And there is a woman in bast shoes and linen skirt, just like mother at home ——

Are they really going to shoot at them?

God knows what each soldier will do during this last moment. One slightest indication as to its not being right, above all as to the possibility of not doing it, one such word, one hint, will be sufficient, in order to stop them.

All men who are travelling on this train will, when they proceed to execute the deed for which they have set out, be in the same position in which a hypnotized person would be, who has received the suggestion to chop a log, and, having walked up to what has been pointed out to him as a log and having raised the axe to strike, suddenly sees or is told that it is not a log, but his sleeping brother. He may perform the act suggested to him, and he may wake up before its performance. Even so all these men may awaken, or not. If they do not, as terrible a deed as the one in Orél will be done, and in other men the auto-suggestion and the suggestion under which they act will be increased; if they awaken, such a deed will not only not be performed, but many others, upon finding out the turn which the affair has taken, will be freed from that suggestion in which they are, or at least will approach such a liberation.

But if not all men travelling on this train shall awaken and refrain from doing the deed which has been begun, if only a few of them shall do so and shall boldly express to other men the criminality of this affair, these few men even may have the effect of awakening all the other men from the suggestion, under which they are, and the proposed evil deed will not take place.

More than that: if only a few men, who do not take part in this affair, but are only present at the preparations for the same, or who have heard of similiar acts previously committed, will not remain indifferent, but will frankly and boldly express their disgust with the participants in these matters, and will point out to them their whole senselessness, cruelty, and criminality, even that will not pass unnoticed.

Even so it was in the present case. A few persons. participants and non-participants in this affair, who were free from suggestion, needed but at the time when they were getting ready for this affair boldly to express their indignation with tortures administered in other places, and their disgust and contempt for those men who took part in them; in the present Túla affair a few persons needed but to express their unwillingness to take part in it; the lady passenger and a few other persons at the station needed but in the presence of those who were travelling on the train to express their indignation at the act which was about to be committed; one of the regimental commanders, a part of whose troops were demanded for the pacification, needed but to express his opinion that the military cannot be executioners, — and thanks to these and certain other, seemingly unimportant, private influences exerted against people under suggestion, the affair would take a different turn, and the troops, upon arriving on the spot, would not commit any tortures, but would cut down the forest and give it to the proprietor. If there should not be in certain men any clear consciousness as to their doing wrong, and if there should be, in consequence of this, no mutual influence of men in this sense, there would take place the same as in Orél. But if this consciousness should be even stronger, and so the amount of the interactions even greater than what it was, it is very likely that the governor and his troops would not even dare to cut down the forest, in order to give it to the proprietor. If this consciousness had been even stronger and the amount of interactions greater, it is very likely the governor would not even have dared to travel to the place of action. If the consciousness had been stronger still and the amount of interactions even greater, it is very likely that the minister would not have made up his mind to prescribe, and the emperor to confirm such a decree.

Everything, consequently, depends on the force with which the Christian truth is cognized by every individual man.

And so, it would seem, the activity of all the men of our time, who assert that they wish to continue to the welfare of humanity, should be directed to the increase of the lucidity of the demands of the Christian truth.

4

But, strange to say, those very men, who in our time assert more than any one else that they care for the amelioration of human life, and who are regarded as the leaders in public opinion, affirm that it is not necessary to do that, and that for the amelioration of the condition of men there exist other, more efficacious means. These men assert that the amelioration of human life does not take place in consequence of the internal efforts of the consciousness of individual men and the elucidation and profession of the truth, but in consequence of the gradual change of the common external conditions of life, and that the profession by every individual man of the truth which is not in conformity with the existing order is not only useless, but even harmful, because on the part of the power it provokes oppressions, which keep these individuals from continuing their useful activity in the service of society. According to this doctrine, all the changes in human life take place under the same laws under which they take place in the life of the animals.

Thus, according to this doctrine, all the founders of religions, such as Moses and the prophets, Confucius, Lao-tse, Buddha, Christ, and others preached their teachings, and their followers accepted them, not because they loved truth, elucidated it to themselves, and professed it, but because the political, social, and, above all, economic conditions of the nations among whom these teachings appeared and were disseminated were favourable for their manifestation and diffusion.

And so the chief activity of a man wishing to serve society and ameliorate the condition of humanity must according to this doctrine be directed, not to the elucidation of the truth and its profession, but to the amelioration of the external political, social, and, above all else, economic conditions. Now the change of these political, social, and economic conditions is accomplished partly by means of serving the government and of introducing into it liberal and progressive principles, partly by contributing to the development of industry and the dissemination of socialistic ideas, and chiefly by the diffusion of scientific education.

According to this teaching it is not important for a man to profess in life the truth that has been revealed to him, and so inevitably be compelled to realize it in life, or at least not to do acts which are contrary to the professed truth; not to serve the government and not to increase its power, if he considers this power to be deleterious; not to make use of the capitalistic structure, if he considers this structure to be irregular; not to show any respect for various ceremonies, if he considers them to be a dangerous superstition; not to take part in the courts, if he considers their establishment to be false; not to serve as a soldier; not to swear; in general, not to lie, not to act as a scoundrel, but, without changing the existing forms of life, and submitting to them, contrary to his opinion, he should introduce liberalism into the existing institutions; coöperate with industry, the propaganda of socialism, the advancement of what is called the sciences, and the diffusion of culture. According to this theory is it possible, though remaining a landed proprietor, a merchant, a manufacturer, a judge, an official, receiving a salary from the government, a soldier, an officer, to be, withal, not only a humane man, but even a socialist and revolutionist.

Hypocrisy, which formerly used to have a religious foundation in the doctrine about the fall of the human race, about redemption, and about the church, in this teaching received in our time a new scientific foundation, and so has caught in its net all those men who from the degree of their development can no longer fall back on the religious hypocrisy. Thus, if formerly only a man who professed the ecclesiastic religious doctrine could, considering himself with it pure from every sin, take part in all kinds of crimes committed by the government, and make use of them, so long as he at the same time fulfilled the external demands of his profession, now all men, who do not believe in the church Christianity, have the same kind of a worldly scientific basis for recognizing themselves as pure, and even highly moral men, in spite of their participation in the evil deeds of the state and of their making use of them.

There lives — not in Russia alone, but anywhere you please, in France, England, Germany, America — a rich landed proprietor, and for the right which he gives to certain people living on his land, to draw their sustenance from it, he fleeces these for the most part hungry people to their fullest extent. This man's right to the possession of the land is based on this, that at every attempt of the oppressed people at making use of the lands which he considers his own, without his consent, there arrive some troops which subject the men who have seized the lands to tortures and extermination. One would think that it is evident that a man who lives in this manner is an egotistical being and in no way can call himself a Christian or a liberal. It would seem to be obvious that the first thing such a man ought to do, if he only wants in some way to come near to Christianity or to liberalism, would be to stop plundering and ruining men by means of his right to the land, which is supported by murders and tortures practised by the government. Thus it would be if there did not exist the metaphysics of hypocrisy, which says that from a religious point of view the possession or non-possession of the land is a matter of indifference as regards salvation, and that from the scientific point of view the renunciation of the ownership of land would be a useless personal effort, and that the coöperation with the good of men is not accomplished in this manner, but through the gradual change of external forms. And so this man, without the least compunction, and without any misgivings as to his being believed, arranges an agricultural exhibition, or a temperance society, or through his wife and children sends jackets and soup to three old women, and in his family, in drawing-rooms, committees, the press, boldly preaches the Gospel or humane love of one's neighbour in general, and of that working agricultural class in particular which he constantly torments and oppresses. And the men who are in the same condition with him believe him, praise him, and with him solemnly discuss the questions as to what measures should be used for the amelioration of the condition of the working masses, on the spoliation of whom their life is based, inventing for the purpose all kinds of means, except the one without which no amelioration of the people's condition is possible, of ceasing to take away from these people the land, which is necessary for their maintenance.

A most striking example of such hypocrisy is to be found in the measures taken last year by the Russian landed proprietors in the struggle with the famine, which they themselves had produced, and which they immediately set out to exploit, when they not only sold the corn at the highest possible price, but even sold to the freezing peasants as fuel the potato-tops at five roubles per desyatína.

Or there lives a merchant, whose whole commerce, like any commerce, is based on a series of rascalities, by means of which, exploiting the ignorance and need of men, articles are bought of them below their value, and, again exploiting the ignorance, need, and temptation of men, are sold back at prices above their value. It would seem to be obvious that a man whose activity is based on what in his own language is called rascality, so long as these same acts are performed under different conditions, ought to be ashamed of his position, and is by no means able, continuing to be a merchant, to represent himself as a Christian or a liberal. But the metaphysics of hypocrisy says to him that he may pass for a virtuous man, even though continuing his harmful activity: a religious man need only be believed, but a liberal has only to coöperate with the change of external conditions, — the progress of industry. And so this merchant, who frequently, in addition, performs a whole series of direct rascalities, by selling bad wares for good ones, cheating in weights and measures, or trading exclusively in articles which are pernicious to the people's health (such as wine or opium), boldly considers himself, and is considered by others, so long as he in business does not directly cheat his fellows in deception, that is, his fellow merchants, to be a model of honesty and conscientiousness. If he spends one-thousandth of the money stolen by him on some public institution, a hospital, a museum, an institution of learning, he is also regarded as a benefactor of those very people on the deception and corruption of whom all his fortune is based; but if he contributes part of his stolen money to a church and for the poor, he is regarded even as a model Christian.

Or there lives a manufacturer, whose whole income consists of the pay which is taken away from the workmen, and whose whole activity is based on compulsory, unnatural labour, which ruins whole generations of men; it would seem to be obvious that first of all, if this man professes any Christian or liberal principles, he must stop ruining human lives for the sake of his profit. But according to the existing theory, he is contributing to industry, and he must not — it would even be injurious to men and to society — stop his activity. And here this man, the cruel slaveholder of thousands of men, building for those who have been crippled while working for him little houses with little gardens five feet square, and a savings-bank, and a poorhouse, and a hospital, is fully convinced that in this way he has more than paid for all those physically and mentally ruined lives of men, for which he is responsible, and quietly continues his activity, of which he is proud.

Or there lives a head of a department, or some civil, clerical, military servant of the state, who serves for the purpose of satisfying his ambition or love of power, or, what is most common, for the purpose of receiving a salary, which is collected from the masses that are emaciated and exhausted with labour (taxes, no matter from whom they come, always originate in labour, that is, in the labouring people), and if he, which is extremely rare, does not directly steal the government's money in some unusual manner, he considers himself and is considered by others like him to be a most useful and virtuous member of society.

There lives some judge, prosecutor, head of a department, and he knows that as the result of his sentence or decree hundreds and thousands of unfortunate people, torn away from their families, are lingering in solitary confinement, at hard labour, going mad and killing themselves with glass, or starving to death; he knows that these thousands of people have thousands of mothers, wives, children, who are suffering from the separation, are deprived of the possibility of meeting them, are disgraced, vainly implore forgiveness or even alleviation of the fates of their fathers, sons, husbands, brothers, — and the judge or head of a department is so hardened in his hypocrisy that he himself and his like and their wives and relatives are firmly convinced that he can with all this be a very good and sensitive man. According to the metaphysics of hypocrisy, it turns out that he is doing useful public work. And this man, having ruined hundreds, thousands of men, who curse him, and who are in despair, thanks to his activity, believing in the good and in God, with a beaming, benevolent smile on his smooth face, goes to mass, hears the Gospel, makes liberal speeches, pets his children, preaches to them morality, and feels meek of spirit in the presence of imaginary sufferings.

All these men and those who live on them, their wives, teachers, children, cooks, actors, jockeys, and so forth, live by the blood which in one way or another, by one class of leeches or by another, is sucked out of the working people; thus they live, devouring each day for their pleasures hundreds and thousands of work-days of the exhausted labourers, who are driven to work by the threat of being killed; they see the privations and sufferings of these labourers, of their children, old men, women, sick people; they know of the penalties to which the violators of this established spoliation are subjected, and they not only do not diminish their luxury, do not conceal it, but impudently display before these oppressed labourers, who for the most part hate them, as though on purpose to provoke them, their parks, castles, theatres, chases, races, and at the same time assure themselves and one another that they are all very much concerned about the good of the masses, whom they never stop treading underfoot; and on Sundays they dress themselves in costly attire and drive in expensive carriages into houses especially built for the purpose of making fun of Christianity, and there listen to men especially trained in this lie, who in every manner possible, in vestments and without vestments, in white neckties, preach to one another the love of men, which they all deny with their whole lives. And, while doing all this, these men so enter into their parts that they seriously believe that they actually are what they pretend to be.

The universal hypocrisy, which has entered into the flesh and blood of all the classes of our time, has reached such limits that nothing of this kind ever fills any one with indignation. Hypocrisy with good reason means the same as acting, and anybody can pretend, — act a part. Nobody is amazed at such phenomena as that the successors of Christ bless the murderers who are lined up and hold the guns which are loaded for their brothers; that the priests, the pastors of all kinds of Christian confessions, always, as inevitably as the executioners, take part in executions, with their presence recognizing the murder as compatible with Christianity (at an electrocution in America, a preacher was present).

Lately there was an international prison exhibition in St. Petersburg, where implements of torture were exhibited, such as manacles, models of solitary cells, that is, worse implements of torture than knouts and rods, and sensitive gentlemen and ladies went to look at all this, and they enjoyed the sight.

Nor is any one surprised at the way the liberal science proves, by the side of the assumption of equality, fraternity, liberty, the necessity of an army, of executions, customhouses, the censorship, the regulation of prostitution, the expulsion of cheap labour, and the prohibition of immigration, and the necessity and justice of colonization, which is based on the poisoning, plundering, and destruction of whole tribes of men who are called savage, and so forth.

People talk of what will happen when all men shall profess what is called Christianity (that is, various mutually hostile professions); when all shall be well fed and well clothed; when all shall be united with one another from one end of the world to the other by means of telegraphs and telephones, and shall communicate with one another by means of balloons; when all the labourers shall be permeated with social teachings, and the labour-unions shall have collected so many millions of members and of roubles; when all men shall be cultured, and all shall read the papers and know the sciences.

But of what use or good can all these improvements be, if people shall not at the same time speak and do what they consider to be the truth?

The calamities of men are certainly due to their disunion, and the disunion is due to this, that men do not follow the truth, which is one, but the lies, of which there are many. The only means for the union of men into one is the union in truth; and so, the more sincerely men strive toward the truth, the nearer they are to this union.

But how can men be united in truth, or even approach it, if they not only do not express the truth which they know, but even think that it is unnecessary to do so, and pretend that they consider to be the truth what they do not regard as the truth.

And so no amelioration of the condition of men is possible, so long as men will pretend, that is, conceal the truth from themselves, so long as they do not recognize that their union, and so their good, is possible only in the truth, and so will not place the recognition and profession of the truth, the one which has been revealed to them, higher than anything else.

Let all those external improvements, of which religious and scientific men may dream, be accomplished; let all men accept Christianity, and let all those ameliorations, which all kinds of Bellamys and Richets wish for, take place, with every imaginable addition and correction — but let with all that the same hypocrisy remain as before; let men not profess the truth which they know, but continue to pretend that they believe in what they really do not believe, and respect what they really do not respect, and the condition of men will not only remain the same, but will even grow worse and worse. The more people shall have to eat, the more there shall be of telegraphs, telephones, books, newspapers, journals, the more means will there be for the dissemination of discordant lies and of hypocrisy, and the more will men be disunited and, therefore, wretched, as is indeed the case at present.

Let all these external changes take place, and the condition of humanity will not improve. But let each man at once in his life, according to his strength, profess the truth, as he knows it, or let him at least not defend the untruth, which he does, giving it out as the truth, and there would at once, in this present year 1893, take place such changes in the direction of the emancipation of men and the establishment of truth upon earth as we do not dare even to dream of for centuries to come.

For good reason Christ's only speech which is not meek, but reproachful and cruel, was directed to the hypocrites and against hypocrisy. What corrupts, angers, bestializes, and, therefore, disunites men, is not thieving, nor spoliation, nor murder, nor fornication, nor forgery, but the lie, that especial lie of hypocrisy which in the consciousness of men destroys the distinction between good and evil, deprives them of the possibility of avoiding the evil and seeking the good, deprives them of what forms the essence of the true human life, and so stands in the way of every perfection of men.

Men who do not know the truth and who do evil, awakening in others a sympathetic feeling for their victims and a contempt for their acts, do evil only to those whom they injure; but the men who know the truth and do the evil, which is concealed under hypocrisy, do evil to themselves and to those whom they injure, and to thousands of others who are offended by the lie, with which they attempt to conceal the evil done by them.

Thieves, plunderers, murderers, cheats, who commit acts that are recognized as evil by themselves and by all men, serve as an example of what ought not to be done, and deter men from evil. But the men who commit the same act of thieving, plundering, torturing, killing, mantling themselves with religious and scientific liberal justifications, as is done by all landed proprietors, merchants, manufacturers, and all kinds of servants of the government of our time, invite others to emulate their acts, and do evil, not only to those who suffer from it, but also to thousands and millions of men, whom they corrupt, by destroying for these men the difference between good and evil.

One fortune acquired by the trade in articles necessary for the masses or by corrupting the people, or by speculations on 'Change, or by the acquisition of cheap land, which later grows more expensive on account of the popular want, or by the establishment of plants ruining the health and the life of men, or by civil or military service to the state, or by any means which pamper to the vices of men — a fortune gained by such means, not only with the consent, but even with the approval of the leaders of society, corrupts people incomparably more than millions of thefts, rascalities, plunderings, which are committed outside the forms recognized by law and subject to criminal prosecution.

One execution, which is performed by well-to-do, cultured men, not under the influence of passion, but with the approval and coöperation of Christian pastors, and presented as something necessary, corrupts and bestializes men more than hundreds and thousands of murders, committed by uncultured labouring men, especially under the incitement of passion. An execution, such as Zhukóvski proposed to arrange, when men, as Zhukóvski assumed, would even experience a religious feeling of meekness of spirit, would be the most corrupting action that can be imagined. (See Vol. VI. of Zhukóvski's *Complete Works.*)

Every war, however short its duration, with its usual accompanying losses, destruction of the crops, thieving, admissible debauchery, looting, murders, with the invented justifications of its necessity and its justice, with the exaltation and eulogizing of military exploits, of love of flag and country, with the hypocritical cares for the wounded, and so forth, corrupts in one year more than do millions of robberies, incendiarisms, murders, committed in the course of hundreds of years by individual men under the influence of the passions.

One luxurious life, running temperately within the limits of decency, on the part of one respectable, so-called virtuous, family, which, none the less, spends on itself the products of as many labouring days as would suffice for the support of thousands of people living in misery side by side with this family, corrupts people more than do thousands of monstrous orgies of coarse merchants, officers, labouring men, who abandon themselves to drunkenness and debauchery, who for fun break mirrors, dishes, and so forth.

One solemn procession, Te Deum, or sermon from the ambo or pulpit, dealing with a lie in which the preachers themselves do not believe, produces incomparably more evil than do thousands of forgeries and adulterations of food, and so forth.

We talk of the hypocrisy of the Pharisees. But the hypocrisy of the men of our time far surpasses the comparatively innocent hypocrisy of the Pharisees. They had at least an external religious law, in the fulfilment of which they could overlook their obligations in relation to their neighbours, and, besides, these obligations were at that time not yet clearly pointed out; in our time, in the first place, there is no such religious law which frees men from their obligations to their neighbours, to all their neighbours without exception (I do not count those coarse and stupid men who even now think that sacraments or the decision of the Pope can absolve one from sins): on the contrary, that Gospel law, which we all profess in one way or another, directly points out these obligations, and besides these obligations, which at that time were expressed in dim words by only a few prophets, are now expressed so clearly that they have become truisms, which are repeated by gymnasiasts and writers of feuilletons. And so the men of our time, it would seem, cannot possibly pretend that they do not know these their obligations.

The men of our time, who exploit the order of things which is supported by violence, and who at the same time assert that they are very fond of their neighbours, and entirely fail to observe that they are with their whole lives doing evil to these their neighbours, are like a man who has incessantly robbed people, and who, being finally caught with his knife raised over his victim, who is calling for aid in a desperate voice, should assert that he did not know that what he was doing was unpleasant for him whom he was robbing and getting ready to kill. Just as this robber and murderer cannot deny what is obvious to all men, so, it would seem, it is impossible for the men of our time, who live at the expense of the sufferings of oppressed men, to assure themselves and others that they wish for the good of those men whom they rob incessantly, and that they did not know in what manner they acquire what they use as their own.

It is impossible for us to believe that we do not know of those one hundred thousand men in Russia alone, who are always locked up in prisons and at hard labour, for the purpose of securing our property and our peace; and that we do not know of those courts, in which we ourselves take part, and which in consequence of our petitions sentence the men who assault our property or endanger our security to imprisonment, deportation, and hard labour, where the men, who are in no way worse than those who sentence them, perish and are corrupted; that we do not know that everything we have we have only because it is acquired and secured for us by means of murders and tortures. We cannot pretend that we do not see the policeman who walks in front of the windows with a loaded revolver, defending us, while we eat our savoury dinner or view a new performance, or those soldiers who will immediately go with their guns and loaded cartridges to where our property will be violated.

We certainly know that if we shall finish eating our dinner, or seeing the latest drama, or having our fun at a ball, at the Christmas tree, at the skating, at the races, or at the chase, we do so only thanks to the bullet in the policeman's revolver and in the soldier's gun, which will at once bore a hole through the hungry stomach of the dispossessed man who, with watering mouth, is staying around the corner and watching our amusements, and is prepared to violate them the moment the policeman with the revolver shall go away, or as soon as there shall be no soldier in the barracks ready to appear at our first call.

And so, just as a man caught in broad daylight in a robbery can in no way assure all men that he did not raise his hand over the man about to be robbed by him, in order to take his purse from him, and did not threaten to cut his throat, so we, it would seem, cannot assure ourselves and others that the soldiers and policemen with the revolvers are all about us, not in order to protect us, but to defend us against external enemies, for the sake of order, for ornament, amusement, and parades; and that we did not know that men do not like to starve, having no right to make a living off the land on which they live, do not like to work underground, in the water, in hellish heat, from ten to fourteen hours a day, and in the night, in all kinds of factories and plants, for the purpose of manufacturing articles for our enjoyment. It would seem to be impossible to deny that which is so obvious. And yet it is precisely what is being done.

Though there are among the rich some honest people, — fortunately I meet more and more of them, especially among the young and among women, — who, at the mention of how and with what their pleasures are bought, do not try to conceal the truth, and grasp their heads and say, "Oh, do not speak of it. If it is so, it is impossible to go on living;" though there are such sincere people, who, unable to free themselves from their sin, none the less see it, the vast majority of the men of our time have so entered into their rôle of hypocrisy, that they boldly deny what is so startlingly obvious to every seeing person.

"All this is unjust," they say; "nobody compels the people to work for the proprietors and in factories. This is a question of free agreement. Large possessions and capital are indispensable, because they organize labour and give work to the labouring classes; and the work in the factories and plants is not at all as terrible as you imagine it to be. If there are some abuses in the factories, the government and society will see to it that they be removed and that the work be made still more easy and even more agreeable for the labourers. The working people are used to physical labour, and so far are not good for anything else. The poverty of the masses is not at all due to the ownership of land, nor to the oppression of capital, but to other causes: it is due to the ignorance, the coarseness, the drunkenness of the masses. We, the men of state, who are counteracting this impoverishment by wise enactments, and we, the capitalists, who are counteracting it by the dissemination of useful inventions, we, the clergy, by religious instruction, and we, the liberals, by the establishment of labour-unions, the increase and diffusion of knowledge, in this manner, without changing our position, increase the welfare of the masses. We do not want all men to be poor, like the poor, but want them to be rich, like the rich. The statement that men are tortured and killed to compel them to work for the rich is nothing but sophistry; troops are sent out against the masses only when they, misunderstanding their advantages, become riotous and disturb the peace, which is necessary for the common good. Just as much do we need the curbing of malefactors, for whom are intended the prisons, gallows, and hard labour. We should ourselves like to do away with them, and we are working in this direction."

The hypocrisy of our time, which is supported from two sides, by the quasi-religion and the quasi-science, has reached such a point that, if we did not live in the midst of it, we should not be able to believe that men could reach such a degree of self-deception. The people have in our time reached the remarkable state when their hearts are so hardened that they look and do not see, that they listen and do not hear or understand.

Men have long been living a life which is contrary to their consciousness. If it were not for hypocrisy, they would not be able to live this life. This order of life, which is contrary to their consciousness, is continued only because it is hidden under hypocrisy.

The more the distance is growing between reality and the consciousness of men, the more does hypocrisy expand, but there are limits even to hypocrisy, and it seems to me that in our time we have reached that limit.

Every man of our time, with the Christian consciousness, which is involuntarily acquired by him, finds himself in a situation which is exactly like that of a sleeping man, who sees in his sleep that he must do what he knows even in his sleep is not right for him to do.

He knows this in the very depth of his heart, and yet, as though unable to change his position, he cannot stop and cease doing what he knows he ought not to do. And, as happens in sleep, his condition, becoming more and more agonizing, finally reaches the utmost degree of tension, and then he begins to doubt the reality of what presents itself to him, and he makes an effort of consciousness, in order to break the spell that holds him fettered.

In the same condition is the average man of our Christian world. He feels that everything which is done by himself and about him is something insipid, monstrous, impossible, and contrary to his consciousness, that this condition is becoming more and more agonizing, and has reached the utmost limit of tension.

It cannot be: it cannot be that the men of our time, with our Christian consciousness of the dignity of man, the equality of men, which has permeated our flesh and blood, with our need for a peaceful intercourse and union among the nations, should actually be living in such a way that every joy of ours, every comfort, should be paid for by the sufferings, the lives of our brothers, and that we, besides, should every moment be within a hair's breadth of throwing ourselves, like wild beasts, upon one another, nation upon nation, mercilessly destroying labour and life, for no other reason than that some deluded diplomatist or ruler has said or written something stupid to another deluded diplomatist or ruler like himself.

It cannot be. And yet every man of our time sees that it is precisely what is being done, and that the same thing awaits him. The state of affairs is getting more and more agonizing.

As the man in his sleep does not believe that what presents itself to him as reality is actually real, and wants to awaken to the other, the actual reality, so also the average man of our time cannot in the depth of his heart believe that the terrible state in which he is, and which is getting worse and worse, is the reality, and he wants to awaken to the actual reality, the reality of the consciousness which already abides in him.

And as the man asleep needs but make an effort of his consciousness and ask himself whether it is not a dream, in order that what to him appeared as such a hopeless state may be at once destroyed, and he may awaken to a calm and joyous reality, even so the modern man needs only make an effort of his consciousness, needs only doubt in the reality of what his own and the surrounding hypocrisy presents to him, and ask himself whether it is not all a deception, in order that he may immediately feel himself at once passing over, like the awakened man, from the imaginary, terrible world to the real, to the calm and joyous reality.

This man need not perform any acts or exploits, but has only to make an internal effort of consciousness.

5

Cannot man make this effort ?

According to the existing theory, indispensable for hypocrisy, man is not free and cannot change his life.

"Man cannot change his life, because he is not free; he is not free, because all of his acts are conditioned by previous causes. No matter what a man may do, there always exist these or those causes, from which the man has committed these or those acts, and so man cannot be free and himself change his life," say the defenders of the metaphysics of hypocrisy. They would be absolutely right, if man were an unconscious being, immovable in relation to truth; that is, if, having once come to know the truth, he always remained on the selfsame stage of his cognition. But man is a conscious being, recognizing a higher and still higher degree of the truth, and so, if a man is not free in the commission of this or that act, because for every act there exists a cause, the very causes of these acts, which for conscious man consist in his recognizing this or that truth as an adequate cause for his action, are within man's power.

Thus man, who is not free in the commission of these or those acts, is free as regards the basis for his acts, something as the engineer of a locomotive, who is not free as regards the change of an accomplished or actual motion of the locomotive, is none the less free in determining beforehand its future motions.

No matter what a conscious man may do, he acts in this way or that, and not otherwise, only because he either now recognizes that the truth is that he ought to act as he does, or because he formerly recognized it, and now from inertia, from habit, acts in a manner which now he recognizes to be false.

In either case the cause of his act was not a given phenomenon, but the recognition of a given condition as the truth and, consequently, the recognition of this or that phenomenon as an adequate cause of his act.

Whether a man eats or abstains from food, whether he works or rests, runs from danger or is subject to it, if he is a conscious man, he acts as he does only because he now considers this to be proper and rational: he considers the truth to consist in his acting this way, and not otherwise, or he has considered it so for a long time.

The recognition of a certain truth or the non-recognition of it does not depend on external causes, but on some others, which are in man himself. Thus with all the external, apparently advantageous conditions for the recognition of truth, one man at times does not recognize it, and, on the contrary, another, under all the most unfavourable conditions, without any apparent cause, does recognize it. As it says in the Gospel: "No man can come to me, except the Father draw him" (John vi. 44), that is, the recognition of the truth, which forms the cause of all the phenomena of human life, does not depend on external phenomena, but on some internal qualities of man, which are not subject to his observation.

And so a man, who is not free in his acts, always feels himself free in what serves as the cause of his actions, — in the recognition or non-recognition of the truth, and feels himself free, not only independently of external conditions taking place outside him, but even of his own acts.

Thus a man, having under the influence of passion committed an act which is contrary to the cognized truth, none the less remains free in its recognition or non-recognition, that is, he can, without recognizing the truth, regard his act as necessary and justify himself in its commission, and can, by recognizing the truth, consider his act bad and condemn it in himself.

Thus a gambler or a drunkard, who has not withstood temptation and has succumbed to his passion, remains none the less free to recognize his gambling or his intoxication either as an evil or as an indifferent amusement. In the first case, he, though not at once, frees himself from his passion, the more, as he the more sincerely recognizes the truth; in the second, he strengthens his passion and deprives himself of every possibility of liberation.

Even so a man, who could not stand the heat and ran out of a burning house without having saved his companion, remains free (by recognizing the truth that a man must serve the lives of others at the risk of his own life) to consider his act bad, and so to condemn himself for it, or (by not recognizing this truth) to consider his act natural, and necessary, and to justify himself in it. In the first case, in recognizing the truth, he, in spite of his departure from it, prepares for himself a whole series of self-sacrificing acts, which inevitably must result from such a recognition; in the second case, he prepares a whole series of egotistical acts, which are opposed to the first.

Not that a man is always free to recognize every truth, or not. There are truths which have long ago been recognized by a man himself or have been transmitted to him by education and tradition, and have been taken by him on faith, the execution of which has become to him a habit, a second nature; and there are truths which present themselves to him indistinctly, in the distance. A man is equally unfree in the non-recognition of the first and the recognition of the second. But there is a third class of truths, which have not yet become for man an unconscious motive for his activity, but which at the same time have already revealed themselves to him with such lucidity that he cannot evade them, and must inevitably take up this or that relation to them, by recognizing or not recognizing them. It is in relation to these same truths that man's freedom is manifested.

Every man finds himself in his life in relation to truth in the position of a wanderer who walks in the dark by the light of a lantern moving in front of him: he does not see what is not yet illuminated by the lantern, nor what he has passed over and what is again enveloped in darkness, and it is not in his power to change his relation to either; but he sees, no matter on what part of the path he may stand, what is illuminated by the lantern, and it is always in his power to select one side of the road on which he is moving, or the other.

For every man there always are truths, invisible to him, which have not yet been revealed to his mental vision; there are other truths, already outlived, forgotten, and made his own; and there are certain truths which have arisen before him in the light of his reason and which demand his recognition. It is in the recognition or non-recognition of these truths that there is manifested what we cognize as our freedom.

The whole difficulty and seeming insolubility of the question about man's freedom is due to this, that the men who decide this question present man to themselves as immovable in relation to truth.

Man is unquestionably not free, if we represent him to ourselves as immovable, if we forget that the life of man and of humanity is only a constant motion from darkness to the light, from the lower stage of the truth to the higher, from a truth which is mixed with errors to a truth which is more free from them.

Man would not be free, if he did not know any truth, and he would not be free and would not even have any idea about freedom, if the whole truth, which is to guide him in his life, were revealed to him in all its purity, without any admixture of errors.

But man is not immovable in relation to truth, and every individual man, as also all humanity, in proportion to its movement in life, constantly cognizes a greater and ever greater degree of the truth, and is more and more freed from error. Therefore men always are in a threefold relation to truth: one set of truths has been so acquired by them that these truths have become unconscious causes of their actions, others have only begun to be revealed to them, and the third, though not yet made their own, are revealed to them with such a degree of lucidity that inevitably, in one way or another, they must take up some stand in relation to them, must recognize them, or not.

It is in the recognition or non-recognition of these truths that man is free.

Man's freedom does not consist in this, that he can, independently of the course of his life and of causes already existing and acting upon him, commit arbitrary acts, but in this, that he can, by recognizing the truth revealed to him and by professing it, become a free and joyous performer of the eternal and infinite act performed by God or the life of the world, and can, by not recognizing the truth, become its slave and be forcibly and painfully drawn in a direction which he does not wish to take.

Truth not only indicates the path of human life, but also reveals that one path, on which human life can proceed. And so all men will inevitably, freely or not freely, walk on the path of life: some, by naturally doing the work of life destined for them, others, by involuntarily submitting to the law of life. Man's freedom is in this choice.

Such a freedom, within such narrow limits, seems to men to be so insignificant that they do not notice it: some (the determinists) consider this portion of freedom to be so small that they do not recognize it at all; others, the defenders of complete freedom, having in view their imaginary freedom, neglect this seemingly insignificant degree of freedom. The freedom which is contained between the limits of the ignorance of the truth and of the recognition of a certain degree of it does not seem to men to be any freedom, the more so since, whether a man wants to recognize the truth which is revealed to him or not, he inevitably will be compelled to fulfil it in life.

A horse that is hitched with others to a wagon is not free not to walk in front of the wagon; and if it will not draw, the wagon will strike its legs, and it will go whither the wagon goes, and will pull it involuntarily. But, in spite of this limited freedom, it is free itself to pull the wagon or be dragged along by it. The same is true of man.

Whether this freedom is great or not, in comparison with that fantastic freedom which we should like to have, this freedom unquestionably exists, and this freedom is freedom, and in this freedom is contained the good which is accessible to man.

Not only does this freedom give the good to men, but

it is also the one means for the accomplishment of the work which is done by the life of the world.

According to Christ's teaching, the man who sees the meaning of life in the sphere in which it is not free, in the sphere of consequences, that is, of acts, has not the true life. According to the Christian teaching, only he has the true life who has transferred his life into that sphere in which it is free, into the sphere of causes, that is, of the cognition and the recognition of the truth which is revealing itself, of its profession, and so inevitably of its consequent fulfilment as the wagon's following the horse.

In placing his life in carnal things, a man does that work which is always in dependence on spatial and temporal causes, which are outside of him. He himself really does nothing, — it only seems to him that he is doing something, but in reality all those things which it seems to him he is doing are done through him by a higher power, and he is not the creator of life, but its slave; but in placing his life in the recognition and profession of the truth that is revealed to him, he, by uniting with the source of the universal life, does not do personal, private works, which depend on conditions of space and time, but works which have no causes and themselves form causes of everything else, and have an endless, unlimited significance.

By neglecting the essence of the true life, which consists in the recognition and profession of the truth, and by straining their efforts for the amelioration of their lives upon external acts, the men of the pagan life-conception are like men on a boat, who, in order to reach their goal, should put out the boiler, which keeps them from distributing the oarsmen, and, instead of proceeding under steam and screw, should try in a storm to row with oars that do not reach to the water.

The kingdom of God is taken by force and only those who make an effort get hold of it, — and it is this effort of the renunciation of the change of the external conditions for the recognition and profession of truth which is the effort by means of which the kingdom of God is taken and which must and can be made in our time.

Men need but understand this: they need but stop troubling themselves about external and general matters, in which they are not free, and use but one hundredth part of the energy, which they employ on external matters, on what they are free in, on the recognition and profession of the truth which stands before them, on the emancipation of themselves and of men from the lie and hypocrisy which conceal the truth, in order that without effort and struggle there should at once be destroyed that false structure of life which torments people and threatens them with still worse calamities, and that there should be realized that kingdom of God or at least that first step of it, for which men are already prepared according to their consciousness.

Just as one jolt is sufficient for a liquid that is saturated with salt suddenly to become crystallized, thus, perhaps, the smallest effort will suffice for the truth, which is already revealed to men, to take hold of hundreds, thousands, millions of men, — for a public opinion to be established to correspond to the consciousness, and, in consequence of its establishment, for the whole structure of the existing life to be changed. And it depends on us to make this effort.

If every one of us would only try to understand and recognize the Christian truth which surrounds us on all sides in the most varied forms, and begs for admission into our souls; if we only stopped lying and pretending that we do not see that truth, or that we wish to carry it out, only not in what it first of all demands of us; if we only recognized the truth which calls us and boldly professed it, we should immediately see that hundreds, thousands, millions of men are in the same condition that we are in, that they see the truth, just as we do, and that, like us, they are only waiting for others to recognize it.

If men only stopped being hypocritical, they would see at once that the cruel structure of life, which alone binds them and which presents itself to them as something firm, indispensable, and sacred, as something established by God, is shaking already and is holding only by that lie of hypocrisy by means of which we and our like support it.

But if this is so, if it is true that it depends on us to destroy the existing order of life, have we the right to destroy it, without knowing clearly what we shall put in its place? What will become of the world, if the existing order of things shall be destroyed?

"What will be there, beyond the walls of the world which we leave behind?" (Herzen's words.)

"Terror seizes us, — the void, expanse, freedom. . . . How can we go, without knowing whither? How can we lose, without seeing any acquisition?

"If Columbus had reflected thus, he would never have weighed anchor. It is madness to sail the sea without knowing the way, to sail the sea no one has traversed before, to make for a country, the existence of which is a question. With this madness he discovered a new world. Of course, if the nations could move from one *hôtel garni* into another, a better one, it would be easier, but unfortunately there is no one to arrange the new quarters. In the future it is worse than on the sea, — there is nothing, — it will be what circumstances and men make it.

"If you are satisfied with the old world, try to preserve it, — it is very decrepit and will not last long; but if it is unbearable for you to live in an eternal discord between convictions and life, to think one thing and do another, come out from under the whited mediæval vaults at your risk. I know full well that this is not easy. It is not a trifling matter to part from everything a man is accustomed to from the day of his birth, with what he has grown up with from childhood. Men are prepared for terrible sacrifices, but not for those which the new life demands of them. Are they prepared to sacrifice modern civilization, their manner of life, their religion, the accepted conventional morality? Are they prepared to be deprived of all the fruits which have been worked out with such efforts, of the fruits we have been boasting of for three centuries, to be deprived of all the comforts and charms of our existence, to prefer wild youth to cultured debility, to break up their inherited palace from the mere pleasure of taking part in laying the foundation for the new house, which will, no doubt, be built after us?" (Herzen, Vol. V., p. 55.)

Thus spoke almost half a century ago a Russian author, who with his penetrating mind even at that time saw very clearly what now is seen by the least reflecting man of our time, — the impossibility of continuing life on its former foundations, and the necessity for establishing some new forms of life.

From the simplest, lowest, worldly point of view it is already clear that it is madness to remain under the vault of a building, which does not sustain its weight, and that it is necessary to leave it. Indeed, it is hard to imagine a state which is more wretched than the one in which is now the Christian world, with its nations armed against each other, with the ever growing taxes for the support of these ever growing armaments, with the hatred of the labouring class against the rich, which is being fanned more and more, with Damocles's sword of war hanging over all, and ready at any moment to drop down, and inevitably certain to do so sooner or later.

Hardly any revolution can be more wretched for the great mass of the people than the constantly existing order, or rather disorder, of our life, with its habitual sacrifices of unnatural labour, poverty, drunkenness, debauchery, and with all the horrors of an imminent war, which is in one year to swallow up more victims than all the revolutions of the present century.

What will happen with us, with all humanity, when each one of us shall perform what is demanded of him by God through the conscience which is implanted in him? Will there be no calamity, because, finding myself entirely in the power of the Master, I in the establishment built up and guided by Him shall do what He commands me to do, but what seems strange to me, who do not know the final ends of the Master?

But it is not even this question as to what will happen that troubles men, when they hesitate to do the Master's will: they are troubled by the question as to how they could live without those conditions of their life which they have become accustomed to, and which we call science, art, civilization, culture. We feel for ourselves personally the whole burden of the present life, we even see that the order of this life, if continued, will inevitably cause our ruin; but, at the same time, we want the conditions of this our life, which have grown out of it, our arts, sciences, civilizations, cultures, to remain unharmed in the change of our life. It is as though a man living in an old house, suffering from the cold and the inconveniences of this house, and knowing, besides, that this house is about to fall in, should consent to its rebuilding only on condition that he should not come out of it: a condition which is equal to a refusal to rebuild the house. "What if I leave the house, for a time am deprived of all comforts, and the new house will not be built at all or will be built in such a way that it will lack what I am used to?"

But, if the material is on hand and the builders are there, all the probabilities are in favour of the new house being better than the old one, and at the same time there is not only a probability, but even a certainty, that the old house will fall in and will crush those who are left in it. Whether the former, habitual conditions of life will be retained, whether they will be destroyed, or whether entirely new ones, better ones, will arise, it is inevitably necessary to leave the old conditions of our life, which have become impossible and pernicious, and to go ahead and meet the future conditions.

"The sciences, arts, civilizations, and cultures will disappear!"

All these are only different manifestations of the truth, and the imminent change is to take place only in the name of an approximation to truth and its realization. How, then, can the manifestations of the truth disappear in consequence of its realization? They will be different, better, and higher, but they will by no means be destroyed. What will be destroyed in them is what is false; but what there was of truth in them will only blossom out and be strengthened.

6

Come to your senses, men, and believe in the Gospel, in the teaching of the good. If you shall not come to your senses, you will all perish, as perished the men who were killed by Pilate, as perished those who were crushed by the tower of Siloam, as perished millions and millions of men, slayers and slain, executioners and executed, tormentors and tormented, and as foolishly perished that man who filled up his granaries and prepared himself to live for a long time, and died the same night on which he wanted to begin his new life. "Come to your senses and believe in the Gospel," Christ said eighteen hundred years ago, and says now with even greater convincingness, through the utter wretchedness and irrationality of our life, predicted by Him and now an accomplished fact.

Now, after so many centuries of vain endeavours to

make our life secure by means of the pagan institution of violence, it would seem to be absolutely obvious to everybody that all the efforts which are directed toward this end only introduce new dangers into our personal and social life, but in no way make it secure.

No matter what we may call ourselves; what attires we may put on; what we may smear ourselves with, and in the presence of what priests; how many millions we may have; what protection there may be along our path; how many policemen may protect our wealth; how much we may execute the so-called revolutionary malefactors and anarchists; what exploits we ourselves may perform; what kingdoms we may found, and what fortresses and towers we may erect, from that of Babel to that of Eiffel, — we are all of us at all times confronted by two inevitable conditions of our life, which destroy its whole meaning: (1) by death, which may overtake any of us at any moment, and (2) by the impermanency of all the acts performed by us, which are rapidly and tracklessly destroyed. No matter what we may do, whether we found kingdoms, build palaces, erect monuments, compose poems, it is but for a short time, and everything passes, without leaving a trace. And so, no matter how much we may conceal the fact from ourselves, we cannot help but see that the meaning of our life can be neither in our personal, carnal existence, which is subject to inevitable sufferings and inevitable death, nor in any worldly institution or structure.

Whoever you, the reader of these lines, may be, think of your condition and of your duties, — not of the condition of landowner, merchant, judge, emperor, president, minister, priest, soldier, which people temporarily ascribe to you, nor of those imaginary duties, which these positions impose upon you, but of that real, eternal condition of existence, which by somebody's will after a whole eternity of non-existence has issued forth from uncon sciousness, and at any moment by somebody's will may return to where you come from. Think of your duties,— not of your imaginary duties as a landowner to your estate, of a merchant to your capital, of an emperor, minister, official to the state,— but of those real duties of yours, which result from your real condition of existence, which is called into life and is endowed with reason and love. Are you doing what is demanded of you by Him who has sent you into the world, and to whom you will very soon return? Are you doing what He is demanding of you? Are you doing what is right, when, being a landowner, manufacturer, you take away the productions of labour from the poor, building up your life on this spoliation, or when, being a ruler, a judge, you do violence to people and sentence them to capital punishment, or when, being a soldier, you prepare yourself for wars, and wage war, plunder, and kill?

You say that the world is constructed that way, that this is unavoidable, that you are not doing this of your own will, but that you are compelled to do so. But is it possible that the aversion for human sufferings, for tortures, for the killing of men should be so deeply implanted in you; that you should be so imbued with the necessity for loving men and the still more potent necessity of being loved by them; that you should clearly see that only with the recognition of the equality of all men, with their mutual service, is possible the realization of the greatest good which is accessible to men; that your heart, your intellect, the religion professed by you should tell you the same; that science should tell you the same,— and that, in spite of it, you should be by some very dim, complex considerations compelled to do what is precisely opposed to it? that, being a landowner or a capitalist, you should be compelled to construct all your life on the oppression of the masses? or that, being an emperor or a president, you should be compelled to command troops, that is, to be the leader and guide of murderers? or that, being a government official, you should be compelled by violence to take from poor people their hard-earned money, in order to use it yourself and give it to the rich? or that, being a judge, a juror, you should be compelled to sentence erring men to tortures and to death, because the truth has not been revealed to them? or that, — a thing on which all the evil of the world is chiefly based, — you, every young man, should be compelled to become a soldier and, renouncing your own will and all human sentiments, should promise, at the will of men who are alien to you, to kill all those men whom they may command you to kill?

It cannot be.

Even though men tell you that all this is necessary for the maintenance of the existing structure of life; that the existing order, with its wretchedness, hunger, prisons, executions, armies, wars, is indispensable for society; that, if this order should be impaired, there would come worse calamities, — it is only those to whom this structure of life is advantageous that tell you this, while those — and there are ten times as many of them — who are suffering from this structure of life think and say the very opposite. You yourself know in the depth of your heart that this is not true, that the existing structure of life has outlived its time and soon must be reconstructed on new principles, and that, therefore, there is no need to maintain it, while sacrificing human sentiments.

Above all else, even if we admit that the existing order is necessary, why do you feel yourself obliged to maintain it, while trampling on all better human sentiments? Who has engaged you as a nurse to this decaying order? Neither society, nor the state, nor any men have ever asked you to maintain this order, by holding the place of landowner, merchant, emperor, priest, soldier, which you now hold; and you know full well that you took up your position, not at all with the self-sacrificing purpose of maintaining an order of life which is indispensable for the good of men, but for your own sake, — for the sake of your greed, love of glory, ambition, indolence, cowardice. If you did not want this position, you would not be doing everything it is necessary for you to do all the time, in order to keep your place. Just try to stop doing those complex, cruel, tricky, and mean things, which you are doing without cessation in order to keep your place, and you will immediately lose it. Just try, while being a ruler or an official, to stop lying, committing base acts, taking part in acts of violence, in executions; being a priest, to stop deceiving; being a soldier, to stop killing; being a landowner, a manufacturer, to stop protecting your property by means of the courts and of violence, — and you will at once lose the position which, you say, is imposed upon you, and which, you say, weighs heavily upon you.

It cannot be that a man should be placed against his will in a position which is contrary to his consciousness.

If you are in this position, it is not because that is necessary for anybody, but because you want it. And so, knowing that this position is directly opposed to your heart, your reason, your faith, and even to science, in which you believe, you cannot help but meditate on the question as to whether you are doing right by staying in this position and, above all, by trying to justify it.

You might be able to risk making a mistake, if you had time to see and correct your mistake, and if that in the name of which you should take your risk had any importance. But when you know for certain that you may vanish any second, without the slightest chance of correcting the mistake, either for your own sake or for the sake of those whom you will draw into your error, and when you know, besides, that, no matter what you may do in the external structure of the world, it will disappear very soon, and just as certainly as you yourself, without leaving any trace, it is obvious to you that you have no reason to risk such a terrible mistake.

This is all so simple and so clear, if only we did not with hypocrisy bedim the truth which is revealed to us.

"Share with others what you have, do not amass any wealth, do not glorify yourself, do not plunder, do not torture, do not kill any one, do not do unto others what you do not wish to have done to yourself," was said, not eighteen hundred, but five thousand years ago, and there could be no doubt as to the truth of this law, if there were no hypocrisy: it would have been impossible, if not to do so, at least not to recognize that we ought always to do so, and that he who does not do so is doing wrong.

But you say that there also exists a common good, for which it is possible and necessary to depart from these rules, — for the common good it is right to kill, torture, rob. It is better for one man to perish, than that a whole nation should perish, you say, like Caiaphas, and you sign one, two, three death-warrants, load your gun for that man who is to perish for the common good, put him in prison, take away his property. You say that you do these cruel things, because you feel yourself to be a man of society, the state, under obligation to serve it and to carry out its laws, a landowner, a judge, an emperor, a soldier. But, besides your belonging to a certain state, and the obligations resulting therefrom, you also belong to the infinite life of the world and to God, and have certain obligations resulting from this relation.

And as your duties, which result from your belonging to a certain family, a certain society, are always subordinated to the higher duties, which result from your belonging to the state, so also your obligations, which result from your belonging to the state, must necessarily be subordinated to the duties which result from your belonging to the life of the world, to God.

And as it would be senseless to cut down the telegraph-posts, in order to provide fuel for the family or society, and to increase its well-being, because this would violate the laws which preserve the good of the state, so it would be senseless, for the purpose of making the state secure and increasing its well-being, to torture, execute, kill a man, because this violates the unquestionable laws which preserve the good of the world.

Your obligations, which result from your belonging to the state, cannot help but be subordinated to the higher eternal duty, which results from your belonging to the infinite life of the world, or to God, and cannot contradict them, as Christ's disciples said eighteen hundred years ago: "Whether it be right in the sight of God to hearken unto you more than unto God, judge ye" (Acts iv. 19), and, "We ought to obey God rather than men" (Acts v. 29).

You are assured that, in order not to violate the constantly changing order, which was yesterday established by some men in some corner of the world, you must commit acts of torture and murder separate men, who violate the eternal, invariable order of the universe, which was established by God, or by reason. Can that be?

And so you cannot help but meditate on your position as a landowner, merchant, judge, emperor, president, minister, priest, soldier, which is connected with oppression, violence, deception, tortures, and murders, and you cannot help but recognize their illegality.

I do not say that, if you are a landowner, you should at once give your land to the poor; if you are a capitalist, you should at once give your money, your factory to the labourers; if you are a king, a minister, an official, a judge, a general, you should at once give up your advantageous position; if you are a soldier (that is, occupy a position on which all violence is based), you should, in spite of all the dangers of a refusal to obey, at once throw up your position.

If you do so, you will do the very best possible; but it may happen — and this is most likely — that you will not have the strength to do so: you have connections, a family, inferiors, superiors; you may be under such a strong influence of temptations that you will not be able to do so, — but you are always able to recognize the truth as a truth, and to stop lying. Do not assert that you remain a landed proprietor, a manufacturer, a merchant, an artist, a writer, because this is useful for men; that you are serving as a governor, a prosecutor, a king, not because that gives you pleasure and you are used to it, but for the good of humanity; that you continue to be a soldier, not because you are afraid of punishment, but because you consider the army indispensable for the security of human life; you can always keep from lying thus to yourself and to men, and you are not only able, but even must do so, because in this alone, in the liberation of oneself from the lie and in the profession of the truth, does the only good of your life consist.

You need but do this, and your position will inevitably change of its own accord. There is one, only one thing in which you are free and almighty in your life, — everything else is beyond your power. This thing is, to recognize the truth and to profess it.

Suddenly, because just such miserable, erring people like yourself have assured you that you are a soldier, emperor, landed proprietor, rich man, priest, general, you begin to do evil, which is obviously and unquestionably contrary to your reason and heart: you begin to torture, rob, kill men, to build up your life on their sufferings, and, above all, instead of doing the one work of your life, — recognizing and professing the truth which is known to you, — you carefully pretend that you do not know it, and conceal it from yourself and from others, doing thus what is directly opposed to the one thing to which you have been called.

And under what conditions do you do that? You, who are likely to die at any moment, sign a sentence of death, declare war, go to war, sit in judgment, torture, fleece the labourers, live luxuriously among the poor, and teach weak, trustful people that this must be so, and that in this does the duty of men consist, and you are running the chance that, at the moment that you are doing this, a bacterium or a bullet will fly into you, and you will rattle in your throat and die, and will for ever be deprived of the possibility of correcting and changing the evil which you have done to others and, above all, to yourself, losing for nothing the life which is given to you but once in a whole eternity, without having done the one thing which you ought unquestionably to have done.

However simple and old this may be, and however much we may have stupefied ourselves by hypocrisy and the auto-suggestion resulting from it, nothing can destroy the absolute certainty of that simple and clear truth that no external efforts can safeguard our life, which is inevitably connected with unavoidable sufferings and which ends in still more unavoidable death, that may come to each of us at any moment, and that, therefore, our life can have no other meaning than the fulfilment, at any moment, of what is wanted from us by the power that sent us into life and gave us in this life one sure guide, — our rational consciousness.

And so this power cannot want from us what is irrational and impossible, — the establishment of our temporal, carnal life, the life of society or of the state. This power demands of us what alone is certain and rational and possible, — our serving the kingdom of God, that is, our coöperation in the establishment of the greatest union of everything living, which is possible only in the truth, and.

therefore, the recognition of the truth revealed to us, and the profession of it, precisely what alone is always in our power.

"Seek ye the kingdom of God and His righteousness and all these things shall be added unto you." The only meaning of man's life consists in serving the world by coöperating in the establishment of the kingdom of God; but this service can be rendered only through the recognition of the truth, and the profession of it, by every separate individual.

"The kingdom of God cometh not with observation: neither shall they say, Lo here! or, Lo there! for, behold, the kingdom of God is within you."

Yásnaya Polyána, May 14, 1893.